Henry Craven St. John

Notes and sketches from the wild coasts of Nipon

With chapters on Cruising after pirates in Chinese waters

Henry Craven St. John

Notes and sketches from the wild coasts of Nipon
With chapters on Cruising after pirates in Chinese waters

ISBN/EAN: 9783337141813

Printed in Europe, USA, Canada, Australia, Japan

Cover: Foto ©Andreas Hilbeck / pixelio.de

More available books at **www.hansebooks.com**

NOTES AND SKETCHES

FROM THE

WILD COASTS OF NIPON

WITH CHAPTERS ON CRUISING AFTER PIRATES IN CHINESE WATERS

By CAPTAIN H. C. ST. JOHN, R.N.

EDINBURGH: DAVID DOUGLAS
MDCCCLXXX

To the Memory of

MY FATHER,

WHO, FROM MY EARLIEST CHILDHOOD,

INSPIRED IN ME THAT LOVE OF NATURAL HISTORY

AND TRUE SPORT

WHICH HAS ENABLED ME TO PASS SO MANY HOURS

OF THOROUGH ENJOYMENT

IN WILD COUNTRIES FAR FROM HOME,

I dedicate this Book.

STOKEFIELD, THORNBURY,
GLOUCESTER, *Nov.* 1880.

PREFACE.

It is with much hesitation I offer this volume of rough sketches to the public.

Many friends have so often suggested that I should put my Notes into some order, that at last I have endeavoured to do so. But although I inherit my father's love for natural history, his charm of writing, I fear, has not equally descended to me.

During my last seven years in the East, when surveying in Japan, I always had the winter months fairly free from duty, and was then able to enjoy many a good ramble in quest of game, as well as to collect objects of nature.

My work lay almost entirely on ground never visited by Europeans, and therefore amongst the natives, who were still unbitten with the mania for Western civilisation, ideas, etc. etc. I was also obliged to meet prince and peasant, the latter more particularly; and it is of him I principally speak, and through him that I judge the Japanese as to character and disposition.

I am only a lover and an observer of nature, and not in any way scientific. One thing those who read this book may feel assured of: everything I have stated came under my own observation, except in those cases I have particularly mentioned.

I constantly kept a dredge at work; nothing is more simple or easy, and nothing will bring to light more objects of natural history, full of wonder, interest, and beauty. I was fortunate in picking up many new things in the way of crustacea and mollusca, which are now in the British Museum. I only wish I had the opportunity of again visiting the eastern coasts of Yesso and the Kuril Islands.

All this locality being washed by the cold arctic current abounds with life, and here a field still remains full of riches to the naturalist and explorer.

As for those rough weather-beaten Kuril Islands, I envy the man who has a chance of examining and exploring the southern and largest of the group.

Nov. 1880.

ANCHORAGE AT AWA SIMA, INLAND SEA.

AINO WOMAN CARRYING CHILD

CONTENTS.

CHAPTER I.

ROUND YESSO.

Wild Geese—Sea Lions—At Cape Yerimo—Cachalots—Cold and warm Currents—Aino Settlement—At Akishi Bay—Swans—Solitary Aino—Spruce Grouse—Anchorage at Hamanaka—More Ainos—Eagles on Island—Cape Noyshap—Nemero Island—Weather in May and June—Herring—Mode of Fishing—Snipe (*Gallinago australis*)—Yesso Brown Bear—Inquisitive Crows—Kunashir Island—Grey Plover—Seals—Eagle's nest in Fir-tree—Trees—Albatross—Prevalence of Fogs—A pet Bear on Board—Flowers—Oteranai—Salmon-Fishery on the Iskari—Enormous quantity caught—Average temperature of South-west Coast—Coal—The Ainos—Their Habits and Customs—Wreck of the *Eliza Corry*—Kinndess of the People . . . . . Pages 1-36

CHAPTER II.

SEARCH FOR SPIDER-CRAB, THE INLAND SEA REVISITED, OCTOPUS, ETC.

The Inland Sea, a fairy region—Its Islands—The Spider-Crab its Scarcity—Efforts to procure it—A trip to Enosima—Kamakura and its Temples—A very hot Bath—Arrival at Enosima—Relics of the Crab—Cave—Hot Sulphur Spring—Painted

Butterflies—The Crab at last—Octopus—Teredo—Channels leading from the Inland Sea—The Naruta—Difficult Navigation—"You never went so fast in a Ship before"—The Captain of the Mail Steamer—"The 'Recommendation' removed"—Deer and Ponies—Awadji Island—Plants and Fungi—Soza-Sima, the largest island—A favourite place for Deer-stalking—The French Gun-boat—"Gros Monkeys"—Seldom molested—Japanese Beaters—A good Stag—A miss—"Such things will happen"—Effects of Slug—An Afternoon Stalk—Deer going down stream—Dog and Deer—A good Head—Inland Sea in May—Harvesting Operations—Flowers and Trees—A slice of hill swept away by water—The Bingo Nada—An Island Deer-Preserve cleared—Hime Sima—Straits of Simonosaki—Obliging our Neighbour—Our Squadron in the Straits—The Street of Simonosaki—Gardens—Houses—Candlemaking—Trade—Rice cultivation—Snakes and Frogs—Hirado—A cover for Deer—A grand sight
Pages 37-63

CHAPTER III.

CURRENTS AND TYPHOONS.

The "Kuro Siwo" or Black Stream—Course of the Warm Currents—Climate of South-East Nipon—In the North—Erratic movements of "Kuro Siwo"—Its effects upon Navigation before Lighthouses were erected—Excellence of the Lighthouse Department—The cold Current—Its Course—Colour and Temperature—Meeting of the cold and warm Currents—Missing the port—Where could the place be ?—A Dilemma—A chase, and capture of a Pilot—Forty miles south of our Reckoning—Now easily accounted for—The Cold Current rich in animal life—Probable bifurcation of the Great Arctic Current—A pleasant change from the Mackau Group—From

the Kuril Islands to the Coast of Korea—Comparatively new
ground for Dredging—Overfalls and Tide-rips—An excited
Captain—Course of Typhoons in Japanese waters—Effects on
the Kii Peninsula—Body of the Storm follows the stream—
Typhoons easily foretold—The Barometer—Other warnings
—If Port cannot be reached, get well away from coast—A
good ship badly managed—Storms frequently travel in pairs—
A Beach after a Storm—The vitreous Sponge—The *Camilla*
lost in a Typhoon—Dangerous in running before the wind—
Sailing in a circle—Average speed of the Storm—A friendly
Typhoon—Probable thickness—Horizontal diameter of a
Cyclone . . . . Pages 64-80

CHAPTER IV.

DEER-SHOOTING AND OTHER MATTERS.

Cervus Sika abundant in North and South—Grasses—Size of
Antlers—Hunters' mode of luring—Damage done by the
Deer—The Hunter of the Old School and of the New—Kingkosan—Shrine—The Modern Priest—Deer plentiful—Best
mode of working the Coverts—A Day's Sport among the
Kobe Hills—Pheasants—Deer—Various kinds of Trees—
Keenness of Spaniel after Deer—Hind and Fawn—Native
Dogs—Keenness of Scent—Their Silence and Tenacity—Terror
of Deer—Swimming Powers of Deer—Wild Boar and Badger
—The Japanese Fox—The tables turned—The Nigou—Diffi-
cult to find—Horns generally broken—Young Nigou cap-
tured—Its Fierceness—A true Antelope—Birds—White-
tailed, white-headed Eagle—Falcon and Snipe—Water-Ouzel
—House-Martin—Sparrow—Lark—Crow—Its Familiarity—
Wildness of Birds outside the Town—Arctic Goose—Man-

darin Ducks—Harlequin Garrot—Robin—Bullfinch and **Wren**—Blue Crane—Kingfisher—Pheasants—Pigeon—**Gulls**—Finches   Pages 81-108

CHAPTER V.

A WALK IN KIUSIU.

Morning in the Village—Snakes—Cottage in the Valley—Trouts in the Well—The Maiden—Green Pheasants and Pigeons—Butterflies and Flowers—Bewildered Hare—Trout Stream—Large Camphor Tree—Mulberry Shrubs—Wax Tree—Adders—White Storks—Comfort—Swallows and Tomtits—Pack-bullocks and Ponies—An unlucky spill—Sulphur Bath—Pines—Resin-collecting—Girls early set to work—The "Red Bird"—"Alcedo"—Evening—A Fisherman at work   .   .   Pages 109-122

CHAPTER VI.

THE KII COAST.

The Kii Coast—Its Extent and Character—Towns and Villages—Whaling—Mode of Capture—Whale's Flesh as Food—Katzura Mineral springs: extremely efficacious—Marvellous Cure—Katzura Waterfall—Cedar and Camphor Avenue—Matoya Harbour—Wonderful locality for Game—Ospreys—Their mode of carrying Fish—Edible Seaweed—Women Divers—Winter Months on the Kii Coast—Earthquakes—Mountains—Odai Yama—Wild Boar and Deer—Excursion to Odai Yama—Character of the Ascent—First night's halt—A good Trout stream—The Honey-bee—A nice Bath-house—

Second day and Third day—Bear and Nigou—Beautiful View—Charm of Atmosphere—Puzzled Wolf—Oaks and Chestnuts—Four days' Observations—Birds and Beasts on the Mountains—Courtesy of the People—Temples—Beauty of the Miniature Gardens—Houses of the poor invariably clean—Children's Games—Baby Nurses—Baby Mortality—The strong ones survive—A young Smoker—Effects of Civilisation—Gentle Manners of the Natives disappear under the bad influence of Western Nations — Missionaries — Roman Catholics and Protestants—Forests of the Kii Coast—One species of Deer—Four kinds of Snipe—Pheasants—Osprey—Falcon and Sea Eagle—Sheep—Kindly act   Pages 123-149

CHAPTER VII.

INSECTS.

Insects—Little Blood-suckers—A troublesome Fly—Spider's Web—Hornets and their Nests—Centipedes—Mosquitoes — Horse-Fly— Ant-Lion — Pit, and mode of capturing his prey — Tree Frog — Salamander — Fossil Elephant's Tooth   .   .   .   Pages 150-159

CHAPTER VIII.

SHOOTING, ETC.

A day's sport in Yesso—Bamboo Grass—Good Cover for Big Game—Can it be a Bear?—Waiting for Duck—Otter attacking Retriever—Twilight—Flight of Birds—A white patch on the Muzzle—Wood Grouse—A good country for Black

Cock and Capercailzie—Dense Brake-fern covers—Watch-houses—Wild Boar—Damage done to crops—Savage native Ponies . . . . Pages 160-170

CHAPTER IX.

SINGING-BIRDS AND FLOWERS, ETC.

A Proverb—Singing Birds in the Goto Islands—Warblers—Hedge Sparrow—Scarcity of Song-Birds—Pursuit of a Bear—Pursuit of a Bear interrupted by the Queen of the Primroses—Lily of the Valley—Magnolia-tree—Beautiful White Lily—Jasmine—Lotos—Camellia-trees—Grafting—Violets—Miniature Gardens—Chrysanthemums—Fruits—Women—Stature of the race . . . . . . Pages 171-182

CHAPTER X.

JAPANESE CUSTOMS AND HABITS, ETC.

The Japanese an unromantic people—A solitary exception—Marriage Ceremony—Polygamy—Truthfulness—Kindness—Domestic Animals—Treatment of Children—The Governor's Present—Whale's flesh—A delicate Pickle—Buddhist Temple—Shintoism—Yamato—Professional singing-girls—Opposite ways of doing things: Sandpaper and Saws—Open-air Toilets—Baths—Hairdressing—Cleanliness—Games—Archery—Tobacco—Tea—Love of Art—Education—Toys and Fish—Duck-hunting . . . . . Pages 183-201

CHAPTER XI.

PAST AND PRESENT.

Harbour Regulations in 1855—Action at Kagosima—A Friend in need—A consultation in the cabin—A run down the

coast—An honest Landlady—English Books and European Fashions—Kindness of the country people—Taxing in kind and taxing in money—The great Nobles' change of life —Their slavish imitation of European costume—The Empress—Entertainment given by the Prince of Kii—A Day's Shooting in a Preserve—Courtesy and Manner of the People—Bathing Arrangements—Natives—Corrupted by Foreigners—Picnics—Tea-houses—Fare—Quarrels—Burials and Burial-places—Feasts—Population—Mortality—No Lunatic Asylums nor Poor-houses—Diseases—Endurance— Children—Reservoirs—Houses—Domestic Fowls—Moderation—Sobriety—A jovial Priest—Missions and Missionaries —The Romish Priest—Protestant Missionaries—Drunkenness and Civilisation—Evil effects of European example
Pages 202-234

CHAPTER XII.

KOREA.

Korea, Russian—An inhospitable reception—The *Sylvia* sent to the Korea—Chosan—A couple of hours' sport—A new bay —An official visit—Surveying under difficulties—A missing Boat—An effective interruption to the Survey—The return of the Boat, and return to Head-quarters—Re-ordered to Korea—The South-west Corner—Surveying under Arms—A polite old Man—A native House—Absence of Temples, etc. —Women—Roughness of the People—Mackau Islands— Scarcity of animal life—Seals at sea and Rats on shore—The Inhabitants, Cattle, Harbour, and Coasts—Goto Islands— An old Christian Colony—A legendary submerged Island— Goatsucker—Swifts—Japanese Nightingale—Nosaki Sima —Difficulty in obtaining Quarters—The obliging Widow
Pages 235-255

CHAPTER XIII.

EXTRACTS FROM JOURNAL.

Kobe—New Year's day—Sozu Sima Peak—Akashi—Tango Sango—Kobe—"The Bear is in your cabin, Sir"—Ape-Foot-marks—Spring—Larks—Mallard and Teal—Violets—Ospreys—Thrush—Woodcock—Bay-tree—Oosima—Awasi Bay—Honest Woman—Osprey's Nest and Eggs—Crested Seal—Taskara Ura—People very poor—Snipe and Mallard—Colony for Vegetables—Buddhist Temples—Toba—Heronry—Ominato—Great Elm-tree—Rich Plain—Number of Osprey Nests—Turtle—Sudden Dip—Barley—Wheat—Rice—Gulls—Brown *Corvus Japonicus*—Women Divers—Spider-crab—Simonosaki—Yuyo Sima Rice-fields—Sandpipers—Pheasants—Plovers—Women and girls on the rocks—Seagulls, etc.—Tsu Sima—Scarlet Kingfisher—Korean Books and People—Inquisitive Crows—Heron—Eagle—Crichton Harbour—Goto Isles—Simonosaki—Rice Junks—Hirosima—Deer Preserve—Wild Boar—Bullfinch—Moon Temple—A Large Deer—Bamboo Plantations—Matoya—Toba—Handicapped tide-watcher . . . . . Pages 256-277

CHAPTER XIV.

CRUISING AFTER PIRATES.

Coast Line in 1864—Hainan—A passage to Swatow interrupted—Eighty-two Passengers and Crew flung overboard—A Boy saved—The Pirates arrested—A narrow Escape—Raising a Blockade—A Capture—The Governor and the Pirates—Tender Mercies—Laughable Incident—Junks and Pirates handed over—Mode of Decapitation—A favourite haunt of

Pirates—A Missionary Priest—An uncomfortable **Neighbour**
—An Ambush—A Bag of Game—A Silent Village—**The
Tiger's Promenade**—News—Under weigh—The Creek—A
Trap and a lucky Escape—A Charge, **and the scuffle well
over**—A Clipper Tea-ship **in** danger—On **the track—An
honest or a pirate** Junk ?—A Capture **and** Disappointment—
Suspected Bribery — Tienpak — A luxurious **Mandarin** —
" Would you like to have us **on** board the Gun-boat ?"—**To**
Nowchow and Hainan—A tiger's footprint—Every Bullet,
etc. . . . . Pages 278-302

CHAPTER XV.

SHOOTING IN CHINA.

Sou-chow Creek—Pheasants in Streams, and Snipe in every Swamp
—A good load for a Blue-jacket—Cormorant-fishing—Game
sent from China to Japan—An Admiral's Sport—Snipe-shooting—An old Sportsman—Orange-legged Partridge—A Sporting Expedition—Friend or Foe!—" Gipsy, ahoy!"—Frog-
fishing—Shooting on the Canton River—A tempting bit **of**
Mud—Some disagreeables of Chinese Shooting-grounds
Pages 303-320

CHAPTER XVI.

MORE CRUISING AFTER PIRATES.

Brigantine attacked—Abduction of **three Girls—Tooni-ang—The**
Headmen made responsible—The judicious effect of the Rope
—The Girls rescued—The New Year—" Puckshui"—Fifteen
Junks—**A** hasty Retreat—Unexpected relief—Charging a
Battery—A fresh Fleet—Friends—The Mandarin's Force, and
how it fared—Macao to Puckshui—Grounded—A coming
Storm—Running **before the Breeze—The last** Shot—A Cap-

ture—Quang-tung Province—Difficulties in sailing among the Islands—Anchored during a Typhoon—Driving on the Rocks—The Gun-boat moves up to her anchors—"The Mother of Winds"—How the Chinese know of its approach—Xavier's Tombstone . . . . . . Pages 321-340

CHAPTER XVII.

THE SAME, AND A FEW INCIDENTS WHICH HAPPENED IN THE LAST CHINA WAR.

Threats from Puckshui and punishments—A great Expedition, and how they managed it—A Charge by a Marine and a Blue-jacket—Why Piracy is practised with impunity—An East Coast Cruise—A successful Ruse—Chinamen no cowards—Female Children exposed—A Ship's pet—Guns and Junks taken during twenty months' time—Regulations at Hong-Kong—Some Incidents of the War of 1856-58—An exciting Trip between Hong-Kong and Canton—A plucky Captain—War Junks in pursuit—Twenty minutes under fire, and well peppered—The Skipper's wrath, and my own Captain's fears . . . . . Pages 341-361

CHAPTER XVIII.

RÉSUMÉ . . Pages 362-384

APPENDIX.

The *Fauna* of Japan . .	Page 387
List of Birds	. 388

LIST OF ILLUSTRATIONS.

ACTION AT KAGOSIMA—*Frontispiece.*

EAGLE'S NEST, YESSO (*Vignette in Title-page, engraved by Amand Durand of Paris*).

AWA SIMA, INLAND SEA	*Page* ix
AINO WOMAN CARRYING CHILD	x
ENTRANCE TO HAMANAKA, YESSO	1
YESSO EAGLE	7
TWO VOLCANOES IN YESSO 8000 FEET HIGH	*to face p.* 18
AINO MAN	20
AINO WOMAN	21
PERPENDICULAR ROCKS, TWO HUNDRED FEET HIGH	36
A FISHERMAN'S HOME, KALANGO ISLAND, INLAND SEA	37
MAP, INLAND SEA	*to face p.* 44
SMALL VILLAGE, INLAND SEA	*to face p.* 52
INLAND SEA FROM THE SOUTH	63

LIST OF ILLUSTRATIONS.

Hornet Rock, Sea of Japan	Page 64
Hind (Cervus Sika)	81
Nigou, Japanese Chamois	96
Scarlet Kingfisher	105
Osprey's Nest in Sutherland, Scotland	108
Do. Do. Taskara Ura, Japan	108
Mutsu	109
Japanese Gentleman	122
Awasi Bay, Kii Coast	123
Matoya Harbour, Kii Coast	126
Map—Kii Coast	to face p. 128
Middy's Tomb in Japanese Burial-ground	149
Roadside Temple—Kii Coast	150
Antlers from South Japan	160
Home of the Nigou, near Awasi Bay	170
Flower Vase	171
Mode of Sleeping, or Japanese Pillow	183
Palanquin	202
Japan	234
Map of Korea	to face p. 234
Stag's Head	235
South Entrance to Sylvia Basin, Korea	to face p. 238

LIST OF ILLUSTRATIONS.   xxiii

Goto Isles, from Hira Sima	Page 250
House in Korea visited	255
Flying Gull	256
Gull (*Larus crassirostris*)	277
Caught Napping	278
Map—Coast of China	to face p. 279
A Trap	290
Capture at Tooni-ang Island	303
Returning to Hong Kong with Three Pirates	284
Entrance to Long Harbour, Mirs Bay	321
The Last Shot	332
Xavier's Tomb	340
Chase and Capture	341
China	361
Homeward Bound	362
Entrance to Nagasaki Harbour	to face p. 370
H.M.S. "Sylvia"	384
Rock in Awasi Bay	386
Eagle's Nest, Kunashir	392
Map of Japan	to face p. 392

CHAPTER I.

ROUND YESSO.

THE ISLAND of Yesso is very little known to Europeans. The Japanese themselves until late years paid scarcely any attention to it.

I first visited Hakodadi in 1855, again in 1863, and now once more in 1871; the place had changed very little. The population had increased from about 6000 to 10,000 in seventeen years. Export trade was chiefly confined to deers' horns and seaweed, both commodities finding a market in China. The former is much relied on by the Chinese as a medicine capable of curing all ailments; the latter as food. I have often used it as a substitute for jelly, and although it certainly requires a good deal of flavouring, with this addition it is exceedingly nice.

I reached Hakodadi towards the latter end of April, and winter was then only breaking up. The hills were white, and snow still lay about in great patches on the plains. Wild geese were plentiful, but only as passers-by, wending their way north; some of the white-fronted I killed were in excellent condition. On the 3d of May the snow had disappeared very much. Bulbous plants and wild vetches were shooting, and large arums and other succulent plants showed their fresh green leaves in every damp corner. The house-martins were busy at their old nests in the Japanese houses, and numerous other birds were pairing.

Two days afterwards I left for the eastward, reaching Cape Yerimo, a remarkable rocky point, the following morning. On the large boulders and smooth rocks which jut out from the cape half a mile into the sea, was a colony of sea-lions. Never before, I suppose, had these great beasts been visited by man; and as I pulled in amongst them, the big bulls kept up a continual roar of indignation; otherwise they appeared in no way concerned at the intrusion. I passed quietly along within a few feet of the rocks on which they lay. Some of the females slipped off into the water, but the old males merely raised their great heads, stared with their great eyes, and roared. As I was watching and admiring these **creatures, a couple of high-finned cachalots came slowly** along, straight towards us, their great scythe-like backfin making graceful curves as they appeared and disappeared under the water. They took no notice whatever of the boat, but passed immediately under it, and I was relieved to see the huge creature rise clear of us a few yards ahead. The water was very deep, right up to the rocks, and beautifully clear, and I could see quite distinctly the huge black mass under the boat; they were evidently feeding, and probably searching for cuttle-fish close along the rocks, which is a favourite food amongst many of the whale tribe. I never came across this particular kind of whale except off the eastern coasts of Yesso, but there they are plentiful. When feeding, or in an undisturbed state, they come constantly to the surface; their great backfin then shows most conspicuously, and I often judged it quite eight feet in length when the animal was about thirty. I have called it the high-finned cachalot (*Physeter tursio*), because it resembles no other species.

The cold arctic stream which rounds the extreme

east cape of the island (Noyshap) flows along the shore to the west as far as Yerimo, after which its influence is not perceptible. The contrary stream of warm water, a portion of the equatorial current which passes through the Korean Straits into the Sea of Japan, and from there branches to the eastward through the Tsuga Strait, reaches Cape Yerimo, where these sea-lions congregate; this cape therefore becomes the blending point of the two streams. Probably this was the reason why these animals congregated here. At any rate I met with them nowhere else. On the 8th we reached Akishi Bay, the only real harbour in the east of Yesso. The bay runs inland for about five miles, and a ship can anchor anywhere throughout, but except right at the head, or in the south-west corner, it is open to the ocean swell. Here I found a settlement of 40 Japanese and 160 Ainos. Seaweed, deers' horns, and fish were collected; the latter being boiled down for manure, and sent to the rice districts in the south, where it is valued by the farmers for their crops. A narrow channel at the very head of the bay connects it with a large lagoon; at the north-west corner of it a river enters. This lagoon, with its numerous dry patches and low grassy islets, was the rendezvous of immense numbers of ducks and waders. Oyster-catchers were busily breeding. I found their eggs surrounded with frozen snow. Ten species of duck, and a few swans and geese, still remained, as if loath to leave this favourite winter resort. I shot one swan, which proved to be *Cygnus musicus,* and excellent eating it was. Numerous skeletons of this bird lay scattered round the margin of the lagoon; **they had been killed by the Ainos for** their downy skins, which were used as part of their winter dress. In exploring the country at the **head of the** lagoon and for some distance up **the river's bank,** I found a solitary Aino living by himself at a part of the river where others of his tribe usually crossed when passing to and fro from the interior. The grass hut this lonely being lived in was filled with the most extraordinary mixture of things possible to imagine. Dried deer's flesh, skins and robes **of the same animal,** horns, fishing-lines made of birch bark, swan's wings, and odds and ends of skins, etc. etc., strewed the ground for some distance round his hut. This aboriginal savage was most polite. He took me out in his log canoe, after some swans which were feeding in the river, saluted my retriever most profoundly, and offered the dog some dried flesh to eat. "Pat" was a source of extreme **wonder** to this queer hairy being, and I shall never forget the expression of the dog's face at being addressed by him.

The country about here is a perfect wilderness of

impenetrable forest, growing on a succession of low hills, the small valleys between being swampy, and thickly covered with rushes, alder, and stunted birch. I shot a couple of spruce grouse, the only birds of the kind I ever saw, not only in Yesso, but anywhere in the East.

I left a party of officers and men to survey the locality, and went on to the eastward, reaching Hamanaka, an anchorage, the same evening. A couple of islands, lying off a deep bend of the coast-line, form this harbour. Here we found another small settlement of Japanese, with about double their number of Ainos. Seaweed collecting, as at Akishi, was their business. Long rank grass covered the islands, with a few stunted, straggling fir-trees. The creeks and sheltered nooks about the rocky shores were swarming with duck. Foxes walked about quite at home and fearlessly. Seals played and fished in the quiet pools, under the cliffs, and seagulls in large numbers revelled in perfect security on the long sandy beach which stretched away to the westward from both islands. On two grass-covered rocky points of the biggest island I found eagles breeding; both nests had a single young one, and in one was an egg. I sat down close to the nest with the magnificent old birds wheeling round my head, the female only a few yards off, but the male kept at a safe distance, only occasionally swooping down within shot. They were in perfect plumage, with the head, upper part of neck, and tail, quite white. Remains of wild-duck covered the ground for many yards round the nest, and my retriever, being enticed to sniff at this débris, was immediately attacked by the female bird, and had a very narrow escape from going over the cliff, which bounded one side of the point.

After examining and fixing the position of this anchorage, we made another start for the eastward, rounding Cape Noyshap, the extreme of the island, and then turning back to the west, kept along the shore until we reached a good anchorage behind an island called Nemero. Here again was a small Japanese settlement, with the usual number of Ainos collected round them. The settlements, although close together, are always distinct from each other. The Japanese despise and keep in most strict subjection and ignorance the unfortunate Ainos, who do by far the greatest portion of the work which these settlements are formed for, collecting seaweed, fish, or deers' horns. They receive no pay in money, but are allowed a certain amount of rice and tea, and some cotton stuff for clothing.

To the eastward of Cape Noyshap several islands extend out twenty miles from the mainland of Yesso. They are the undisturbed homes of albatross, seals, divers, and numbers of waders, none being inhabited by man.

It was the middle of May when we reached Nemero, but the weather was still wintry. Snow lay about in heaps, and on the 19th a heavy fall took place, covering the country to a depth of nine inches. On the 24th, immense masses of floating ice appeared in the straits between Yesso and Kunashir, the southernmost of the Kuril Islands. On the 1st of June the mountain range running to the north-east was white, and at the water's edge snow still lay here and there in patches. The temperature of the water at the surface and bottom was only $36°\cdot 5$. Gales from the eastward were constant, and dense fogs very prevalent. Such was the weather at the beginning of June in the eastern part of the island. By the 13th of the month a great change had taken place, summer had commenced. The buds had burst, the first flowers were showing, succulent grass had sprung up, and the early trees were green in a few days. The transition from almost winter to the first flush of summer was very sudden. On account, however, of the ever-occurring fogs, the sun's rays seldom reached the earth, and in consequence the warmth it receives is comparatively slight. None of the few seeds which the Japanese had sown or endeavoured to cultivate came to anything. The whole country is almost entirely covered with primeval forest, which is chiefly stunted oak and birch. The only tree which appeared to flourish and reach perfection, was the *Pinus jessoniensis*, a grand and lovely species. In the few open glades, single trees, and clumps of half a dozen or so, grew to perfection.

The object of the Japanese settlement here is to collect and cure the hard roe of the herring, and boil down for manure the rest of the fish. In May and June this fish appears in incredible numbers. The straits, bays, and creeks appear alive with them. They are in such numbers, that those nearest the beach are pushed out of the water, and the shore for miles is thus kept constantly replenished with fresh fish; countless numbers of seagulls, eagles, crows, besides foxes, wolves, and bears, find an ever ready meal; and the way the seagulls just picked the tit-bit from the back of the neck, and left the remainder of the fish, showed how well they knew the supply was constant. The Japanese simply ran a net straight out from the shore, 150 or 200 yards along a line of stakes; at the end of the net is a bag, which the fish, on striking the net and working along it, soon find their way into. When required, the fishermen only have to go off, haul the bag up, and opening the end let the fish fall into their boat. This species of herring is both larger and coarser than our own. The temperature of the water in which they appear to flourish to such an extraordinary degree averages 36°, whereas that in which our own fish is found averages 54° to 58°. Salmon are not common at Nemero, nor elsewhere in the east of the island; and they do not enter the rivers until August. Flat fish are very plentiful.

The large snipe *Gallinago australis* was busily breeding in June. It was most interesting to watch these birds flying about during the day, sometimes perching on the dead trees, again wheeling round at a great height, then suddenly swooping down, making a loud drumming noise with their wings. All this time, except when actually in their swoop, they keep up a constant note, like chuck-chuck-chuck. After watching this bird carefully many and many a time, I consider that the drumming noise is made by the rapid vibrations of the wings. Different species of wild-duck and waders were breeding in the small lochs, well away from the coast. I numbered forty-eight different species of birds in June at this place. Most, if not all, of these must have been breeding. Seals were very plentiful, and fearless. They swam about the anchorage and close to the ship quite unconcernedly.

The large brown bear of Yesso is a frequent visitor to the beach at night. Some of their tracks I measured were 14 inches by 10. Unfortunately I never could come across one of those animals. In fact, without dogs it is a mere chance doing so; their sense of hearing and scent being so keen, enables them to slip away on the near approach of danger, long before the cover which they are probably in is entered.

In the end of May I crossed the **narrow strait of** water separating Yesso from Kunashir, the most southerly of the Kuril Islands. The south part of this island is a wilderness of forest and swamp, the resort of bears, wolves, foxes, and several species of martin. On the 25th of May, immense masses of floating ice blocked the bay where the ship was anchored. Thousands of the scaup and velvet scoter, besides albatross, divers, and seals, appeared at the same time. It was very amusing to watch two of the raven-like crows (*Corvus japonensis*), which in the afternoon regularly flew off to the ship. Such a thing they had evidently never seen before, and lighting on the rigging, the two birds would earnestly converse in their own way as they looked down on us; turning their heads so as to search with their sharp eyes every nook and corner on deck. After remaining about the ship for some time, away on shore they would fly, returning next day about the same time. Similar instances of this bird coming off to the ship I had often observed at other places. In one spot where I frequently anchored, a pair of pied wagtails regularly flew on board, and in a perfectly fearless manner hunted the flies about the deck, the cock bird every now and then flying into the rigging, where he would perch for ten minutes or so, singing very prettily.

In the north part of Kunashir Island the sea-otter is common. I shot here the grey plover (*Vanellus griseus*) in perfect summer plumage, and I have no doubt the bird was then breeding. Sea-trout were in the small rivers, and river-trout appeared to flourish in every tiny stream. Herrings of course abounded. The business of the small Japanese settlement on the island, as at Nemero, is to cure the hard roe. Amongst the great numbers of seals everywhere about, both here and in Yesso, I never saw more than one species, which I considered to be *Phoca vitulina*. On the low flat point which, running out four miles, formed the eastern boundary of the bay, stood a single colossal stem of a dead fir-tree, having still two great arms which forked out about thirty feet from the ground. In this fork was an eagle's nest, and judging from the mass of sticks which in repeated layers formed the nest, the birds must have been at work on it for years. I had not the heart to shoot one of the noble birds, which were busily employed rearing their young, but afterwards I regretted not having procured a specimen in the perfect adult plumage.

I only observed thirty different species of birds at this place, but my time was short, as I had to return to Nemero. Excepting in the valleys, the trees were all small; by far the greater portion reach only about twenty feet in height, the tops being either twisted off or broken and bent down. The whole face of the country has the appearance of being swept by strong south-easterly winds. The northern species of albatross, so common about here, breeds, I should think, on some of the low flat islands to the east of Yesso. The young, I believe, are of a blue-black colour, with a flesh-coloured bill; and although I have seen this bird through every month of the year, I never observed one in an intermediate state between the black young bird and the pure white, black-pinioned, buff-necked mature one. Kunashir is an island full of interest to the naturalist, but the climate is far too rigorous for cultivation. The same may be said of the east of Yesso. The temperature of the sea in the hottest month, August, was only 38°, and in June and July a few degrees lower. The cold stream from Behring's Straits flows down along the line of the Kuril Islands, and, washing the north-east and eastern shores of Yesso, is the primary cause of the low temperature and the constant fogs during summer. On ascending the highest hills, which about Nemero or Akishi are not above 300 feet in height, I have, even in that distance or height, got above the dense fog and enjoyed bright sunshine, and on one occasion I did so by only going to the ship's masthead! On leaving Nemero I followed the north-east coast-line of the island for 400 miles before reaching any shelter or anchorage.

Remaining a day or two where a small number of Ainos and Japanese were settled, I went for a long ramble through the oak forests, seeing great numbers of deer. My coxswain, who was a few hundred yards to my right, came across a bear in a tree; he fired a charge of slug at him, which only seemed to tickle the beast, which got down the tree as fast as he could and made off.

A propos of these animals: the Ainos keep the young

ones in cages until they are a year old, then at a great feast they eat them.

Returning from my walk, I exchanged an old pair of trousers for a cub about as large as a big spaniel. The little beast was brought down to the beach by an Aino woman, who, tying it to a post, squatted beside it and began to weep most profusely. Inquiring the reason for such grief, I was told she had brought it up from a very small thing, when its mother was caught and killed in the spring, and that she had suckled it as one of her own children until it was able to manage for itself. This mode of rearing the cub when quite young I afterwards found was quite a common occurrence. It took four of my blue-jackets to secure and carry the cub to the boat, which was not done without many scratches and bites. For two days I kept her tied up, then allowed her to go loose, with a short piece of rope round her neck. For a week or so she took every opportunity of slipping overboard and swimming for the shore. Afterwards she never attempted to do so, but became perfectly happy and playful. On hot summer days she regularly enjoyed a swim round the ship, and would then remain in the screw well, stretched on the bango frame, during the heat of the day. In a year's time she was so large and powerful that I feared mischief might happen, and I therefore gave her a dose of strychnine.

Before leaving Nemero, I see in my notes that on the last day of May I found a sweet-scented little clustering primrose of a most delicate pink colour, also a blue species of foxglove, and that lilies of the valley were shooting through the earth. Raspberries and strawberries, though only of small size, were plentiful; and amongst a few other flowers, a sweet-scented rose grew on the sandy hillocks along the shore.

Oteranai, a settlement on the west coast, is the only other place worth mentioning. Here there is good anchorage, and the country round presents an excellent scope for agricultural enterprise. The Iskari, the largest river in Yesso, enters the sea about fifteen miles north-east of the settlement. For some miles up the river, the bank, in places, and on one side, is prepared for salmon fishing. Long drying-sheds, with a house for the fishermen to live in, are erected just above the artificially sloped banks. The seine used has the bag attached by a slip-line, and on its coming on shore full of fish, is thus easily and quickly slipped off, and another put on immediately. In this way no time is lost. It was the end of July when I visited the river, and no signs of the commencement of fishing were visible. I was told, and from my own observation believe it to be correct, that not until the end of August do the salmon enter the river, and from then until the beginning of November, when the fishing ceases, 6000 tons of salmon are caught and salted on this few miles of river.[1] There are many fabulous stories regarding the quantity of fish that go up the rivers,—that their backs are visible, and that the water rises along the banks as the first rush takes place over the bar at high tide. I believe, however, that there is no doubt about the quantity being correct which I have mentioned as being caught and cured in the short space of time given.

Regarding the agricultural prospects of this southwest part of Yesso, owing to the average moderate temperature, I think almost anything would grow well; but as to the eastern parts of the island, on account of the

[1] This appears an extraordinary quantity of salmon to be caught in such a short time, and in a very limited extent of a single river; but I took great pains to ascertain the correctness of my statement. It is the only river in Yesso that is systematically worked, and actually supplies the whole of Japan with this fish. Not a village that I ever went through, either in the north or south, was at any season of the year without its salted salmon. It is universally a great article of food. When I was at anchor surveying Oteranai, the port from which the Iskari fish are shipped, I counted one day more than two hundred large junks start in a body for southern ports, all laden with salmon. A hundred and more junks remained at anchor waiting for their cargo. This alone bore out the enormous amount of fish that are taken. It must also be remembered that the fleet of junks I thus counted was only a single start, and that many more of such magnitude take place in the season.

very low average temperature, nothing I believe would repay the labour of cultivation and sowing. The cause of this great difference of climate in the east and west of the island is very easily accounted for. The warm equatorial stream, with an almost uniform temperature of 58° to 60°, washes the western shores. The cold arctic current, with its low maximum temperature of 38°, embraces all the eastern part, and not only is the cause of this low temperature for the latitude, 44°, but is also the cause of the constant fog during the summer months, which always takes place when the warm southeasterly wind blowing up from the tropics, and charged with vapour, comes in contact with the cold water. I experienced no real summer in the eastern parts of Yesso. The high land had always snow on it. About three days in a month at most were clear of fog. Gales from all quarters were frequent, and I was told that the straits between Yesso and Kunashir are well frozen across early in the winter.

There are several localities where coal is found on the island. I tried some from the Iwani mine on the west coast, but found it wretchedly bad. The fault of nearly all Japanese coal, I have been told by geologists, is, it is too young. Good timber is abundant in Yesso; amongst deciduous trees, numerous species

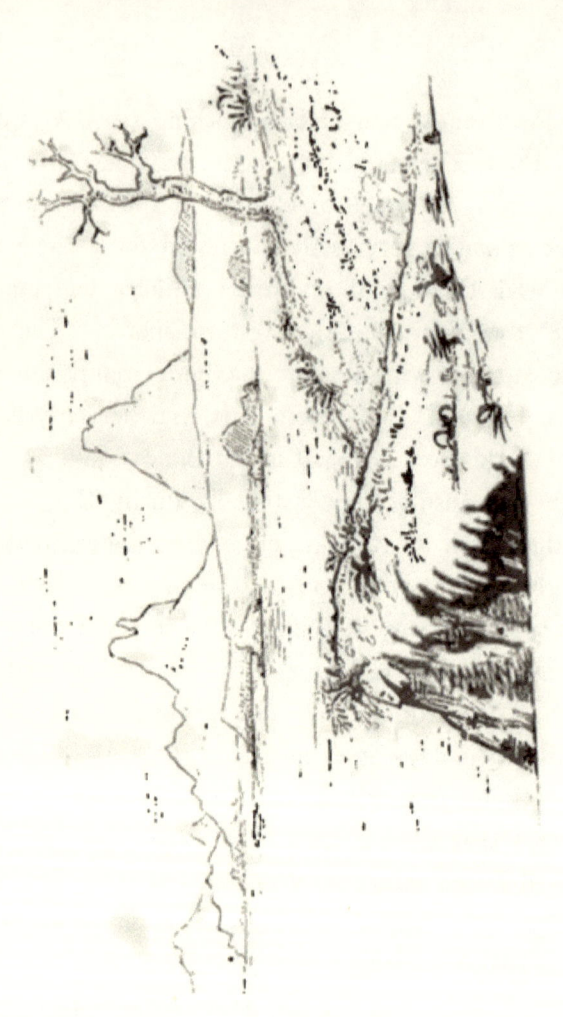

of oak, are prominent; and regarding pines, the *Pinus jessoniensis*, which I have mentioned elsewhere, is certainly a prince of trees.

I must now say something more about the Ainos, the aborigines of Yesso. In days gone by they inhabited the north part of Nipon, as well as Yesso; possibly, going still further back, the whole of Japan. At what date they were driven out of Nipon across the Tsuga Straits I know not. Now at any rate they are only found in Yesso, Saghalien, and the Kuril Islands. I much doubt whether there are any in the interior of Yesso. The Japanese settlements round the coast have pretty well drawn them to these centres, where, although worked and treated much as slaves, they are partially clothed and fed, and not unkindly or harshly dealt with. The race is, I believe, decreasing, and will in all probability become extinct before many generations pass.

In the settlements they live quite distinct from the Japanese. Money they never receive, and a strong objection was always shown to our giving them any thing, even in exchange for deers' heads, etc., and particularly so regarding money. In height, the men average from five feet two to five feet four inches, the women under five feet. Both sexes are spare, light and wiry, stout muscular development being rare, fatness still more so. Men and women do the same work, and seem equally capable of undergoing exposure and toil. The colour of their skin is a copper hue with an olive tint; this with almost constant uniformity, both in the north and south. Occasionally a darker-skinned man appeared, but never a woman. The children vary very little from the parents; their skin had perhaps a cleaner

appearance. Their features are regular and good, and in expression decidedly pleasing; they have neither the high cheek-bone nor oblique upper eyelid peculiar to the Mongolian family. Very many of their faces were certainly intelligent. Their temples are flat; foreheads broad, square, and high; arch of the head flat; entire head round and well-shaped; their lips are full, but not particularly so, eyes very dark, eyebrows straight, and parallel to the axis of the orbits. Their most peculiar characteristic is their hair, which is very coarse, black, long, and straight, and in great profusion in both sexes. The men wear long flowing beards and moustaches. Their entire body is invariably covered with hair, and very frequently to an extraordinary degree. The children are also hairy little things. Few reach the age of fifty; probably the hard, exposed life they lead is the chief cause of this low standard. The women appear to pass from girls into old women almost without any intermediate state; marrying very young, and their life afterwards being a very hard one, soon brings about premature old age. The women wear their great mass of hair flung back over their head and tied behind; ornamentation is not neglected  when they manage to get a few pieces of coloured glass, blue cloth, or beads. The glass is stuck into a band, and on great occasions worn round the head, while with the cloth they trim the collars and cuffs of their deer-skin robes. Great massive ear-rings are also worn by some of them. Besides trimming their deer-skin robe with blue cloth, they work patterns on their other single and simple dress made of the birch bark. The women only tattoo, and this in two ways. On the upper lip of the little girls a small patch of tattooing is seen, which is gradually added to until they marry, when the finishing touch is put to it in the shape of a sharp point on the cheek; the mark then resembles a moustache turned up into a fine point on the face. The other mode consists in marking rings round the arm, commencing at the wrist and working up to the elbow. I think these rings mark certain periods of time, but I never was able to find out for certain what they really meant. As a rule, these people are excessively dirty in their persons. I doubt if they ever wash themselves, and in consequence skin-disease is very prevalent amongst them. In every settlement some are sure to be seen who have lost all the hair from the head. Lime in a state of paste is smeared over the head as a curative, and I daresay this helps to destroy the hair. Small-pox occasionally makes its appearance on the island, generally brought by the Japanese trading to the settlements. The Ainos immediately disperse into the interior when this dreaded disorder reaches them, and break up into small bands until it is over and past. Fish is their chief food; rice and saki (spirits) have both been introduced by the Japanese. During summer and spring a bulbous grass is collected and eaten. I believe this to be the only native plant so used; it shows however that, like other races low in the scale of humanity, they are not indifferent to the benefit derived from esculent plants.

During winter, when fishing is interrupted, or wholly at a stand-still, deer's flesh is resorted to for food. Quantities of these animals are also killed, when the snow lies thick on the ground, merely for their horns. In spring the hinds are persecuted for the unborn fawn, which is considered a dainty dish by Japanese epicures. The price of deers' horns **a few years ago** at Hakodadi was three dollars **for 133 lbs.**, the same quantity or weight selling for forty dollars at Shanghai. *Now* the 133 lbs. is bought for six dollars and sold for nine.

The Ainos' original weapon was the bow and arrow; at the present day, with few exceptions, it remains the same. The bow is about three feet long, **the arrow** twenty inches; they are tipped with a poisoned, hard, spoon-shaped piece of bamboo, bone, or iron. The poison is prepared from the brains of the crow, the ashes of tobacco, and two insects named **yousiki and krombi**; the latter is found in water, attached to stones or sticks. These four ingredients, being mixed together and allowed to become putrid, are then fit for use. Another poison used is a preparation of the deadly nightshade. The Ainos are a good-natured, kind, and obliging people, and always appeared glad to see us strangers; they are neither rude nor inquisitive; on the contrary, they invariably saluted us in meeting. The mode of salutation is far more ceremonious than might be expected amongst such primitive beings. They drop on their knees, make a low obeisance, lifting both hands to a level with their head, stroke their long beards down, and let their hands fall on their knees, palms up. The women raise their hands, and rub their upper lip under the nose with the forefinger of the right hand. Beyond food and clothing their wants are nothing. These being easily procurable, thoughts for the morrow trouble them not. They are consequently, though a grave, yet a happy race. The women, when paddling about, fishing, etc., constantly sing wild queer ditties, which are not without melody. Their dwellings are very rough; grass matted over a square framework of poles, with poles again lashed across outside. These huts are usually about fifteen or twenty feet long by ten or twelve in width, sloping from the base to the top, and have a square, open hole at one end of the upper part to allow the smoke to escape, and generally a smaller opening lower down on the opposite side as a window. The door is always under the chimney end of the hut, and has a porch or small outer chamber, with another door to it. In this compartment they keep their nets and such gear; their dogs also live here. In the centre of the large chamber is the fireplace. The inside of these rude dwellings is black from the smoke rising from the constant wood-fire. Close to every hut is a storehouse of the same material and construction as the dwelling hut, raised eight or ten feet off the ground on poles. Here is kept the winter store of fish and other food. These stores are raised from the ground to be clear of the snow, and out of reach of wolves, foxes, and dogs. The birch bark, besides being woven into a coarse kind of cloth, is used for twine, from which their fishing-nets are made. Log canoes, from twenty-five feet in length to much smaller ones, are still used, although the Japanese have brought to the settlements their own more handy flat-bottomed boats.

Their dead are buried almost anywhere, a short

distance from the huts. A shallow hole is dug, and the body covered over, which very soon becomes food for wolves, foxes, and I believe their own half-wild, wolf-like species of dog. I brought home two Aino skulls, which proved, on examination, very interesting.

Spirit-worship in the following way is observed by them. There is the Spirit of the sky, of the river, mountain, fire, and the fishing Spirit. These spirits are represented by sticks peeled in different ways; at one end of the stick the rind is left on in curls. If the fishing spirit is to be propitiated, the sticks are placed by the water's edge. No shrine or temple, either singly or collectively, is used.

In spring, when they have bear-hunts, for the sake of the skins, very young cubs are often caught; these are handed over to their wives to bring up, who, as a matter of course, suckle them with their own children until little Bruin's teeth get disagreeably long. As many as five bears were in some of the settlements I visited, kept in strong cages. They are kept until about a year old, and then eaten, at the annual autumn feast of bears, a sort of half spirit-worship, half custom feast, held at that time.

They have no written language. In connection with

the Japanese, a mixture of both is used. In explaining the course of a river, situation of a lake, or suchlike, they draw on the sand a rough explanatory sketch. The women are the greatest adepts at this sort of primitive literature, having when young been instructed in the art of pattern-drawing by the oldest women of the tribe.

Some of their customs are noteworthy, and I think peculiar to themselves. A very favourite fish appears in the rivers about May and June, the capture of which is conducted with considerable ceremony. To begin, they observe a sort of fixed ceremonial custom, called "Mon-ou-me," the best explanation of which, or resemblance, more properly speaking, may be found in the 18th chapter of Leviticus. Cleanliness in their person is also then to be attended to, but of this I have very great doubts. However, every preparation being gone through, including placing the spirit-sticks near the scene of action, they sally out and commence operations. Those left at home are forbidden to speak, and the ladies are not even permitted to indulge in music of any description, sweet sounds being greatly objected to by this imaginary inhabitant of the deep. When the first fish is caught and brought home, it is passed with great secrecy through the single opening in the hut, and not by the door. If the latter by chance is used, the other fish still enjoying freedom will, it is believed, disappear. Such is one of their customs, as related to me.

In Saghalien, on the death of the chief of the tribe, his body is laid on a table, close to the door of his hut, his internal parts are removed, and widow and daughters then continue to wash the body clean daily. This unsavoury operation goes on for a whole year, and if at the end of the year the remains are intact, they are placed in a box and interred. The female relatives of the departed receive constant presents of tobacco, clothes, etc. A sad alternative, however, awaits the widow: if, notwithstanding all her labour, she has been unable to *cure* or preserve the remains of her lord and master, she is killed and put under ground before her husband's body is buried.

A capacity for sorrow is supposed to be highly developed in the Aino people. On the death of any one, the neighbours always come and condole with the survivors. Death is considered a very disagreeable subject, and seldom, if ever, mentioned or spoken of. When a man dies, his house is burnt. Husbands appear to be kind to their wives, and well they may, for the woman's part or duty is to save her spouse all trouble and hard work that she can possibly do or undergo herself. Occasionally two wives are kept, and concubines are allowed. Neither of these luxuries, however, is often taken advantage of. The meeting of two friends after the absence of either is to a stranger certainly funny. The one who has remained at home takes the other's hands in his, and rubs them, weeps if possible, and asks after his health. This ceremony completed, business can be entered on.

Feasts are common. The guests, after being seated on mats, are regaled with saki by the host, salutations by rubbing hands going on at the same time. A little of the saki is thrown over the head as an offering to the spirits, before any is drunk.

The Japanese law is publicly read every 15th of November, on which day the girls in the settlement perform a dance, called the "crane dance." Owls are looked upon as very wise creatures. It is considered that only through the great wisdom of this bird was it ascertained how to obtain children. Eagles are kept in cages, in the same way as they keep bears. The Japanese, as I have mentioned, endeavour to keep these people in utter ignorance. They speak of them as beings of a very inferior description to themselves, and place their origin on a very low platform indeed.

According to them, a woman reached the earth from above, and wandered about alone for a very long time, meeting or seeing no living thing. At last, however, far away in the mountains, she met a strange creature in the shape of a dog, the result of which meeting is the Aino race. I have now said enough of these interesting people. Are they Mongolian? If they are, they have none of the characteristics of that race; and if they are not Mongolian, then they are something like a strange drop of oil in the ocean, being surrounded by Mongols, yet *not* of them.

The good feeling and kindness of the Japanese is well illustrated by the following narrative:—

The British brig *Eliza Corry* left Hakodadi on the 9th of January 1871, but, owing to adverse winds, had to anchor under the lee of a point of land until the 16th, on which day she again got away with a fair wind. This, however, was only of short duration, for a strong south-west gale sprang up, soon veering round to the north-west, from which quarter it blew with great violence for three days. The vessel must then have sprung a leak, as she settled in the water, and became unmanageable. The sea now swept over her, and hourly her state became worse. The captain endeavoured to weather Cape Gamaley, and reach once more the Tsuga Straits, but to no purpose. She steadily neared the shore. A very short time now elapsed before the breakers were reached, and the doomed vessel struck heavily on the long sandy beach about four miles north of Noshiro. Everything that could be thought of to save the **lives of** the crew was attempted. The long-boat was got out, but immediately capsized, and the two men in her were seen no more. Some of the crew, lashing themselves to spars, tried to reach the shore, but not one did so alive. One man **was drowned** on the deck; the captain's kangaroo hound was washed away from the ship; Mrs. Graham, the captain's wife, with a life-buoy lashed to her, was dashed about the deck with such violence that the life-buoy was torn from her, and she died almost immediately afterwards in her husband's arms. **The** bulwarks, and everything on deck, were swept clean away. The chief officer and two men, who had steadily refused to leave the captain, were now persuaded to try and reach the shore by swimming. The captain himself, throwing off his coat and boots, jumped into the sea. Fortunately, a spar floating near him, he managed to grasp it, and this without doubt was the means of his life being saved. In a short time he felt the sand with his feet, and almost at the same moment found himself washed high and dry on the beach. The other three men never reached the shore, making in all eleven souls who perished. As soon as Captain Graham gathered his senses together, he looked around in hopes of seeing a habitation, but, excepting a straw hut some distance along the beach, nothing of the kind was in sight. In this shed he remained all night, walking up and down to keep himself warm. Some hours after he had been here, his dog, which had been washed overboard from the wreck, rushed into the hut, wild with delight at again finding his master.

In the morning he managed partially to cover himself with an old mat he found in the hut, and on going a short distance along the sand he saw a man approaching. The man, however, was so astonished at Captain Graham's appearance that he made off as fast as he could. Shortly afterwards he again appeared, and by signs was made to understand what had happened; he at once then led the shipwrecked man to a village a quarter of a mile off, called Tago. Here the natives gave him some warm water to drink, as he was not yet able to eat anything. Then followed a series of acts of kindness and forethought on the part of the natives far too numerous to relate. Some few I will give, but it can only convey a faint idea of the reality.

Tago being an insignificant place, they sent to Noshiro, three miles off, which was the chief town of the district, and in the middle of the night some officials arrived from that town, who wished to remove their guest. He was, however, far too unwell, and for three days afterwards he remained in a state of raving fever, at times wholly unconscious. The doctor was sent for from a distance; and on their finding out he was an Englishman, an official was selected to be with him who spoke a little English. They made clothes for him after the European fashion. When he began to feel better they sent miles away for a chicken, with which they made broth. A Japanese sleeping-dress was procured from a town twenty miles away, and as soon as he could be removed he was taken to Noshiro. Here the natives appeared unable to do enough for him. He was an Englishman, they said, and that was quite sufficient. The interpreter who had been selected to attend him had previously been at Hakodadi, and had seen and mixed with Europeans, which accounts for the following acts. A camp-stool was made for him to sit on. A table, a fork, and a large and small spoon of copper were also made. After a short time they got a wideawake hat, apologising on giving it him because it was second-hand. Captain Graham kept a journal;

but the natives observing he found it difficult to write with one of their hair pencils, they procured a black lead pencil for him. The master of a junk arriving from Hakodadi brought him three Californian apples, three sheets of foreign note-paper, and a pocket-knife.

At Noshiro he was lodged in the best house; even a room was set apart for his dog, with an attendant to wait upon the animal, with orders to feed the dog as his master directed. Whilst here, a severe cold and spitting of blood again laid Captain Graham prostrate; every possible remedy was procured, and impossible ones invented and tried. The officials sent miles for chickens and fresh eggs, and when potatoes were obtained they were served as a delicacy. A comb and a looking-glass were found for him. One day the officers came to him in great glee: they had found a European neck-comforter. His legs had swollen considerably, and on this abating they became exceedingly thin and weak, seeing which, the natives made boots out of oiled paper lined with wadded silk. Here should be mentioned that seven bodies, part of the crew of the ill-fated *Eliza Corry*, had been found by the Japanese washed up on the beach, who buried them most decently near Noshiro. When fit to be removed, which was not until he had been twenty days at Noshiro, he was placed in a sort of travelling-box, made purposely for his comfort, seven feet long by three feet high, carried by relays of natives. Another large case had been also made to carry provisions, and what little clothes he had. The interpreter and another official went with him, and in this way he was carried across the country to Hakodadi. Messengers were always sent on ahead to make ready for his comfort at the next halting-place. Even the poor villagers came out to welcome him with offerings of sweetmeats, sugar, and tea. It would be impossible to relate the innumerable acts of kindness and forethought that he experienced from those good people during the eight days it took to cross the country from Noshiro to Awormouri. His attendants were particularly instructed, if from fatigue or sickness the invalid was unable to cross the straits, they were at once to send to the English Consul at Hakodadi for proper medicine, and that they were to take special and good care of him whilst he was detained at Awormouri. On reaching Hakodadi the Japanese officials would not accept any remuneration for all the trouble and expense they had been put to. They would listen to no such proposal, and it was with difficulty that our Consul persuaded the chief official, who accompanied Captain Graham, to accept a silver watch as a token of regard.

PERPENDICULAR ROCKS TWO HUNDRED FEET HIGH.

CHAPTER II.

SEARCH FOR SPIDER-CRAB, THE INLAND SEA REVISITED, OCTOPUS, ETC.

THE Inland Sea I consider a sort of fairy region. It runs east and west for 240 miles, varying in width from thirty miles to 400 feet. Islands of all dimensions are scattered over the surface of the water, clustering thickly in some places, and forming numerous narrow channels. In height they vary from 2500 feet to twenty-five or thirty. Nearly all are inhabited. Life here is very enjoyable. I refer particularly to the natives, but found it equally so myself. During the summer the climate is exceedingly pleasant, July and August being alone rather too hot to be agreeable for out-of-door work. The clear water washes up to the cottagers' doors, and the little urchins spend most of the day swimming and paddling about. Fish are plentiful. Springs of good water are everywhere found. Millet, wheat, and rice grow round the villages, and wood for firing on all the uncultivated hillsides. Many of the islands were, during the old *régime*, not taxed. On these rare spots villages were numerous, besides houses straggling away, in twos and threes, wherever a tiny valley would permit cultivation.

Some years ago the large species of spider-crab, *Inachus Kaempferi*, was common, and constantly to be seen in the markets and fish-shops. A native generally bought part of a limb, a yard long, or more, which was quite enough food for the whole family for a couple of days. When I returned in 1874 I at once set to work to procure a specimen. I constantly visited the markets and fish-shops in all the principal towns. I set people to search. I left most earnest requests, offered rewards, and left no stone unturned for three whole years; but not a vestige of the creature could I ever hear of. My hopes of procuring a specimen had reached a very low ebb, when I decided on a short walking trip to Enosima, which I had heard was noted for them, as a sort of forlorn hope. My track lay through a very beautiful part of the country, bordering one of the great gulfs (the Uraga Gulf) which runs up fifty miles from the outer coasts. Kamakura, the site of the ancient capital of Japan, lay *en route*, and I again visited it. Here a group of half a dozen very fine Buddhist temples still remain in perfect condition. A long avenue from the sea leads up to them. At the temple end of this avenue you pass over a curious high-arched bridge of solid slabs of stone; on either side is a pond surrounded by beautiful firs, *Cryptomaria elegans*. A few years before I had leant over this bridge and watched the mallard, widgeon, and numerous other wild-ducks as they swam about on those tiny lakes. Fearlessly, for they were never molested, these birds lived here, and picturesque and beautiful they looked amongst the lovely water-lilies and other aquatic plants. But now they were no more. The stranger, in the shape of all kinds of foreigners, had taken to visit this quiet spot, stones had been flung at them, and guns let off indiscriminately. Frogs, water-beetles, and fresh-water shells still remained, but the ducks were elsewhere. Passing over this bridge, you enter an open space, with the largest temple facing you. In a shady grove on the right is a large block of stone, resorted to by married women for the same reason as that which drew the Athenian ladies to the marble slab on Mars' Hill. To obtain the efficacious help of the Japanese precious stone, a short prayer is addressed to the figure on its surface. An elderly lady, when I was there, toddled up, flung her small coin into the box placed beside the stone—this money oblation goes to the priest,—and went through the usual ceremony. Leaving Kamakura, I passed through Dyboots, where the great bronze figure of Buddha, fifty-three feet high, rests on his haunches. It is made in seven castings, and, being hollow, the inside of the figure is used as a temple. So much, however, has already been written about this huge bronze figure, I need not stop to describe it. Ten miles from this we came out on the sandy beach of the gulf. In a village opposite Enosima,—an island sacred to Buddha,—I put up for the night. Selecting a clean inviting-looking tea-house, I was at once taken in charge of by two pretty damsels, whose first care was to remove my boots and bathe my tired feet in warm water. I was almost boiled later in the evening when plunging too hastily into the great wooden bath; and if not for the timely assistance of the two muzumees, who rushed to my rescue, each with a bucket of cold water, I should at least have resembled a boiled lobster for some time afterwards. On visiting the island next morning, I found, amongst other marine curiosities, which women and children collected at low tide, and presented for sale, as souvenirs of the sacred spot, several backs of the big crab I was in search of,—so many, in fact, that they were used as receptacles for sponges, shells, etc. This was encouraging. On inquiry, I found that formerly they were frequently caught attached to the fishing-lines, and also to the nets; but alas! for a long time not one had been seen. A cave goes right into the heart of the island from the south side. About eighty yards from the entrance a clear hot sulphur spring runs down the side of the cave and forms a deep well on the flooring. The water of this spring, being good for cutaneous affections, is much prized by the people in the neighbourhood. From the number of rest-houses, temporary tea-houses, and sheds which were erected on the island, it evidently was a favourite resort of the Japanese. The following day I turned homewards, taking a long round through the lovely country. The weather was charming, bright, clear, and cool, with a warm sun. I saw a fresh bright-painted lady-butterfly fluttering about the bare rock in a sunny, sheltered spot. A small yellow species of butterfly I have often seen throughout the winter months on bright days. It was late in the afternoon when I reached the ship, and what was my delight to find a crab, the long-looked-for crab, actually tied to a rope's end and sprawling in the water! What a colour the animal was! No paint could produce the crimson that in great splatches spread over a bright yellow ground. This one measured eleven feet six inches from tip to tip, and I am quite sure it was by no means one of the largest. I soon set to work and disjointed my crustacean, and, washing each joint out with carbolic acid diluted with water, afterwards had the satisfaction of sending the big fellow to my old friend Mr. John Hancock, who most kindly mounted it and presented it to the Museum at Newcastle-on-Tyne, where it now is. Some fishermen, thirty miles from the ship, had caught the creature and brought it to me. It took two men to carry it overland.

In the Inland Sea the octopus is very common. It is brought to the surface when clinging to bait or the fishermen's lines. It is greatly relished by the natives, being considered both agreeable and nutritious. I can imagine it possessing the latter quality, being such a gelatinous creature, but I should think it very tasteless. I never saw a large one; but an incident was told me by a native, whom I believed, of one of those curious creatures flinging an arm over a boat in which a man was quietly fishing. He was so utterly taken aback and astonished, that overboard he jumped, making a tremendous row, and, swimming for the nearest boat, related his story. Three or four fishermen returned, armed with an axe, to the boat, and found it still in the clasp of the monster. They soon chopped the arm in two, and saw nothing more of the animal. The part left in the boat was as thick as a man's thigh. Returning to England on one occasion, I put into the Seychelles, a group of islands off the east coast of Africa, in latitude about 5° N. Here I heard of two instances of men being caught by these diabolical creatures. One man, when searching amongst the rocks at low tide for shell-fish, was seized by an octopus, and retained in the animal's hold, until the tide came up and drowned him. He was afterwards found dead in the creature's grasp. The other case was similar, only that the man, being in a less lonely part of the coast, managed to make himself heard, and was rescued.

There is a most determined species of teredo, or boring-worm, in the waters of the Inland Sea. If the smallest atom of copper became detached, the ship's bottom was certain to be attacked in a few hours. The native craft have an extra planking or false bottom, and this is frequently charred by burning grass and light brushwood underneath, which prevents in some measure the attacks of the worm.

Four channels lead out of the Inland Sea, and, from their narrowness, the tides rush through at great speed. The Naruta, or "whirlpool," between the island of Awadji and Sikok, is very narrow; through here the ebb and flood tide literally falls eight feet in 200 yards. In passing through in a ship, you feel as if rushing to something unknown. Very few people venture to take this channel, and wisely; but from being intimately acquainted with the tides, rocks, and locality generally, I often took it with perfect confidence in ordinary weather. In fact, after getting within the influence of the rush of water, you are carried through in safety *nolens volens*. When deer-shooting once, on the Sikok side, and passing close to the rocky point which formed the boundary of the pass on that side, we were not a little surprised to see one of our men-of-war approaching from the Inland Sea, but after watching her through in safety, we thought nothing more of the circumstance or of her bold captain until, meeting him

THE INLAND SEA.

a month afterwards, I found he had hardly recovered from the effects of passing the Naruta.

"Why did you take that channel?" I asked him.

"Because it was recommended on the chart; but you will never catch me there again. As I neared it, I could see nothing but rocks, breakers, and foam; wished myself out of it, and put the helm hard down; but although the ship was going twelve knots through the water, she would not answer the helm a bit. In another moment I was through, and being whirled about in the eddies in a most horrible manner. In fact, the ship was out of all command."

"Well," I said, "I rather expect you never went so fast in a ship before."

"Never," he replied. "Why, I must have been going at least twenty-five knots over the ground."

Another man, the captain of one of the American mail steamers, I knew well, took his ship once through the Naruta, and but once. He hardly liked to speak about it; his rudder-chains were carried away when approaching, and the steamer passed the narrows in the most erratic manner, whirling and twisting about entirely at the mercy of the waters, which waters, as I said before, took you through safely enough if you allowed them. After my friend's little "adventure,"

I had the "recommendation" removed from the charts.

Deer were very abundant in the fir woods at this corner of Sikok, which is, in fact, an island, cut off from the mainland by a narrow boat's channel, partially artificial. Here two or three houses reposed on the bank of a deep bight of blue water. A more lovely spot can hardly be imagined, and is beyond any attempt at description. I lived here with the natives for some time. These kind people were in charge of the Prince of Awa's pony-breeding establishment. The animals had the whole island to roam about on; and the place being kept quite quiet, deer, as I have said, abounded. I found deer at pony-breeding establishments in other parts of the country also, and came to the conclusion that these two animals get on well together. It was a fact, however, that very few ponies were ever seen; certainly not one-tenth that of the number of deer. Awadji island is almost all wild country in the south. In roaming over the mountains, I found for the first time the bay-tree growing in profusion; several species of myrtle also flourished, one of which, when in flower, has the most obnoxious smell imaginable. The first spring plant that shows a blossom in Nipon is our own *Cardamine pratensis*, cuckoo plant. Towards the end of March it is well out in flower. Walking past some swampy ground one day, I saw a number of women and children picking the young shoots of a species of *Equisetum*, and on asking what it was for, was told they boiled it well, and ate it as a vegetable. Almost every kind of fungus is eaten by the Japanese; but although I have tried most myself, I cannot say I appreciated any except the ordinary mushroom.

The largest island in the Inland Sea is Sozu Sima, the first reached after passing through the Naruta. On its south side is a harbour of the most perfect description, and sufficiently large to hold the navies of the world. It was a favourite resort of mine during the winter (the non-surveying season), and I shall ever remember the many delightful days I have spent deer-stalking amongst its rugged mountains and fir woods. A mud wall to protect the crops encloses the cultivated slopes adjoining the few small villages which are dotted round the bay. Sugar-cane is the chief crop, the rough sugar from which is manufactured on the spot. Barley, wheat, and rice are also grown. The French surveyed this locality, and the small gunboat employed for the purpose made the bay her headquarters for three years. The result of such a lengthened stay amongst people so charming and accommodating as the inhabitants of this place, is seen in a slight variation from the general Japanese type in some of the little urchins who play about in the shallow water, and on the white sandy beach. It is curious that, so far, the children born from Japanese and European parents seldom live to their sixth year.

I was strongly urged to go well armed when I went into the woods.

"Why?" I asked my informant, the captain of the French gunboat.

"Ah, my very good friend," he answered, "you do not know, you have not seen the monkeys. Mon Dieu! such very gros monkeys—so big as me—as myself—quite, I assure you. I am most afraid, fearful of my life; therefore, for protection to my person, I do always go accompanied by des marins, armed with le chassepot and the cutlass."

I often came across families of these apes. The old patriarchs of the community were about the size of my Irish retriever,—grey, grizzly-looking fellows, who never hurried themselves when suddenly come upon, but very leisurely walked off, seeing their wives and children well ahead before they thought of moving. From never being molested by the natives, doubtless they consider themselves quite safe. It is the only species of Quadrumana in Nipon, and, being well known, I never troubled them.

On one occasion in January—my favourite month for shooting here—I took about half-a-dozen Japanese beaters, and a lot of their pariah dogs; and sending them to beat a part of the thick fir woods, where a warm, sunny aspect made it likely we should find deer, struck away with my **coxswain—who always accompanied** me—for an opening on the other side of the cover. **We** had hardly gone three **hundred yards when a stag**, with his fine head thrown back, dashed past within twelve yards. He had evidently been disturbed by some early wood-cutter, and had accidentally crossed my path. I never felt more sure of an animal in my life, as I pulled first one trigger, then the other, both barrels loaded with slug, at his broadside; and I could hardly believe, on the smoke **clearing away, that it was the** same animal I saw bounding along as if nothing whatever had happened. Such things will happen, however, and after examining his track for a short distance, to see if there were any spots of blood on the ground, on we went. Slug is most uncertain; sometimes the charge goes just as you wish it, and **is** then terribly effective, but, as often, there is no knowing where the shot goes: it seems to spread all over the place. The beaters were now at work, but after standing still for an hour, and no deer appearing, I moved on again half a mile ahead of the Japanese and their dogs. No success following this move, and trying once more, I got tired of so much waiting; so bidding the men adieu, I started to try some ground on the way home. It was late in the afternoon, and I knew the deer ought to be well on their feed, and very likely not far from the mountain streams. Examining the banks carefully as we came upon the clear pools, I at last found some very fresh tracks. The animals could not have left the spot ten minutes before. Sending my attendant down the stream, I turned up its course, keeping some twenty yards in the cover. In this way I had noiselessly advanced a quarter of a mile, when three shadow-like forms started from a thicket thirty yards ahead. I had just time to pull one trigger before they were gone. There appeared, however, no satisfactory result, and, listening, I could hear the deer dashing along the crest of the hill, making for the higher ranges. No luck to-day, I thought, as I went to examine the spot the animals had started from. The grass and fern showed no signs such as I hoped to find. However, I let my retriever go, and listened. Three or four minutes elapsed, and, to my delight, I heard the good old dog giving tongue *down* the stream. I knew at once he was on a wounded deer's track, and that it was badly wounded I felt certain, by the animal having turned down stream instead of going up with the others. A mortally hurt deer will seldom if ever take up hill; if they try it for a short distance, they are certain to turn down very soon. Away I went as fast as possible, over and through the rough cover. The dog's notes kept every now and then sounding ahead. He was in sight of the deer, I knew by experience, when he barked. On we went in this way for a good mile, when suddenly no more sounds came from "Pat," and directly afterwards I met the dog coming back on his own track. "What's the matter, old man? Have you got thrown off the scent?" Another half-mile down the course of the stream and I came on a sandy patch, and here, to my delight, was imprinted the fresh track of a stag. At the same moment "Pat" was off, and I caught a glimpse of the deer's white stern-patch as he sprang round the shoulder of a rise of ground a little distance ahead. Dog and deer were both out of sight in a moment. Another good half-mile race—still going down hill, most fortunately. I began to feel sure of the poor beast now. The mud-wall I have mentioned was close at hand; I felt almost certain the deer was on his last legs, and reaching the wall, and finding the deer's track on the path which ran along by it, off again I went on better ground. In a couple of hundred yards I turned a sharp angle. At the same moment, fifty yards from me on the path, with antlers flung over his shoulders, and with an unsteady but swinging gallop, came the stag. It was impossible to get out of his way, and he, poor brute, was past caring for what was ahead. A dreaded dog was close behind him, and to keep going was his only chance. Swinging my gun to the shoulder, I fired at his throat when twenty yards off, and he fell dead. His head was the best of many a deer I shot on the island, although several larger animals fell to my gun afterwards.

The scenery in the Inland Sea is in perfection during May. For thirty miles after leaving Soza Sima you pass innumerable islands of all sizes and shapes. The golden patches of ripe corn are now being cut. In Japan harvesting is done very differently from that in England. The neighbours assist one another in cutting, gathering, and threshing, which all goes on at once, and on the spot. No grain is cut here until quite ripe. The whole village, men, women, and children, all do their share of the work. Merrily and quickly the

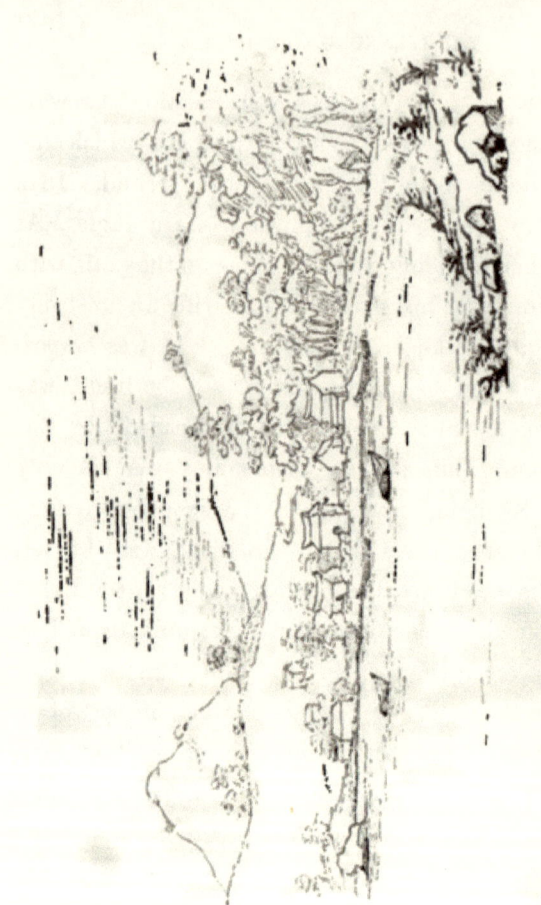

SMALL VILLAGE, INLAND SEA.

harvest is worked out. Threshing is the simplest operation. A gigantic iron comb is erected on a frame, and a handful of corn is pulled through at a time. I often examined and admired the clean way this simple method did its work. Mats are spread under and round the comb, and very few grains are lost. The straw is tied in bundles, and stacked round trees until required for thatching purposes.

Azaleas are in their glory; poppies and a large blue campanula are also in full bloom. These flowers, mixed with the fresh green fronds of the brake fern, form a most charming covering to the banks and hillsides. The young chestnut and oak, now in their richest spring foliage, set off against the dark firs with peculiar brightness, and the picturesque villages, separated only from the clear blue water by the brightest of sandy beaches, combine to form one of the most charming scenes imaginable. Each village has its Buddhist temple, conspicuous by its size and ornamented roof from the rest of the houses, marked out also very frequently by some single tree of great size, or a clump of camellias, and often one or two of that peculiar fern-leafed tree, *Salisburia adiantifolia*, the foliage of which turns a bright yellow in the autumn, when the seeds are collected and eaten by the natives.

When at anchor once between two of these islands, Syako and Hiro Shima, a severe typhoon passed along the Sikok coast. The weather at the time, where the ship lay, was merely very heavy and overcast, wind strong, with sharp gusts, and torrents of rain. The clouds appeared so low that they struck and broke on the island's summit, which was only 650 feet high. Next morning on landing I found a slice of the hill-side had been swept away in a very strange manner. A cut eight feet deep and twelve wide was gone; trees were torn up and swept to the foot of the hill; big boulders, washed clean, had also been brought down; and on each side the height of the water—for this had been done by water—was distinctly marked. I followed the cleft up the hill, and came to its commencement, about 200 feet below the summit ridge. Here the appearance was as if the ground had been scooped out by a volume of water from above. At any rate this occurred on the night of the typhoon, and from the bursting of no spring. In other parts of Japan I have also seen similar marks on the hill-sides.

The Bingo Nada, an open piece of water, separates the thick cluster of islands I am speaking of from the Kurusima Straits. These straits are formed by another mass of islands reaching across the Inland Sea, with numerous narrow channels between them. After passing the Kurusima, more open water is reached, with islands only here and there. One of these, called Uri, a very small grass-covered dumbbell-shaped islet, is right in the track. In days gone by, it was the deer-preserve of a Daimio living on Sikok; but, unfortunately, one of our gallant naval captains heard of the place being well stocked with deer, which was quite sufficient for his sportsmanlike propensities. He anchored his ship close to the island, and landed about a company of blue-jackets armed with Snider rifles. The wretched deer were driven from end to end, backwards and forwards, and nearly all killed or wounded. On hearing of this visit of English sportsmen (!) to his preserve, the owner sent men to the island with orders to exterminate the few remaining animals; but notwithstanding such persecution, when I quitted Japan there were still a few left, and if no more such gallant shooters have been there, doubtless there are now a good many. From Uri to the western end of the sea the water is still more open; all the islands passed lie on the north side, and some way from the usual track. Hime Sima, a cone-shaped island, is famed for a strong mineral spring. A most beautiful species of large butterfly flourishes on the island, which is rare elsewhere, and the peregrine falcon breeds on a patch of red cliff on the south side. Thirty miles from Hime Sima you reach the western entrance to the Inland Sea, the straits of Simonosaki. This entrance is twelve miles in length, winding, and in places very narrow, being in one spot only three cables wide.

In 1864 these narrows were virtually closed by the chieftain of the north side firing at every vessel that approached. A Dutch man-of-war went down, so did an American, and both received the warmest reception. One returned with seven or eight men killed, and two ports knocked into one. This sort of thing could not be tolerated, though one hardly sees why, considering the prince lived in his own castle, on his own ground, and merely wished so to live, without the foreigner's interference or assistance! However, as our friends who had got knocked about by his guns had no force of their own, we were philanthropic enough to take up the cudgels for them. We are often ready to oblige our neighbours, as well as ourselves, when the offending one is of the smallest dimensions, but think over it a good deal if he is more our own size. It is well known how our squadron went to Simonosaki, accompanied by a gallant vessel, a tug, hired for the purpose by the Americans, on which to hoist the insulted flag, the Stars and Stripes. What a picnic our friends had, and how they must have admired us blazing away at 2000 yards! (We had learnt a lesson at Kagosima, and did not try any more point-blank range with these people of the "rising sun.") The smaller ships then took the batteries on their flank. Small-arm companies were landed, and a quantity of ammunition expended by firing into the thick cover. The leading detachments had got half-a-mile ahead to a gap in the hills, where the enemy were supposed to be stockaded, and **ready to** receive us, but none could be seen owing to the thick cover. A nimble young sailor responded to the call for some one who could climb. All sailors, although they are supposed to climb like cats, and even hold on by their eyelids, cannot **manage to get up a tree,**—I ought rather to say not one in a hundred **can.** However, an active youngster was found, **and he was soon** thirty feet from the ground, looking anxiously for the enemy ahead. Just as he was about to give some valuable information, he was hailed by such a shower of bullets from all points (except from the direction of the enemy), and particularly from his friends behind, and further down the path, that down the tree he came a good deal faster than he went up. The stockade was all the same found and captured. The territory on the south side of the straits belonged to a prince who was at enmity with his northern neighbour, which of course was much to our advantage and comfort. When surveying the straits years afterwards, a farmer pointed out the spot where the few men killed in the action were buried. This man had watched the whole affair from his own door on the south side.

The town of Simonosaki chiefly consists of one long street, built along the north shore of the straits for more than a mile. In walking along the street you see through the houses on either side. On the water side you have ever-changing views of junks, with their white sails, boats busily at work carrying merchandise and people to and from the big craft at anchor,— muzumees in blue and scarlet being paddled off to the native craft, where they pass their evenings drinking tea and entertaining their friends on board. The mountains on the south side of the straits form sometimes a grand, but always a pretty, finish to these repetitions of pleasing and happy views. As you walk along, it all resembles many different pictures of similar objects. The other side of the street is quite different. Here the houses are open through as before; but on the further side gardens, green, cool, and fresh, greet your eyes, flowers, miniature mountains, cascades, tiny lakes, white herons, storks, wild ducks, and so on; creepers and ferns, hanging from moss-covered rocks, dripping water, and, in fact, every description of garden peculiar to the Japanese style.

How fresh, green, and cool these tastefully arranged and carefully cared for Japanese homes are! The disposition or nature of people who universally show such taste and love for all that is pleasing and beautiful in nature, cannot, in my own humble opinion, be bad. There must be a considerable amount of inherent kindness, goodness, and gentleness in them; and this, I think, is most strongly shown in the Japanese race.

Simonosaki is a busy place. Rice from the north reaches here in straw bags carried on ponies' backs, and thence is shipped to all parts of the country. In walking along the streets, candle-manufactories are conspicuous. These articles are made from the wax which is extracted from the berries of a species of mulberry-tree, the wick being a rush. The berries are first boiled, under which process the greater part becomes wax, of a substance softer than manufactured beeswax, and lighter in colour. In making the candles, the rush is dipped into the hot wax, pulled out and rubbed smooth with the hand; when hard enough, the same process is gone over again, until sufficient wax has adhered to form the candle. The light given by these articles is not good. They require constant snufling, where no snuffers are to be had, barring those of nature's providing, and make an abominable smell if not so operated on. In short, they exactly resemble the "Purser's Dip," so familiar of old to the naval officer! The ordinary cotton cloth of the country is also made here to a considerable extent. Girls work away at their looms, stripped to their waists in the hot weather, singing and chatting to the passers-by, getting through their tasks with merry contentment. Excellent rice is grown in the neighbourhood. The cultivation of this staple article of food appears very simple, but in reality a very considerable amount of labour is necessary for its production. The seed is sown in March, in small square patches; the fields at the same time are being prepared by hoeing, cleaning, and flooding. In May the young plant is six inches high and ready for transplanting, which is usually done by women and girls. Taking bundles of the young rice from the seed-beds, they pass in line quickly over the fields, dabbing little patches of the plant into the hot, wet mud, about eighteen inches apart. Up to their knees in this slush, with nothing but a rag round their loins, these contented creatures sing and chatter over their work all the day long. A few days after the rice is thus planted, all the flat country has become green. From thence to harvest-time (October), the crops require constant cleaning and attending. Too much water may wash the plants away, too little dry them up. Snakes are very fond of these warm, muddy fields; frogs abound, and on these the snakes feed. When snipe-shooting once, I heard in the tall rice a very peculiar loud note, unlike any bird or animal I knew. I approached cautiously, expecting some winged creature to rise every moment. I got so near at last, that the sound appeared almost at my feet, and on parting the long green plant with my hand, I saw an unfortunate frog in the jaws of a snake. The reptile had seized the frog by the stern, half was already in his jaws, but the frog being large, it was no easy matter to manage the remaining part. Every time the snake gave a gulp at his victim, and another eighth of an inch disappeared, the croak of anguish which had attracted my attention was squeezed out of the poor frog. There are very few species of venomous reptiles in Nipon, and even these, unless trodden on, are harmless.

After passing Simonosaki, the Korean Straits are entered, and following the coast to the south for eighty miles, Hirado, a large island, is reached. It is separated from the mainland by a very narrow pass, through which the tides run like a mill-sluice. The inhabitants of Hirado are considered as foreigners by their brethren on the mainland; "uncouth beings" is the expression applied to them by their compatriots. I never myself observed any such radical difference. In a beautiful harbour on the western side, I often lay snugly at anchor when it was blowing great guns outside. On a point running out between two bays grew a grand cover for deer; it was scarcely a mile in length, the land side terminating on a smooth grass-covered slope, the ridge of which, if viewed from the wood, cut against the sky. Before daybreak one morning I hid myself in some bushes by the edge of the wood, expecting at dawn the deer would return from their feeding-grounds on the open hills beyond. The grey morning light had hardly reached the western side of the hill when a single pair of antlers appeared over the ridge. A fine stag soon stood clear against the sky. He scented no danger, and on he came; twelve more followed, and then a herd so thickly packed I could count no longer. Seventy or eighty stags were now within one hundred yards of me. At this moment, as well as I could judge, as many hinds crossed the ridge and followed the stags towards the cover. It certainly was a grand sight. I had only a muzzle-loader, but if my "express" had been with me I might have made a wonderful **bag**; as it was, I only secured two. Eighteen months after this, not a single deer was to be found here.

INLAND SEA FROM THE SOUTH.

CHAPTER III.

CURRENTS AND TYPHOONS.

THE equatorial current of the Pacific flowing from the south passes between the Ladrone and Philippine Islands, then it has a north-westerly direction; its course afterwards trends more directly to the northward, and by the time it reaches the coast of Japan the body of this great warm stream of water is flowing to the north-east, following the line of the south coast of Japan. The whole of this part of Japan is influenced by the Black Stream or "Kuro Siwo," as the natives call it: a very good name for it, the water being of the deepest blue. After reaching the south-east corner of the islands, instead of turning to the north,—the line the coast takes,—it retains the north-east direction towards Behring's Straits.

CURRENTS AND TYPHOONS.

The climate of the south-eastern parts of Nipon, speaking generally of the group of islands which collectively make up the kingdom of Japan,[1] is so influenced by this warm body of water that it is almost tropical in Kiusiu, their southern extremity. Fish are found on the north coast which could not exist on the southern side. The winter on the north side is most severe and lengthened, whereas on the south it is more a fitful than a regular visitant. The Gulf Stream of the Atlantic and this Pacific current are very similar in origin, course, and influence. Fortunately, we in England are enveloped by the Gulf Stream, otherwise our climate would be hardly bearable. Japan is not so encircled by the " Kuro Siwo," the south side alone being influenced by it. The consequence is, that although so much lower in latitude than England, lying between the parallels of 30 and 45, which includes Yesso, the climate is very much more severe than ours. The stream being interfered with and checked in its northern course by the coast of Japan, is not only driven off, and forced to the eastward with great speed, but is very erratic in its general movements. I remember well when making this coast many years ago, when it was all but a *terra*

---

[1] It may be well to mention that "Nipon" and "Japan" are synonymous.

incognita, how we dreaded this current. In reality, after once getting within its influence, we were never certain, if it came on thick or foggy, or at night, when the coast could not be seen, where we were going, at what speed we were being carried along, or in what dangers and scrapes we were likely to find ourselves entangled. I have heard of vessels being carried dead to windward against a heavy gale of wind at a wonderful speed; other ships, thinking themselves close off the coast, suddenly finding they were far away to the south, being carried hither and thither amongst the islands and rocks. This " Kuro Siwo" was, in fact, a very ugly customer. Time, however, brought wonderful changes. The Japanese erected excellent lighthouses along their coasts, and for several years now all this part has been as well lighted as the coast of England. Of course the navigation of these formerly dangerous seas now became simple enough, and the current so much dreaded before was made of the greatest service in running along the coast. If all the things which the Japanese were persuaded or obliged to take in hand were as well executed, as honestly and straightforwardly carried out, as the construction and working of the lighthouse department has been, they might well be congratulated, and many foreigners have less cause to feel shame.

The counter stream to the Kuro Siwo flows from the north, following in its southerly course the line of the Kuril Islands; part then reaches the sea of Japan, and meets the Kuro Siwo somewhere about the Korean Straits. In this neighbourhood I have seen the meeting of these two streams, which is most remarkable,—**the one so dark and deeply** blue, the other **of** a pale green colour. They don't mix, but rub against each other. So decided is this, that on taking the temperature almost on either side of the ship, the difference was 14°. On one occasion the ship I was in left Shanghai for Nagasaki. We of course steamed straight for the intended port, only about four hundred miles distant, and made the land the second morning at daylight; but strange to say, **the** entrance to the harbour could not be seen. **Where could the place be? was the question.** No one could tell. In such a short distance it appeared very strange that we should **not have hit** it off most accurately. There was then no lighthouse **to** mark the entrance, and our experience of the currents was simply *nil*. I was the only one **on board** who had ever been to Nagasaki before, but that **was** ten years previously, when I was a youngster, and before I took much notice of these things, and could in the present instance give no useful information. **We steamed to** the **south,** thinking **we had through** some unknown cause made too much of a northerly course. After going about ten miles in this direction, and seeing nothing like our wished-for port, we again stopped, and began to think the place must have suddenly disappeared. Just then a fishing-boat was caught sight of. Here was a chance. We made at once for the boat, but on seeing us, the occupants made off as fast as oars and sails would take them. A regular chase ensued, which resulted, of course, in the speedy capture of the fishing craft. The scene that then took place was ridiculous. Not a soul on board could speak a single word of Japanese; and the two natives were in such a state of terror that signs and gesticulations were quite useless. Nothing would induce them to leave the boat. A British tar was sent down to carry one up, but he could not even hold the slippery half-dressed native. A rope was then attempted to be got round him, but that also failed. At last some more sagacious being tried a little rum and water, which had the most instantaneous effect: the Japanese was on board the ship at once. By repeating the word Nagasaki with much energy, we got our captured pilot to understand what we wished him to do. He took us straight for the entrance of the harbour, which turned out to be forty miles to the northward of where we then were. How, in such a short run, we could have been set down so far to the south of our course seemed then most strange. Since, however, we have known more about the currents I have mentioned, the circumstance is easily accounted for. On getting well inside the harbour, but not in sight of other ships that might be there, we quietly slipped our friend in need on shore, having tipped him with some silver coin before doing so.

For some years the entrance to Nagasaki has been well marked by an excellent lighthouse, and the existence and peculiarity of these currents known. The cold stream from the north, which I have mentioned as a counter current to the Kuro Siwo, I always look upon as a most interesting body of water. I spent the greater part of a year within its influence, and found it abounding in different objects of natural history,— notably all kinds of cetacea, seals, fish, and duck. In dredging, the bottom of the ocean proved equally prolific of life. Many of the mollusca I collected in this way turned out to be of great interest; some were new species, whilst others came to light which were previously only known to inhabit the North Atlantic. It would seem from this that the great arctic current divides; one part passing through Behring's Straits into the North Pacific, the other by Davis Straits into the Atlantic. On the south coast of Korea a cold current sets regularly to the south-west, doubtless a portion of the arctic stream. When surveying the islands off this peninsula, the difference of temperature of the water in their neighbourhood from that of the Yellow Sea, a few miles to the northward, was found to be very great.

During the hot month of August it was quite refreshing to return from the Makaw group, where the water was warm, to the cool waters so near. The temperature of the atmosphere was influenced so much that at night a blanket was quite enjoyable. The specific gravity of the water in these two localities is the same, proving the cold current to be oceanic, and not from any large river flowing from the interior and emptying its waters into the sea in that neighbourhood. I feel sure that the localities influenced by this arctic current in its southern course must be rich in subjects of natural history, and well worthy the notice of the scientific world. The line of the Kuril Islands, the eastern and north-eastern shores of Yesso, the sea of Japan, and the coast of Korea, are all, comparatively speaking, new ground for examination. The few collectors who have had the opportunity of visiting these localities have scarcely done more than very lightly touch the ground with the dredge. Not only the opportunity must be obtained, but time is a necessary adjunct; and this I, with so much other work on hand, could seldom spare. I often wished when in the north, and in this current, that I had a few months to devote entirely to collecting the numerous objects so plentifully distributed around me.

As this body of warm water, the Kuro Siwo, flows along the southern coasts of Nipon, its north-easterly course is frequently interrupted by strong contrary winds and gales, as well as by numerous points, capes, and peninsulas.

The results of such interruptions are manifold and perplexing; but the chief peculiarity, perhaps, is the formation of numerous overfalls and tide-rips. They sometimes take place in calm weather, when their appearance is startling, and by no means inviting to the mariner.

The calm sea suddenly seems lashed into fury. The waves rise like walls, breaking in angry foam along their crest, and as suddenly fall again. These wall-like waves are so near together that a vessel has no time to rise and fall, but has to flounder through in the most uncomfortable manner. Large ships have their decks washed, and their engine-gear severely tested. Small ones get literally thumped and knocked about. If an unlucky sailing ship gets drifted into one of these troublesome patches in a calm, she is very roughly handled; and to small vessels they are exceedingly dangerous. New-comers have often been sorely puzzled by these rough patches suddenly appearing in their course, and innumerable reports used to come to me of dangerous shoals having been discovered.

When these overfalls occur so far from the land as to be out of the influence of local disturbance, probably they are the effect of the diurnal tide-wave acting in opposition to the course of the main stream.

The worst part of the coast for tide-rips is in the vicinity of Rock Island, at the entrance to the Gulf of Yedo. Nine times out of ten, in passing here, these disagreeable things will be met with. I remember a friend of mine going out to look for a ship which was reported to have been seen dismasted in this neighbourhood. On his returning, after five days' search, I went on board at once to hear the result, and shall not easily forget his appearance. On asking him where he had been to, he answered, "Been to?—the Lord knows! I hardly know myself; in fact I don't know. I was here, there, everywhere. Thought myself in one place safe as a church, away from those abominable islands, when, to my horror, on the mist lifting, I was bang on the top of them. There is only one place I have not been to—bed. Talk about currents! Mill-sluices is the proper name. And as for the ship, of course I **never** saw her. I am only precious glad I see my own at this present moment." He certainly looked considerably ruffled, and in want of a good night's rest.

The typhoons which occur in Japanese waters are, I believe, always distinct from the China storms. Originating in tropical latitudes, their first course is to the north-west, the same as that of the Kuro Siwo. It appears they then pass over the same ground, gradually turning to the north with the warm current, striking the south coast of Japan just as they incline away to the north-eastward. Their northern disc now becomes flattened in against the high mountain ranges, which form an almost insurmountable barrier to their further progress across the country. The general north-east direction of the coast is then followed until the southeast corner of Nipon is reached, when they pass out to the open Pacific until their force is expended. The result of these circular storms becoming flattened on **their** northern semi-diameter is, that easterly winds prevail during their passage along the coast. This may be easily understood by pushing an indiarubber ring, lying flat on the table, against any stationary object. The part which comes in contact is no longer round, but flattened out. The Kii peninsula, which drops down alone and unprotected into the ocean, feels the effects of these storms more than other parts. The centres frequently pass close to the south point, and sometimes over it. Enormous blocks of rock are moved to new resting-places; lanes are cut in the woods as if by a scythe; cliffs give way and disappear into the deep water; mouths of rivers are entirely changed, besides villages wrecked and valleys inundated. I have seen all this after the passage of one of these storms, and it was as wonderful, in showing the extraordinary force of wind and water combined, as it was pitiable in the way of destruction and misery brought on the inhabitants.

The body of the storm, I have said, passes to the north-east, or with the Kuro Siwo; but the wind prevails from the eastward (until the centre of the typhoon has passed), or exactly against the course of the current. The result of two such strong forces meeting is a horribly confused sea, alike trying to man and ship.

From long experience it became easy to foretell the approach of these disagreeable visitors. First, as a never-failing indicator, the barometer stands unrivalled. It must, however, be thoroughly understood before reliance on it can be felt, the ordinary rising and falling of the mercury being quite insufficient. Speaking generally, a falling barometer with the wind between north-west and east (through north) is a bad sign. A long heavy swell setting in from the south-east, without any previous wind from the same direction, is another suspicious indication. The sun setting amongst high-banked clouds, and giving out copper-coloured rays, denotes some uncomfortable change. Birds coming steadily in from seaward, as if anxious to be near shelter, is a very certain forerunner of bad weather. If all, or one or two, of these signs are observed at the same time, when the weather is otherwise bright, fine, and everything that is pleasant, my maxim was, "Get to a safe harbour." The falling barometer and the swell setting in, generally gave forty-eight hours' warning, but the other indications were less reliable.

When these storms occur, if a port cannot be reached, the next best thing is to get well away from the coast; at the same time, the land hardly ever becomes a lee-shore, owing to the course the storms almost invariably take; and in any case, if hove-to on the right tack—according to her position in regard to the storm—a good ship, properly managed, ought to weather it well. I remember one vessel, through want of knowledge of the general laws of circular storms, getting well into the centre of a typhoon, which proved as much as the good old ship could well stand. This, however, was not all; for it had no sooner passed over and cleared, than the unfortunate vessel was steered right in front of its track, and for the second time the centre passed over her. This was simply inexcusable, and as blamable as running, in broad daylight, on a rock well out of water. It is a strange peculiarity of these storms that they frequently travel in pairs. On two occasions I experienced this in a most remarkable and unmistakeable way. On both occasions I was snugly at anchor, with two anchors well ahead, steam up, and in good harbours. The interval in each case between the passage of the storms was three and four days.

It is quite a marvellous sight to walk along a stretch of beach after a typhoon has passed and gone. Shells, crabs, fish, and sponges are washed up in great quantities; most, of course, broken or damaged, but some few perfect. Amongst the most curious things I ever picked up in this manner was a very strange species of vitreous sponge (*Hyalonema Lusitanicum* is, I believe, its proper name). It must be very plentifully distributed towards the head of the Uraga Gulf, and it was on the sand at the extreme head of this gulf I found it. I afterwards got from the natives some beautiful specimens, which had been obtained by trawling in the bay, but at what depth I could not ascertain. It looks like a small cup-shaped ordinary sponge pierced through the centre by a number of clear glass fibres twisted together into a column eight or twelve inches long. It seemed to me as if the sponge, with the cup uppermost, rested on the sand, the glass-like spiral column being imbedded in the sand or mud, similarly to the roots of a plant, a small portion of the glassy-looking column being above the cup, and to this part bits of seaweed and tiny shells were often attached.

A typhoon passed along the south coast, in September 1862 (I think), and on reaching the south-east extreme of Nipon went away to the eastward into the broad Pacific. The *Camilla*, a man-of-war brig, had left Hakodadi for Yokohama, and must have encountered this storm as it left the coast of Nipon. She was never heard of again. There are more ways than one by which a vessel may get into very serious difficulties or come entirely to grief, if overtaken by one of these circular storms, particularly if something of the law of storms is not understood by the man in command. The act of running before the wind is tempting enough, when your course is the right one; but it is far from being the safest to adopt. If continued, a vessel will, of course, keep sailing in a circle, and in so doing pass in front of the centre, possibly get into it. Again, a vessel may run on for so long that, although her commander is well aware she ought to be hove-to, it has become a very hazardous evolution. She may, when in the act of coming to the wind, be struck by a heavy sea, broach to, and be taken aback, and go down stern foremost.

I remember well on one occasion being in a ship which was kept before the wind, until to round her to, and bring her to the wind, was out of the question. There was nothing left but to continue to scud before it. The ship—a big one and a Symonite—became very difficult to manage. Sometimes she was all but broadside on; then rushing before it, and the next minute whirled round with her other side to the wind. Our boats were washed away or destroyed, and the vessel strained. If we had lain-to, and allowed the gale to pass, no damage whatever would have occurred.

On the other hand, with a good ship, and perfect

confidence as to the position and track of the storm, a fair wind may be sometimes made of it, or it may be absolutely necessary to run, at any rate, for a time, to escape the centre of the storm, which may be approaching directly on your position. After being in a great many of these typhoons, I found the average speed of the whole body of the storm to be about eighteen miles an hour.

It once happened that after running along for several days with a fair wind, which was not more than a good strong breeze, I came to the conclusion that we were in the outer circle of a cyclone. I ran on some more days, feeling still more certain we had at last met with a *friendly* typhoon. Our destination was a point in the Indian Ocean where I had to commence a line of deep soundings. By the time we reached this place I had determined in my own mind that the cyclone would, on our stopping, overtake us, and the centre pass a little to the northward; then the storm would take a south-westerly course. On reaching my position I immediately furled all square-sails, and set a couple of storm ones. The wind now increased, the sails were split to ribbons, a boat was smashed by the sea, and altogether we spent a rough and uncomfortable night. Next day was beautifully fine, and, after getting the sounding, we went away in a south-west course, the same as I believed the cyclone to have taken. The barometer at once began to fall, and the following day we overtook the storm, which was plainly visible ahead. The barometer had been falling since we left the sounding-spot and bore away to the south-west. I again hove-to, and the barometer at once began to rise. After allowing sufficient time for the cyclone to get well ahead, we went on once more.

I give this as an instance of a slow-travelling cyclone of large diameter. I do not think these storms are ever of great height,—seldom, I imagine, does their thickness extend over a mile; their horizontal diameter varies from a couple of hundred miles to a thousand or more. The more limited the storm is in its range, the greater the violence. I only once saw through the thick vapour which is blown along by the violent wind, and then I saw the blue sky and bright sun. It was but for a moment; a sort of rent in the dense cloudy shroud.

Electricity is frequently very prevalent, but I never heard thunder during the passage of a true cyclone storm.

CHAPTER IV.

DEER-SHOOTING AND OTHER MATTERS.

THERE is only one species of deer in Japan (*Cervus Sika*). This animal, however, is very abundant, both in the extreme north and south. Owing to the **great** difference in climate in the extremes of the island, or more properly islands, the herbage varies immensely, being succulent and nutritious in the north, but coarse, rank, and indifferent in the south. Nearly all the grasses found in the southern parts are rough-edged or saw-toothed. On account of this great difference of herbage the deer vary very much in size, a hundred pounds being above the average in **the south,** but in the north two hundred to two hundred and fifty pounds weight is not uncommon. The antlers of those in the north are finely formed, large, and well grown, but in the southern parts are stunted, and often quite imperfect. I have never seen any species of deer so regular in their points: there are always four, except where malformation has occurred in the early stages of the horns' growth. The horns are shed in March or beginning of April, and by the end of July they are full-grown, and clean from velvet by the middle of August. The rutting season is in September, and all October, and many a fine stag then comes to grief by the wily Japanese hunter, who, waiting concealed near some stream or pond, imitates the call of the female so accurately, by means of a small instrument made out of the horn of the deer, and covered by the skin of the same animal, that the stags, who are at that season following the hinds, are easily attracted to within a few yards, and then shot. These deer are very timid and shy; but at night they often break through the mud-wall, or other fence, which invariably surrounds the cultivated ground, and do a lot of mischief in a very short time, as much by trampling the standing corn or rice as by eating it. In some of the more unfrequented parts the natives feel very seriously the result of these nocturnal visits, and notwithstanding that either a man or woman remains in the fields all night howling, rattling sticks together, firing off matchlocks, or pulling a number of rattles at the same time, in different directions, by means of strings led away from their centre post, so pertinacious are these animals during the dark hours that by some means they manage to get in, and eat and destroy all before them. During the day they take to the large woods and thick coverts, but I have also very frequently come across them in the open, and at midday, grazing in, no doubt, a feeling of perfect security on these mountain slopes. The inhabitants of some parts of the Goto Islands told me they seldom got half their crops of corn and sweet potatoes in before the other half or more was destroyed by deer, wild boar, and pheasants; and I do not think they were much wrong in their calculation. In days gone by the Japanese hunter was a *rara avis*. He was generally the shoemaker of the village, and lived somewhere on the skirts of his native hamlet. He was a blood-taker, a destroyer of life, and consequently tabooed from the society of his fellows. This is Buddhism. The skin of the animal was what he wanted to make the sole of a strong walking sandal. Now-a-days the huntsmen—or perhaps sportsmen they ought or expect to be called—are common, for every one shoots who likes, and eats the spoils of the chase afterwards. In former times deer would often be met with just outside the houses of a village, and the early riser was sure to see some strolling up and down the street. Fond of hunting deer as I am—in fact, I think there is no sport like it when they are really wild, wary animals,—nothing would have induced me to kill one of these beautiful creatures which by kind treatment, and being unmolested by usually their bitterest enemy, man, had become more than half-tame.

I landed once on the island of Kingkosan, a sacred locality on the east coast. An ancient temple still stands on a beautiful spot, clustered round with grand old trees, patriarchs of the surrounding forest. No woman was ever allowed to put her dainty foot on the island. The shrine was to be visited by man alone; but since Western ideas had been so profusely introduced, even this spot, so far away from the centres of new enlightenment, had fallen sadly from its time-honoured customs; and instead of the shrine being visited by crowds of pilgrims, and the place being kept up in its ancient order and neatness, it was allowed to fall into disuse and decay. The priests of old were represented by a being dressed in a black suit of cast-off garments, which had done many a day's duty on the person of some Western grogshop-keeper or merchant skipper. This deluded mortal was very proud of a few words of English which he had picked up, and would keep airing them for my benefit. If he had known the feeling of pity and regret which I had for him, as well as for the whole of his nation, he would have kept to his native language. This was but an ever-recurring instance of the change which has come over these people. Flinging from them their old customs, particularly the good ones, and snatching eagerly at new ideas from the West, civilisation—or what is usually understood by that term—had cast its shadow over this fairy land some time before I visited Kingkosan. Of this, however, I may say something hereafter. So to return to the island: Quantities of deer were feeding on the open slopes, and being hard up for fresh meat, I asked my friend in the old black suit if he objected to my shooting one or two. "Certainly not," he answered. "Although they were once, and still really are, sacred, yet *now* we don't mind. Shoot away." I roamed over the lovely undulating ground, and reached the conical peak of the island, 1000 feet high, and from here had a grand view. On my return I shot a hind, and when my men were

carrying her down, fired at a copper pheasant and
another hind almost at the same moment. The latter I
killed, and found the addition to our larder of two deer
very acceptable. Often when surveying the coasts, particularly the out-of-the-way localities, it was difficult to
get fresh meat, and at such times a deer or some pheasants, or a wild boar, came in very much to the purpose.
The abruptness of the mountain-sides, the deep, narrow
valleys, gorges, great masses of rock, impenetrable
coverts, and interminable woods, of which the country
is made up, afford such shelter for these animals, that,
plentiful as they are, it is no easy matter to fall in with
them, and when this is done it is difficult enough to
shoot them. I found the best way to succeed was by
working the coverts and woods with a couple of dogs, a
spaniel and an Irish retriever. I had taught these dogs
to go with whom I pleased, particularly one or two of
my men who had been trained by me how to work the
woods. Picking out the way which I considered most
likely for the deer to take if the dogs stuck to them, I
almost always bagged one, and very frequently two, in
the day.

The following narrative of a day amongst the hills
behind Kobe will give a general idea of this kind of
work. It was early in November, before the rutting

season had ended, and the hinds were still calling all over the higher ranges. A cup of coffee about two in the morning, and then off with the dogs and one attendant. The first mile is perfectly flat, then the mountains rise like a wall to about 1000 feet, gaining height as ridge after ridge follows each other, until they reach 2500 feet, about a mile back from where they spring from the plain. The whole of this endless range of mountains runs right away into the interior of the country. Valleys, some large, but mostly quite small, intersect the country, and on these rice is almost invariably grown. Following a woodcutters' path back from the first line of ridges, half a mile or so, we reached a well-known and favourite deep cleft in the hills, where the matted cover was sufficient to shelter any number of deer. It was quite dark, and not a leaf stirred, so still was the morning air. We remained perfectly quiet for a quarter of an hour, when a cold, grey sort of light began to steal over the black hill-sides. A cock pheasant crowed far away to the eastward, another immediately answered him, then several all round. Ten minutes elapsed, and the note of a warbler came from the cover on the opposite hill-side. At this moment I heard several raps on the stem of a fir-tree not forty yards below where I stood. I knew at once it was a stag rubbing and knocking his horns, and feeling sure of his whereabouts, and that I should be able to find him later in the day, I passed on to another valley three-quarters of a mile off. Turning the shoulder of a hill, which opened the valley, the first thing I saw was the head and neck of a hind, and immediately afterwards two more hove in sight. Nothing like a stag was to be seen anywhere, and making certain, as I thought, of the best hind, I fired. The report appeared to echo, first on one side, then on the other, and go repeating itself far away up valleys and over ridges, reaching the very furthest mountains; but what was my chagrin to see a great stag, black with mud and water, springing from a wet hole almost under my feet, and before I could do more than pull the second trigger in a hurry, he was over the ridge, and out of sight! Following the ridge round, I took up a commanding position, and had my spaniel put on his track. Away the little dog went, and was soon lost to view in the tall grass and tangled cover. Out of this she found it hard to drive the stag; he dodged backwards and forwards for some time, trying in vain to throw the dog off; but at last he had to show himself, and face whatever might await him. He was 150 yards below me, a difficult shot; so hoping he would turn to the left, and pass nearer, or on a level, I did not fire. Instead of taking the direction I expected, he took just the opposite, and, turning the shoulder of the hill, was gone, and I saw him no more that day. Some months afterwards, however, I had the satisfaction of seeing him again, and this time I brought the fine animal on board. His head **was** the finest I ever got in the south. Taking up another station, I sent my dogs to the extreme end of the valley in which I expected the frightened hinds (for frightened only, it appeared, they were) had gone. In a few minutes they were in full cry, but it took a lot of working to make them show. In half an hour a hind stole away, coming straight for me; on came my spaniel, sticking to her track capitally, and as the hind passed, I fired where I thought her shoulder would be, as her head and neck was all that topped the grass. Taking a plunge, she disappeared in a sort of break-neck cleft, covered with tangled creepers. Feeling sure she was dead, I remained still, watching my hound-like spaniel; on she came without a check, passing me, and disappearing where the deer did. To my astonishment, on she went (this I knew by her notes), and watching the valley far down, I saw the hind stealing away towards the stream at the bottom. Making the best haste I could, I followed, and on reaching the stream, found the dog at fault. Soon, however, I got the track of the deer in the bed of the stream, still going down. We followed it for a good mile in this direction, and then got utterly at fault, and I was in the act of turning up the hills again in despair, when up jumped the poor beast out of some low firs growing on a patch of dry sand, and off went the dogs in full cry. A sharp run of a quarter of a mile down the stream brought me ahead of both deer and dogs, who were struggling through the long bamboo grass on the edge of the stream. Another half-mile, and an open spot presented itself on the face of the hill, and knowing that here they must show, I stood still against a huge boulder. In five minutes the hind came struggling along, and hesitating for a moment which way to turn, my bullet passed through her heart, and she rolled down the hill-side to my feet. Her shoulder was broken by the first shot, high up. Cleaning her out, and giving the dogs a taste of liver, I returned to the higher grounds, and waited for a friend who was to join me after breakfast. We beat the same valley and bagged another hind, enjoying a charming day's sport altogether. It was then too late to return to the stag I had first heard in the morning.

It is impossible to give but the very faintest idea of

the lovely scenery, the bright, fresh, exhilarating air, that gives such a wonderful charm to these interminable mountains and valleys. No description can convey the beauty of the autumn foliage. The chestnut, oak, and maple present at this season the richest and most varied colours. Numerous species of fir spring in clumps and single trees among the golden and russet tints of the first-mentioned trees and shrubs. Masses of grey rocks, and clear rushing streams, add to the great beauty and wildness of the scenery.

The spaniel I had was without exception the keenest dog after deer I ever saw. I have pointed to the track of a stag in the sand which I had noted passing over the spot two hours and a half before, and she started the animal after following the scent through thick cover and over rocks for half a mile. She would take to the water after a deer without a moment's hesitation; and I remember her once coming up with a dying stag which had swum off into the sea, and scrambling on to its back. Three or four hours was nothing for her to stick to the scent, there appeared no tiring or shaking her off. If she got thrown off the scent, the little creature would pick out a conspicuous ridge or peak on her way back to where she had left me, and, sitting on her haunches, would bark in quite a different way from what she did when on the animal's track. She knew perfectly well I should follow up in the direction the deer had gone, and evidently learned from constant work that it saved herself a great deal of trouble, this letting me know where she was, instead of returning on her own track to the spot I had been left in, and finding me gone, having then to follow me up, perhaps a good many miles. In June once, when walking over an island, a hind springing from some thick cover, I shot her dead with my rifle, and regretted it immediately afterwards on finding she had a fawn somewhere near. One of my dogs very soon found it, and I took the beautiful little thing on board. It must have been about a week old. On showing it to my spaniel, the dog went into the most extravagant delight, licking and whining over it; and if the other dog came near she growled and was quite ready to fly at her. I firmly believe if she had been in a state to act as wet-nurse, that she would have endeavoured to save the fawn from a premature death.

Frequently I took several natives—anything between twenty and half a dozen, and as many of their half-wild mongrel brutes of dogs. A more motley lot could hardly be imagined. Placing myself in some clearing, if possible on a ridge, the Japanese with their animals would take a sweep round, and enter the cover or woods a mile off. Then turning towards me, and letting go the dogs, all would work very slowly through the woods. The dogs pay no attention to their masters, but work together and amongst themselves in a silent, cunning, and most deadly manner. These pariahs almost always killed one or two deer alone and unaided. They have such keen scent, that once on the track of deer or boar, no hound could stick better to the quarry. It always struck me the poor timid animal got far more put out, and at a loss to know what to do when chased by these silent persistent enemies, than by dogs giving tongue. I have watched the deer steal quickly away, and, hearing no sound, stop and listen; suddenly a white wolfish-looking animal would appear from the cover, at the same spot the deer had left it; away would bound the nervous animal—again coming to a stop a few hundred yards off; suddenly, as before, the white-like shadow would emerge on the track, always perfectly silent; dashing off once more, to undergo the same horror of being followed, the poor beast, if not shot, would very soon plunge into the water—be it sea or lake,—and swim not unfrequently two or three miles to some other point or cover. Deer almost invariably take to the water after a time. It is extraordinary how well deer can swim. No dog can come near this sharp-footed thin-legged animal in the water. This they evidently are aware of, and hence the cause of their taking to an element apparently so very unsuitable to them.

Wild boar don't pay much attention to these dogs; they run at first, but an animal of any size soon turns and faces his persecutors. Many a time I have seen the dogs beaten off, and not unfrequently badly hurt. Badgers are very numerous, and are not the nocturnal creature they are in Scotland. It was a very common occurrence to meet them walking about the edges of the paddy-fields any time during the day, and on observing my dogs or self they only shuffled off into the cover, remaining close to, and were easily turned out and shot. In the winter their skin makes a nice mat, but during the summer their fur gets very thin, and their skin is then not worth a charge of powder. Of all the most impudent animals, I think none comes up to the Japanese fox. I believe it to be identical with our own; in size, colour, and habits, it certainly very closely resembles the British species. They are very common, and perfectly bold and fearless. In fact, to kill a fox is considered very unlucky. It offends the spirit of the animal, which spirit is capable of visiting the family of the life-taker with all kinds of trouble and evil. At the same time, the natives rejoiced to see one of their farm robbers knocked on the head, and had no compunction afterwards in enjoying a hearty meal on the carcass. Many a time have I been amused watching these creatures, squatting on their haunches on some open hillock, and on my dogs getting near their locality, setting up a barking of indignation without any appearance of alarm. Japanese dogs don't like them, and avoid their resorts. Neither did I ever see a native dog follow them either by sight or scent. It was different with my spaniels, and this Reynard would soon find out and take to his legs; he would only run a short distance ahead, however, and then turn round and bark at the dogs. I remember one day I saw a fox sitting on a bare sand hillock, and started a pointer after him; away went both fox and dog, the latter in full cry with excitement and being in such close proximity to a tempting brush. The chase lasted only a hundred yards or so, when the tables were turned by the fox facing round and chasing the dog back to where I stood, barking sharply at him. I have known them come in through the paper windows of the houses at night, and clean the plates of all scraps which were left out in the cooking apartment.

There are several species of martens and weasels. One of the former is of a most rich yellow golden colour, and has a good fur. The common otter is exceedingly plentiful; and many species of seal. The bladder-nosed seal also I have seen in the south. The Japanese chamois (*Antilope crispa*) is a very difficult animal to find, and to bag when found; they keep to the highest mountains, and to the highest and most rugged peaks of these ranges. I have hunted them with the  natives, and with their dogs, and this often; and yet only once, although often close to the creatures, have I had a glimpse of one, much less a shot. On one occasion I was lucky enough to see one, and this was by mere accident, and when not in search of game. I have often been told fabulous stories about the Nigou, the native name for this wary animal. They were supposed to have but one horn, and to use this single frontal ornament as a means of hanging on to trees as well as in self-defence. After some years of anticipation and endeavour to get even a dead specimen, I got a couple, and then, strange to say, several others were brought to me. A young male, alive, was caught, after its mother was shot. Only one specimen of all that were brought to me by the native hunters had both their horns intact—always one, and often both, being more or less broken. In hunting them with dogs, it soon became evident why this was so generally the case. The Japanese, who knew the animal's habits intimately, invariably placed me near some huge bare slab of rock, on which the Nigou, when pressed by the dogs, was expected to appear, and on looking at these slippery sloping platforms, I tried to conjecture —when waiting for the animal to appear—where, if I knocked one over, it would tumble, and what shape or form it would be in by the time it stopped. I could then easily understand why the horns were usually so damaged. I have no doubt also they often caught in the bushes or trees by the slightly turned-back horns, on their falling and reaching the foot of these rocks, hence the origin of the story of their holding on to the trees. The young one which was brought to me alive was the most fierce little thing I ever saw. **Any dog,** large or small, that approached its cage, down went its head, and with a quick sudden spring the creature invariably came bang up against the wooden bars. Its horns were about two inches long, as sharp as needles, and quite capable of inflicting a very nasty wound. The colour of the Nigou is a brownish slate; the older they get, the lighter coloured they become. Until I actually had one in my hands, I was unable to decide whether they had a beard or not, and was pleased to find they do not possess this ornament—therefore they are true antelopes, and not goats.

The birds of Japan are more interesting than the quadrupeds. In the first place, there is a far greater variety, and many are so nearly allied to our own, whilst others are also so nearly connected with those found in India, that very little difference, and sometimes none, can be detected. A few of those which are, I believe, identical with the British bird of the same species, I will note, mentioning how sometimes they do in some way or another differ. To begin with the beautiful white-tailed white-headed eagle.[1] This bird is exceedingly common in the north. Stray birds are found in the south, but I never saw a single mature specimen. The natives believe they get the white tail the second year, and the white head the third. I have frequently seen them with the white tail only, but never with the head only white, which corroborates the Japanese opinion. The osprey is common throughout the whole of Nipon, and breeds on the pinnacle rocks and in the

---

[1] See sketch of this bird, p. 7.

forks of old fir-trees. I consider this bird to be identical with our own, excepting in size. The Japanese bird is, I think, a little smaller than his Western congener.

The peregrine falcon is also plentiful. Shooting one day in a marshy patch of ground, a snipe rose, and before I could fire, something darted past my head, and the snipe dropped into the rushes. A male peregrine had sprung from some firs not far off, and swooped at the snipe. I put the frightened thing up four or five times, the falcon each time dashing at the bewildered bird; during the interval he flew round and round my head, within five-and-twenty yards. The snipe at last refused to rise, and my retriever brought it to me uninjured. Thinking the bird had gone through enough to entitle it to another chance, I let it go, and the poor little creature may be still enjoying life. No enemies with guns at any rate are likely to visit the locality. A snipe is a favourite bird with epicures of the hawk kind, and particularly with the peregrine; I have often seen one of these birds dart after a snipe that I had started, and excepting in the instance mentioned, the snipe has invariably gone away with the wind, and kept rising to get above the hawk. The kestrel, sparrow-hawk, hen-harrier, and a species of buzzard, come next as to general distribution. The three first named are, I believe, similar in every way to our own species. The water-ouzel (*Cinclus Pallasii*) is found in all the mountain streams. It differs from the British bird by having no white mark on the breast. I have watched this most interesting bird while feeding or otherwise undisturbed, and always observed that its habits were just the same as in the mountainous streams at home. Where trout exist, the ouzel are particularly plentiful, appearing to prefer the young of this fish to that of the more common Japanese white silvery fish, which is very tasteless, and inferior to the trout. The house-martin is a great favourite with the natives. The bird becomes very tame, building its nest on the cross-beams in the houses, within a couple of feet of the inmates' heads. When sitting at the open street-side of the shops, these birds keep passing in and out, within a few inches of your face. A small board is placed under the nest, to prevent any mess reaching the clean-matted floor. The nests are never destroyed, and year after year the birds return. If they do not, or if they forsake their nests, it is considered very unlucky. The house-sparrow (*Fringilla domestica*) does not exist in Japan; but the tree-sparrow (*F. montana*) takes its place in every way. It is in Japan exactly what the house-sparrow is to us in England. It lives in the streets, and breeds in the thatched roofs and holes in the walls. The Japanese **boys** amuse themselves by putting bird-lime on the top joint of an old bamboo-rod, and then cunningly stalk the sparrows as they sit perched on the eaves of the houses.

There are numerous birds that have prolonged notes or even a kind of short spasmodic song; but from my own experience over many years spent in the country, I consider there is but one real songster, and that is our own species of lark (*Alauda arvensis*). To see this bird rise from the ground, and go soaring up until almost out of sight, singing during the time, just, in fact, as the bird does from an English field **in** spring or summer, is more than interesting. **There is something** very charming, very home-taking, when so **far** away—as far away in reality as can be reached by sea or land—in thus being reminded of home scenes and associations. The common Japanese crow (*Corvus japoniensis*) is found everywhere. They roost in certain set places, generally in the clumps of trees, **which** invariably surround the temples, and which are close to or in the villages; here they congregate **in great** numbers every evening. They breed, however, raven-**like, in** single trees, and far from each other; or in rocks, cliffs, and suchlike places, partaking, as it were, partly of the habits of the raven and partly of the rook. They are most impertinent birds. I remember once being very much amused watching a girl washing some plates outside a cottage-door. Six or eight of these cool inquisitive birds were on the ground, not two feet from her hands, and every now and then two or three would hop in and pick at something which fell from the dishes, the girl constantly switching her cloth at the black birds to keep them from pecking her fingers. The coolness of these kindly-treated feathered friends of the Japanese is everywhere the same. They do good particularly in the fishing villages, by picking up remains of fish, and anything of such nature, that finds its way into the streets.

Many a good bag of geese I have made on the flat rice plains outside Tokio (the capital), and wild and difficult were these birds to approach; but walking on into the capital, and in the heart of the great city, there the very birds—swan, geese, and all kinds of ducks—which outside on the plains had got up wild and wary, were congregated in the moat surrounding the palace grounds. Hundreds of people keep passing up and down within half a stone's-throw; yet here, from time immemorial, have these birds flown in, and remained during the day, feeling quite secure from harm; but if met with outside the city on the fields how different they appear! Such may the wildest and most timid bird become by kind treatment and protection. It was always a matter of fact, that whatever new ground I visited where Europeans and guns had never been, the duck and geese knew at once I was not a Japanese, and therefore not to be trusted. I used to carry a native loose jacket and white head-tie, and on seeing a flock of geese feeding in the open rice stubble, would slip these two articles on over my shooting-jacket and cap; a little straw stuck on the end of my gun completed my disguise. In this way, and imitating the short, shuffling walk of the Japanese, I used to walk straight up to geese whilst feeding, and often have a right and left at very easy range.

The arctic goose used to be very common during the winter in the southern big plains, and two kinds of the white-fronted, grey-lag, bean, and Shanghai species are so still. There is a greater variety of ducks than any other genus. The most lovely in plumage, and without exception the best-flavoured, is the mandarin duck. This bird is particularly fond of the acorn of the *ilex*, and is often found far up the hillsides feeding under this shrub. It appears quite as much at home on the branches of big trees as in the water. It is neither wild nor wary, and except for the sake of having a specimen of one's own shooting—or, alas! for one's own eating!—it is a pity to kill such a marvellously beautiful creature. The female is of a dull slate colour, with nothing at all remarkable in her plumage, excepting that she has a decided crest, which she can elevate like the male. The harlequin garrot (*Anas histrionica*) is very common along the northern shores of Yesso; I once saw it as far south as Yedo Gulf, in latitude 35°. There were only about six in all; they had probably been driven so far south by hard weather. The male is an exceedingly pretty bird. They evidently breed about Kunishir and the north-eastern coasts of Yesso, as it was in the summer I saw them so constantly and in such numbers.

The robin (*Sylvia rubicula*) I have seen, but only on the mountains. The bull-finch (*Pyrrhula orientalis*) is common throughout Japan. Although this bird is classified as a different species from our own (*P. vulgaris*), I consider it the same bird. In habits, note, and plumage there is not the slightest difference, with the single exception that the red in the Japanese bird only extends over the throat, whereas in ours it runs down on to the breast.

The little common wren (*Troglodytes vulgaris*) is, I think, somewhat smaller in Japan than at home. There is no **finer** bird in Nipon than the great blue **crane**. With what majestic strides he walks across the paddy-fields, as if all he surveyed belonged to him; and his strong harsh croak, which is invariably sounded as one approaches him, always appeared to **me most** suitable to the wild scenery which generally surrounds the favourite feeding-grounds of the birds. Though sacred in ancient days, I have even **then eaten** them at the princes' tables, and very good eating they **were**.

A beautiful species of kingfisher (*Halcyon coromanda major*), although rare, is to be found on the southern and western parts of Japan. It evidently **breeds** there, as I have shot both male and female in the heart of summer. It is a lovely bird, almost entirely of a red scarlet colour, with a blue patch over the tail. It inhabits the cool shady places, in the very densest woods, often far from water; its chief, if not only, food is the smaller kinds of grasshoppers. I believe the bird is a native of India as well as Nipon.

There are only two species of pheasant indigenous to the country, the common green bird (*Phasianus versicolor*) and the copper bird (*P. Sömmeringi*). As a rule, the former is found on the lower country, in the plains, and near and amongst cultivation, whilst the latter sticks chiefly to the hills and mountainous districts. In the north one may often shoot the two birds right and left; still, you certainly find the copper pheasant on the very highest mountains, where its food is mainly wild raspberries and other diminutive fruit, and where the green bird never goes. They appear never to cross in breeding. Both are equally good to eat; but the copper bird is more difficult to shoot; he is more wary, and gets away quicker, and altogether is far more satisfactory sport. The metallic hues as the sun shines on its plumage are beautiful. The Japanese keep them in confinement, but they never appear to become tame or domesticated as the green bird easily does.

The large black species of pigeon (*Carpophaga*

janthina) is most common on the western islands—in fact, I never saw one on the mainland. I think it is a bird which lives almost, if not entirely, on fruit. Although by no means rare, it was years before I saw one. I accounted for this by finding it was a shy wary bird, and almost always remained in the trees that grew on the very steepest banks on the sides of the islands. Amongst the numerous gulls which either visit or reside on the coasts, *Larus crassirostris* is, I think, the most interesting. All large species of gull that I know of when mature have the tail white; this bird is an exception, having a broad black band across the otherwise pure white feathers. I found them breeding on the low rocks which surrounded an island at the entrance to Awari Gulf. There is a species of finch found in the north, *Pyrrhula rosea*, Tem., which (both male and female) has a very pretty plumage. I called it the scarlet-finch for want of a better name. The head feathers are of a rosy-red hue, with the end of each feather tipped silvery white; breast red, back much the same, the ground-colour being a rich brown. I kept a couple of these birds in a cage for a considerable time, but fearing they would not retain the rosy tint if allowed to moult twice, I killed them for their skins. Another bird, the little rose-coloured bull-finch, has also a very silvery head, and rose-tinted plumage, but after keeping this bird through a couple of moultings, and finding he lost the lovely rosy hue on the second moulting, and never got it again, I feared that the finches would do the same. One of the bull-finches I brought to England, where the reader may possibly meet it, as it escaped and never returned!

OSPREY'S NEST IN SUTHERLANDSHIRE, SCOTLAND.
Rock eight feet high.

OSPREY'S NEST AT TABKARA URA, JAPAN
Rock twelve feet high.

CHAPTER V.

A WALK IN KIUSIU.

For some days it had rained with little intermission, but on the 15th of June it cleared, and the sun shone out brightly. I knew the country would be fresh and tempting for a good walk, so as early as possible after breakfast I started. The little village, which ran for a couple of hundred yards just behind the clean sandy beach, was first passed through. How busy all the womenkind were, airing their clothes, attending to their flowers, washing rice, and so on! The men were long since at their work in the fields. At the further end of the village, and a little way back from the path, was the Buddhist temple. Two very fine specimens of the fern-leaved tree grew on either side of the entrance.[1] They were in their fresh, green foliage, and looked extremely well in contrast with the dark Sugi (*Cryptomeria*), and other pines, which surrounded on three sides this very neat and pleasant spot.

I followed the path up the valley. The young rice was looking very well. The great lotus plant, with its beautiful pink flower, here and there broke up the monotony of the paddy-fields. Snakes kept constantly gliding off the path into the grass or rice cover. They were all the common harmless species, and were evidently bent on enjoying the warm sun. My spaniel every now and then made a dash at one, and succeeded occasionally in nipping it through the back. For some reason, she had lately taken the most inveterate hatred to these creatures, and never lost an opportunity of waging war against them. I think she must have been bitten by one of the venomous species, for, on one occasion, her face had swollen up very much, evidently from the sting or bite of something poisonous.

Half a mile up the valley I passed a cottage standing near the pathway. The little garden in front was a mass of flowers, among which there was a large plant of the oleander in full bloom, and a perfect

[1] *Salisburia adiantifolia.*

hedge of the big jessamine (*Olea fragrans*), which scented the whole atmosphere. Cucumbers were growing over the side path and hedge, and a great vegetable-marrow plant had run all over one end of the roof of the cottage. A few tea shrubs were in full bloom in the garden. This useful species of camellia is both pleasant to the eye and to the taste. A pair of little bantams pecked about the garden, and one of the tailless cats peculiar to this country basked in the sun. A pretty girl worked away at her loom under the shade of the broad verandah; a cloth round her waist was her sole attire, and was doubtless enough, for the day by this time had become very warm, although the thermometer stood only at about 78°.

The elderly lady of this comfortable little home was busy amongst her pots and pans. Two or three smaller bairns were playing with a kitten, and a baby strapped on its tiny sister's back was enjoying itself in profound slumber, notwithstanding the perpetual motion of its nurse. I could not help contrasting this comfortable happy-looking labourer's home—by no means an exceptional one—with many of our own dirty, uncared-for, squalid cottages, belonging to the same class of people.

A little way further on I came to the well from

whence these cottagers got their water. Looking in at the beautiful clear water, which was about four feet deep, I saw two fine trout swimming about. They appeared quite tame, coming to the surface as if they expected to be fed, and just then a nice-looking girl coming for water, I asked her why they kept the trout there.

"To eat the insects," she answered. "They keep the water perfectly free from anything of the kind."

"What a capital plan!" I remarked; "and I see they are very tame."

"Oh yes! They know we won't hurt them, and we often bring them a few grains of rice."

"Can you tell me the way to yonder mountain, the one with the smooth peak, like a cup upside down, and a little knob on the very top?" I asked.

"If you follow this path you cannot go wrong; it will take you to the foot of the Maiden," she answered.

"The Maiden," I said; "is that the name of the mountain? Why is it called so?"

"Because the top of it is so like a maiden's breast," she replied, looking at her own.

"Well," I said, laughing, "so it is. Good-bye. Perhaps I'll come in and have a cup of tea on my way home."

"Do so; we shall be glad to see you, and you will be hot and tired by that time, and glad to rest. A pleasant walk to you."

Soon afterwards I reached the head of the valley. I observed the barley was nearly all cut, and that the other crops of sweet-potatoes and cotton looked very promising. Half-a-dozen green pheasants were pecking away at the potatoes. One fine old bird, standing on a mound, crowed every now and then, and immediately afterwards flapped his wings violently, as pheasants always do, making a peculiar drumming noise. This is a challenge to all comers; but none of the other four or five cocks appeared the least inclined to accept it. A pair of the beautiful light-green pigeons passed across in front of me, their bright yellow necks shining like gold in the sun. The rough path now entered the fir wood, which ran down on each side of the valley I had come up. Just before the trees closed over the path, I looked over the high bank of the reservoir, which is invariably found at the head of all cultivated valleys, and observed a small flock of mandarin ducks swimming about by the edge of the alder shrubs which hung over the water from the wood side. The drake of this species is, as I have already said, the most beautiful of all the duck tribe I know.

As I passed through the wood, numbers of a little yellow butterfly were flitting to and fro, constantly lighting on the damp spots of ground, and sucking the moisture up greedily. The wood was quite narrow at this spot, and as I emerged from it on the hill-side, a beautiful copper pheasant cock rose at my feet, and went off like a rocket for the cover. The path skirted round the hill, leaving the wood on the right and the grassy hill-side on the left. Sweet-scented yellow lilies were everywhere scattered about, and pretty blue-bell-shaped flowers, besides the scented jessamine, and azaleas in profusion, carpeted the ground. My spaniel, who had evidently been tracking something for some way, here entered a clump of thorn bushes, and immediately a tremendous commotion ensued therein. Out jumped a stupid, bewildered-looking hare, which appeared too astonished and confused to decide what to do. I nearly knocked it over with my stick; and my dog rushing headlong at it, got entangled in some creeping plant, and tumbled head over heels on to the creature. This appeared to rouse it somewhat, for it now made off in great bounds, as if making up for lost time.

I soon came to a clear stream running down the hill-side, in the deepest pools of which trout five or six inches long were plainly seen against the dark rocky bottom. As I stood watching them, a little green kingfisher dashed suddenly into the water ten yards up the stream, and immediately appeared with a trout about two inches in length. The bird was not the least put out by my presence, but returned to the dead branch overhanging the water, on which he had been watching for his prey. Numbers of the painted-lady butterfly appeared about the banks of the stream, attracted, I suppose, by the warm surface of the great rocks.

The path in a short time again entered the wood, which was more open underneath, and the lovely ferns which grew in profusion were more easily seen. Here I came upon a gigantic camphor-tree. It must have been of great age, for the two or three branches that were left appeared the size of large trees. The stem of this patriarch I carefully measured, and found it to be fifty-three feet in circumference at four feet from the ground; it was long past its prime, and very decayed and hollow. Thirty feet round is not a very unusual size for this tree when still in the prime of life.

I soon entered another valley, and passed through small groves of mulberry shrubs, and the wax tree, which is also a species of mulberry. In the autumn this tree turns a bright red; the berries then are picked and ground, and run into wax by the assistance of heat.[1] An adder lay coiled in the path, and positively refused to move, but instead bit viciously at the end of my stick. My dog was very anxious to fly at it, but I preferred knocking the wicked-looking reptile on the head. I only know two species of venomous snakes in Japan, though the natives say there are others.

Passing over a sharp rise I found myself in a large valley which ran up amongst the hills at right angles to the general direction I had been coming, and as it was now very warm I decided to give up the "Maiden," and stick to the lower country. A broader path led up the left side of this big valley. Great fir-trees here and there towered high over everything. When these isolated trees are found growing along or by the road-side, it generally indicates some main highway. A few white storks were feeding in the rice-fields, and grand birds they looked. Although they evidently breed in the country—in fact were then probably breeding—I never succeeded in finding where they nested. Coming to a tea-house about noon I decided to rest half-an-hour. No sooner had I sat down under the grateful shade of the overhanging roof than a pleasant smiling girl appeared, and begged to be allowed to take off my boots while I had some tea.

[1] See remarks on candle-making, chap. ii.

"You look very warm and tired," she said; "pray let me bathe your feet; it is most refreshing, I can assure you."

While I remained here a couple of swallows kept flying in and out, passing within a foot of my face. Their nest was under the roof close within two or three feet of where I sat, and the little young ones' heads peeped out over the edge, anxiously watching for each return of the old birds with food.

"Do these birds always build here?" I asked.

"Oh yes, every year; if they did not, we should consider it very unlucky."

"I did not know you people were so superstitious," I remarked.

"Ah, but we are; besides, we are fond of birds."

"I know that," I said. "I see you have one of those curious restless tomtits, which is continually jumping to the top of his high cage, turning over backwards when there, and lighting again on his perch."

From the tea-house I kept up the valley, meeting every now and then natives, with their patient well-conditioned old bullocks, laden with rice, charcoal, and other articles. These slow-going carriers plod along quietly, but surely, for great distances. They are shod with straw shoes, but as these things soon wear out, each animal has a dozen pair or so strapped to the rest of its baggage. I met ponies also laden with similar goods, and wearing the same kind of straw shoe. One of these ponies not only had a good load of merchandise on its back, but perched on the top of all was a woman. The whole erection appeared very shaky, and as if very little would bring goods and female to the ground. Just as I was thinking so, something startled the animal, which swerved to one side so suddenly that everything was unshipped; down came the whole load, the unfortunate girl lighting on her head, and then rolling over on the ground. To rush to her rescue and to hear she was not hurt was the act of a moment. She was more amused at her little adventure than otherwise, and wishing me a pleasant walk she proceeded on her journey.

I trudged on to the village near the top of the valley, meaning to have a dip in the sulphur spring which I knew existed there. Going straight to the large shed which was built over the water for the comfort and convenience of visitors, I found the bath, which was only about four feet square, already occupied by an elderly gentleman and lady, a young damsel and a youth. Not wishing to interfere with this happy but peculiar quartet, I gave up the idea of a bath and went on. The path now led directly into an extensive range of hills covered with wood. Numerous species of fir, oak of small size, maple of several kinds, alder, Spanish chestnut, and birch, were the principal trees. The *Pinus Massoniana*, which is the most hardy of all the coniferæ that grow in Japan, flourishes as well in the sand close to high-water mark, as it does high up on the mountain-sides, or in the valleys where the soil is deep. The forest here became so open underneath, and looked so tempting, I left the path and kept ascending for some distance. I came upon a number of the largest "mats,"—the native name for the pine just mentioned,—with notches cut in the bark, always on the north side of the tree. A little box was suspended just below the lower notch, and some of the boxes were half full of resin, which had trickled down from notch to notch, until it reached the box. On inquiring, I was told it took about a fortnight to fill these receptacles. As I stood by one of these trees, examining this simple process of collecting the gum, a badger came shuffling along, and got quite near before he observed me. When he did, the beast appeared very little astonished, only altering his course slightly as he passed by. In this country animals are not persecuted, and are consequently far less in fear of man than is generally the case.

Myrtles and azaleas grew on all the more open places; the latter being in full blossom, and forming a rich and beautiful carpet. Presently I heard some laughing voices coming from the higher ground, and almost immediately afterwards five girls hove in sight each carrying a bundle of sticks. The two smallest, who were only about three feet high, certainly had very tiny bundles, of about half-a-dozen sticks apiece, but the elder girls had enormous loads on their heads. They rested a little, and told me they had come from the village early in the morning.

"You don't mean the village where the sulphur spring is?" I said.

"Yes, that's the one," they answered.

"And these little things too, did they come all that way?" I remarked.

"Oh yes."

"Why, it's one rii" (three miles), I said.

"I think so," they answered.

I candidly own the heap of sticks these girls carried I could hardly move, except by rolling them along the ground; and to observe the way they again got them on their heads was both instructive and curious. Kneeling down in front of the bundles, they got their head underneath them by some extraordinary working, and then gradually rose to their feet. Of course, beginning so early, all the muscles which come into play by carrying weights on the head are very much developed. These girls told me they had seen some "*skha*" (deer) just before they met me, adding I should probably see them as I went on. About a quarter of a mile further on a red bird like a gigantic butterfly started from a branch as I passed, and after flying twenty yards lit on a low bush. It was the Alcedo (*Halcyon coromanda major*), the very beautiful kingfisher already spoken of. As I was watching this interesting bird, a stag trotted from a clump of bushes and made off up the hill. A fine fellow he was, with the velvet still on his horns though they were full-grown.

Evening was approaching, and I had still some miles to go, so getting again into the path I made the best of my way back.

As I neared the bay, and was passing by the stream that entered the village, I came upon a fisherman sitting net in hand on a stone, quietly watching a mat spread out over the water, just above where there happened to be a slight fall of about eighteen inches. Underneath, the stream was blocked up sufficiently to prevent any fish from passing that way. I had hardly been a minute on the spot when a fine grey mullet sprung from the water, with the intention of overcoming the slight fall, but instead of lighting in the upper pool he found himself landed on the mat. The fisherman at once reached out his landing-net, secured his fish, sat down again, and lit his pipe.

My walk was over; a dozen specimens of butterflies, several beetles, and a few additional ferns were added to my collection.

JAPANESE GENTLEMAN.

CHAPTER VI.

THE KII COAST.

THE Kii coast, embracing 100 miles in a straight line, is one of the most beautiful, as well as the wildest, in Japan. It is very thinly peopled. Narrow valleys, bounded by abrupt rugged mountains, afford the only habitable localities. In most of these small villages are scattered about, generally consisting of twenty or thirty houses, the inhabitants being either fishermen or woodsmen. A few larger villages there certainly are; Singo is one towards the south, which has nearly 4000 inhabitants. It is built on the banks of a large river, down which timber cut inland is floated, until it arrives at the town; where it is collected, and shipped off in junks to different parts of the country.

A little south of Singo is Koza Gawa. Wood, as at the former town, is shipped from here to the large cities. Whale-fishing is also carried on at Koza. The plan of capturing this big creature is so unusual, I will give a short description of the *modus operandi*. Large boats are kept ready for launching, and, when whales are reported, put off, manned by twenty or more men. The boats work in couples, each couple having a strong grass-made net, from 200 to 300 feet in length. These nets are made in squares—the mesh two to three feet—each square being about thirty feet in size, and attached lightly to the next, until the entire length of net is made up. When a whale is seen, the net is dropped across his course, or the animal is surrounded by several nets; on his making off, and striking the net, the square which he comes in contact with is broken away from the rest, and clings round his head and shoulders. The faster he goes the closer it sticks to him. The whale appears soon to get frightened and flurried, as he seldom remains long under water, but returns to the surface, where he flounders and plunges about. The same manœuvre is then repeated by his pursuers, and if a second net is successfully got round him, his capture is certain. Wearying himself by frantic endeavours to get clear of the net, he soon lies exhausted at the surface, and is then put out of his misery by tough spears and other weapons.

Whales' flesh is much esteemed by the natives, and finds its way from these fisheries to all the large cities. During the winter months it may be seen in the provision-shops in Kobe, and a most uninviting kind of food it looks. At Katzura, a small town, where a few boats are kept, the inhabitants told me they had caught fifty whales in one season, and during half-a-century had lost only one man in the pursuit. At this place (Katzura) are several mineral springs, the waters of which are famed for their curative properties, particularly in cutaneous diseases; so much so, that I was assured by the natives seven days were sufficient for all ordinary cases, and fourteen for the most serious. The effect on a friend of mine whom I took there was marvellous; in about ten days an old wound, which had been open for years, was healed. I believe my friend, besides bathing seven or eight times a day, drank as many bottles full of the water, so that a very radical cure might have been anticipated. When he went down to the spring, a mere hole in the rocks above

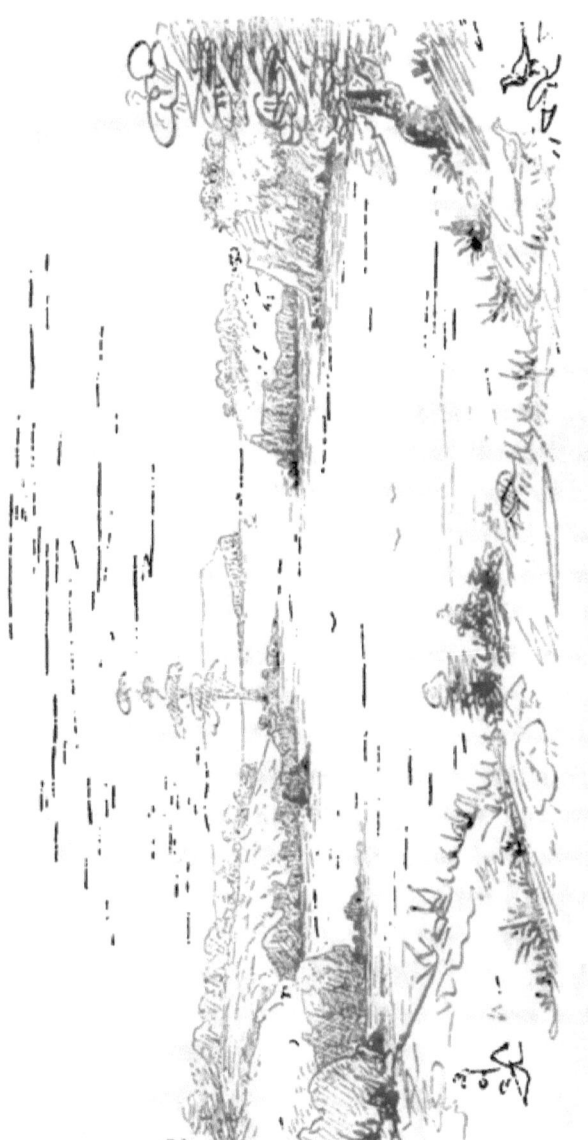

MATOYA HARBOUR, KII COAST.

low-water mark, he found a young lady quietly enjoying the warm bubbling water in the bright sunshine.

There is a very beautiful waterfall six miles inland from Katzura. The river comes over a slab of rock, and falls, without a break, 275 feet into a deep pool, and then runs away between great boulders and masses of rock, along a picturesque valley, to the sea. The beauty of the situation is not thrown away. A famed Shinto[1] temple, built 300 years ago, stands on the slope of the mountain, which curves amphitheatre-like round the waterfall. Pilgrims from all parts of Japan come here to pray to the unseen Spirit for those at sea and far away. A magnificent avenue of cedar and camphor trees leads up to the temple, and then on to the fall. Some of these trees were twenty-five to thirty feet in circumference, and otherwise of grand proportions; but the Government axe, which has been very busy of late years, has fallen even here.

Matoya harbour, eighty miles to the north, is of great value to vessels coasting from the Inland Sea to

---

[1] Some readers may not know that Shintoism and Buddhism are the only two religions of the Japanese. Shinto is never represented by any figure, but is worshipped as the "Unseen Spirit" which pervades everything. Buddha, as is well known, is always represented by a male figure; Shinto, the unrepresented, is supposed to be a female.

Yedo. More particularly was this the case when junks carried all the merchandise. Steamers of late years have taken the place of these ancient craft, and there is now less traffic along the coast; still, large fleets of junks occasionally assemble here, waiting for a fair westerly wind. During the interval the crews enjoy themselves in the tea-houses, which are so attractive as to tell much against a speedy voyage.

A narrow creek runs a couple of miles inland from the harbour of Matoya, opening out to a large shallow lagoon. The surrounding country is undulating; the narrow valleys between the low hills are partly cultivated, and generally terminate in swampy patches. It is a wonderful locality for game. Many an excellent day's shooting I have enjoyed here. Beginning on one side, and taking the country as it came, working up to the head of the lagoon, my bag usually averaged six to ten brace of pheasants, a hare or two, a woodcock, some pigeon, half-a-dozen snipe, a few quail, and often a mallard or a couple of brown duck. On reaching the head, where a clump of large fir-trees grew round the site of a small temple, lunch and an hour's rest was thoroughly appreciated; and here, whilst enjoying the warm sun, I used to watch some ospreys, which invariably were to be seen fishing in the shallow water. The

THE KII COAST

boldness of these birds, when they are not persecuted, is very great. **They used,** for instance, to hunt the water within easy shot, plunging in after their silvery **prey** often not twenty yards from **where I sat.** On capturing a fish, they would make off to some large rocks, a couple of hundred yards **away,** returning again **in a very short time. Whether in a short flight or a** long one, these birds always carry the fish **in their** talons, and always with the head of the fish pointed in the same direction as their own, never crosswise or **tail first. I once** saw one of these birds strike a fish too large for it to lift, and a tremendous struggle for a short time took place. I happened to be in **a boat,** and nearly came up to the combatants before the osprey **let go his hold.**

After lunch, **a few more** pheasants, **and as many snipe as I** pleased from the paddy-fields, which bordered the small river flowing into the lagoon, **besides several** shots at teal, would swell my bag considerably. As the evening closed in, I generally finished up by waiting **for duck, as they flew in** from the open water of the lagoon to feed amongst the rice-fields in the valleys.

The part of the coast **outside Matoya harbour is** famous for a kind **of sea-weed** much esteemed **by the** Japanese for food. It grows in about twelve feet of water, and is collected by women. At low water numbers of boats put out from the villages, having one man and eight or ten women in each. The man manages the boat, while the women strip, and drop quietly into the water. Each woman has a tub, which floats on the surface, until filled by the owner's repeatedly diving, and bringing a handful of weed up at a time. These women remain under water about thirty seconds, and on coming to the surface float about as much at home as a lot of seals, diving again in a very short time. In fact they seem far more like some water-nymphs than bipeds belonging to *terra firma*. During the few seconds they rest they whistle a queer, plaintive note, the effect of which, when there are several score of them together, is very strange. For two hours or more will they stick to this work, then coming on shore stand and squat round a huge fire, lighted on purpose, in some sheltered nook. Here they chat and bake their olive-coloured bodies to a good brick-dust red. If the tide suits, they again go to work for another hour or two, or even longer.

The reason given me by these divers themselves why women, and not men, were always employed in collecting this sea-weed, was rather novel. Formerly, in bygone days, men did dive for it, as the women do now; but on one occasion a man was seriously impaired by some hungry fish, and after this accident the fair sex only were considered fit or suitable for this pursuit. On an island, a couple of miles from the shore, where I frequently had to go, these women used to assemble in numbers, and at first, when my boat appeared, they were rather scared, and ran to some cover; but their fear soon wore off, and they would come tumbling into the surf, and, catching hold of the boat, with a run **and** a laugh, haul her, crew and all, high and dry **out of the** water. They are short-lived, according to their own account. How they stand it at all is a mystery to me; for they not only work during the summer, when the atmosphere is warm and pleasant, **but in** mid-winter as well; at which season the strong **and** constant westerly winds are very sharp and keen, coming off snow-covered mountains, and blowing across this lower land with intense bitterness.

Nothing can be more charming than the winter months in this particular part of Japan. The healthy **bright but cold** winds, the clear atmosphere, the wild grand scenery, coupled with abundance of game, and the nice, polite inhabitants, makes a visit most enjoyable. At least I give those I made a high place among **my** happy memories of Japan.

Shocks of earthquake are frequent throughout Japan. On one occasion, when just going off to sleep, in a Buddhist temple, I heard a rumbling sound like distant thunder, which appeared to come down the valley. I had just time to think it a strange occurrence on a cloudless starlight night, when the temple appeared to receive a sharp violent kick from directly underneath, lifting me nearly off the floor. A cock pheasant at the same moment crowed most energetically, evidently as much surprised as I was. On another occasion, when waiting at the edge of a forest for deer, which I expected would leave the cover towards sunset to feed on the open mountain, the ridge opposite me seemed to sway backwards and forwards, causing a most uncomfortable sensation; but it was really the ground on which I stood that moved, and conveyed the very disagreeable impression. Houses at Kobe were split up by this shock; and the *Sylvia*, lying a quarter of a mile off the shore, quivered as if the cable was running out. The same evening, about a couple of hours afterwards, the temple I was staying in rattled as if it was coming to pieces.

The hills and mountains of this peninsula are covered with wood. The crests of the higher ranges are about 5000 feet above the sea, the highest peak,

Odai Yama, being 5600 feet. These upper **ranges are** clothed with primeval forests of coniferæ, oak, and chestnut; the lower with cedar and fir almost entirely, having thick under-cover of innumerable species of hard, deciduous shrubs. Wild boar and deer abound. At night they descend into the valleys, and notwithstanding the fields are fenced in, and traps, rattles, and watchers **are** there also, they **do a great deal** of damage amongst the rice **and sweet-potato crops.** Wild boar are particularly destructive, trampling down even more than they eat. Pits are used, but with little success. My dogs occasionally got into them; and one of the officers of the *Sylvia*, when out shooting, disappeared suddenly from his companion's sight, much to his own discomfort. It was no easy matter, **I believe,** to get him out. Fortunately the Japanese do not use spikes in these traps. Hunting one day with several Japanese and a number of their dogs, a wild boar was started, and came straight up to another gun placed fifty yards from where I stood. He fired right and left at the animal as it dashed past, not five yards off, without effect. Away went the boar down the steep hillside, into some thick cover at the bottom. Soon, however, he again appeared, and faced the opposite hillside, which was open and bare. On the different peaks

Japanese hunters were placed to mark any game started, and I shall never forget their astonishment and delight when my second shot entered piggie's carcass between the shoulders, killing him stone dead on the spot. The distance and deadliness of the "Express rifle" was always a cause of wonder to the Japanese. This particular boar was about 200 yards off. With their own matchlocks, firing a bullet as large as a big pea, they make excellent shooting up to seventy yards, killing pheasants and other birds, besides boar and deer. The latter are hardly ever killed dead, but are wounded, and run down with dogs. I have already remarked that deer almost always take to the water when hunted by Japanese dogs. I have seen them swim long distances, crossing bays and arms of the sea.

In October 1874 I had to make an excursion to Odai Yama, the high peak before mentioned. Two days were spent in reaching it, and a very hard climb it was. A few hours after we started the first crest was reached, and we looked back towards the east from a height of 3000 feet, while to the west range after range of mountains still rose before us. Shortly afterwards we had descended to only 1000 feet above the sea, but towards evening had again reached the height of 4000 feet. From here the path seemed to tumble headlong down to a few woodmen's huts built on a mere shelf of the mountain. This wild spot was 1500 feet above the sea. A river of the clearest water rushed past just below this cluster of houses. Excellent trout abounded in the pools, affording sport as well as food to the natives. A bamboo rod, silk line, and generally a white fly were used by these people with skill and success. Here I found for the first time in Japan the honey-bee. It appeared smaller than our own, but otherwise identical. The hives were square wooden boxes, placed in rows on stands close to the cottages. The owners assured me they never destroyed the bee in taking the honey. An instance of Japanese politeness is here worth mentioning. The headman of the village, on the coast from where I had started, had begged me to wait three days beyond the time I intended, alleging as a reason for making this request that the best guide, in fact the only man who had ever been up the mountain, was away from home. This guide was to meet me at the village I reached the first evening. The guide was there in readiness; but the object to be gained by my delay of three days was really to give time for a new bath and bath-house, to be built ready for my particular use on the one evening I remained there.

Nothing that I know of is so refreshing after a long and tedious walk as a good bath, in water as hot as you can bear it. Scarcely a cottage in Japan, however poor, is without its bath, particularly in the country, where there are no public bath-houses, as there are in the large towns. They are generally placed in front of the house, in the path, or beside a stream. The goodman first gets in, then his wife and children. If the bath is big enough, two or three at a time soak themselves. Soap has only been used of late, since, in fact, it was introduced a few years ago by foreigners. In the public tea-houses the bath-room is attached to the house, and covered over.

To return to my trip. The following day our course, for there was no path, led up the stream, which, I have mentioned, passed the village. After six miles of this slippery, wet walking, we struck up the face of the mountain, and climbing, scrambling, and sometimes walking in a zig-zag line for several hours, we at last gained the crest; an hour afterwards we reached the camping-ground, a plateau of some extent, where three streams met, which, after flowing a short way west, tumbled down the mountain side in a single river of fair size. These streams were all full of trout of excellent quality. Next morning I left our camp very early for the peak, 1000 feet above our wigwam. I very nearly met a bear as he crossed a tiny stream, and but for my anxiety to reach the top early for the purpose of taking observations, I could easily have followed the animal until I came upon him, probably up an oak-tree enjoying the ripe acorns. A nigou, *Antilope crispa*, the Japanese chamois, passed like a shadow across the tall tree-stems. I fired a couple of snap shots at him, but unsuccessfully. The view from the top was very beautiful. Fusi Yama, the sacred mountain of Japan, rose like a great white mass of sugar out of mist and haze, as the crow flies 150 miles from where I stood. I was able to take angles with the theodolite at objects, such as a single conspicuous tree, fifty miles away. During the time I remained at the summit a wolf, evidently much puzzled at our intrusion on his hunting-grounds, kept howling, scarcely 200 yards off. I remained four days at this wild, elevated spot, returning by a different way, which in distance and time was much the same as that by which I ascended. This upper range of mountains I found to be covered with primeval forest. Oak of large size flourished. Chestnut came the next in quantity. On the very summit itself several species of fir grew in profusion. The Hinoki, *Cryptomeria Japonica*, appeared to take the lead in size and number. *Picea Veitchii* was the next, and many others. Copper-pheasants were common. A single large snipe, *Scolopax australis*, baffled my attempts to get within shot of him. Bears were evidently plentiful, by the marks I saw. Wild boar, deer, nigou, and wolves roamed over these grand mountains unmolested. Our own well-known common wren, *Troglodytes Europæus*, was here. The water-ouzel, *Cinclus Pallasii*, was busily at work in the streams, enjoying the trout spawn. It certainly was most interesting finding these two birds on this high range of mountains so far away from our own shores, and to find their habits and peculiarities were just the same as at home. The Japanese water-ouzel differs in one respect from ours, by having no white horse-shoe patch on the breast.

When surveying this part of Japan, I often lived with the natives for days or weeks at a time. Nothing could exceed their kindness, politeness, and thoughtfulness. Sometimes I put up in the Buddhist temples, at other times in their houses. The accommodation in the former is always exceedingly nice and pleasant. Suites of rooms are usually kept in readiness for travellers, and for a very small daily charge I used to get two or three large rooms, the use of the kitchen, bath-room, etc. These rooms are almost invariably built round a miniature garden, where ponds, **tiny** streams, cascades, small forests, wild scenery and flower gardens, are all represented with wonderful taste and accuracy. Live birds, such as wild ducks and storks, are often introduced. Fish in the ponds come regularly to be fed. Sometimes there are men, women, and children, modelled in china, and arranged in different groups, representing a picnic or pleasure party; others standing on the edge of a cliff or mountain peak, supposed to be enjoying a view of wild scenery; models of temples, with priests attending to the gardens, or sitting down in some favourite nook in the grounds. In fact, the variety of objects represented in these miniature gardens is endless, and all with wonderful accuracy. Oak-trees six or eight inches high, and others in similar proportion. The mandarin duck, with his beautiful plumage, is a favourite bird for these tiny ponds. The stork and white heron appear at once to be at home if caught, pinioned, and turned into however small an enclosure, and scarcely more beautiful objects can be imagined than these graceful birds; the heron with its snow-white plumage, or the stork in his more sombre grey colouring, as they walk quietly about these exquisite little gardens, or stand like a statue by the water's edge.

However poor the Japanese may be, their houses are always neat, clean, and comfortable, and I invariably found the country people most willing and pleased to put me up, turning out of the best room, and placing their clean store of mats for my use, cooking, preparing and making ready the bath on my returning in the evening. The daughters of the family always attended, making tea, taking off one's boots and washing one's feet, bringing in the evening meal, talking and joking in their exceedingly pretty manner during the time, and on their taking leave later on, always wishing one goodnight, and pleasant repose.

The children are full of fun, and have innumerable games of play. The girls have their dolls and dolls' houses; the boys every conceivable kind of top, and kites of all shapes and sizes. They all go to school at the age of six, according to Japanese reckoning, but five of ours, and very soon learn to read and write.[1] The girls take charge of the babies when, in fact, they are but babies themselves, the smaller of the two being strapped on the back of the other. I have often seen the feet of the one being carried only just clear of

[1] The Japanese count the age of their children from nearly a year previous to their actual appearance "into this breathing world."

the ground, so little difference was there in size. It is astonishing how these infantile nurses take care of the little—or littler—ones. Many a time have I been much amused in watching a dozen or more of these children playing together. The baby on its nurse's back either sleeps, as if nothing was going on, or, rousing up, watches the game in the most absurd way. The approach of a stranger, particularly if he has a dog with him, will, in out-of-the-way places, cause quite a panic among the little nurses, who, picking up their charges, if they had happened to place them on the ground, scamper off as hard as they can go. The average number of children to a family is about five, but only two to three come to maturity. As might be expected, the strong alone survive. I have come upon villages where five out of eight had died of small-pox,—this before vaccination was introduced. Women after marrying bear children quickly, and nurse them for years. In fact, I believe from what I have seen that they remain capable of nursing without intermission until they leave off having children entirely. I have seen two children so big that they fought over the favourite breast of their mother. I have also seen them standing on the ground, the mother likewise standing and nursing them without having to stoop.

On one occasion a man, his wife, and boy, came alongside the ship to sell fish. While there the boy took his father's pipe, tobacco, flint, and steel, and in the regular orthodox manner went through the whole process of filling five pipes and smoking them, knocking the ashes out each time. He then quickly returned the pipe, etc., to their leather cases, put his small fists to his eyes, and began to cry. On seeing this the mother took the boy on her lap and suckled him. The boy was five or six years of age. Japanese pipes are quite small things, six or eight good draws emptying them.

I cannot say too much for the goodness and kindness that I always received from the inhabitants of this wild part of Japan. At one or two places only had Europeans ever been seen; and consequently the infatuation for Western manners had not spread amongst them. I always found the further from the open ports I went, the nicer in every way were the people. How is this? Why, because the first European settlers in the shape of traders, shopkeepers, and their parasites, that arrive at a new port, or a new country, are always bad specimens of the country they hail from. Adventurers and scoundrels of all descriptions, who, the chances are, have made the country they leave too hot to hold them, rush from all parts of the world. Then comes the **foreign liquor,**—every description of vile and cheap **poison, got up with gold and** silver tinsel-covered corks, spirits of every denomination and abomination,—Bass's bottled ale in enormous quantities being the least evil. Scores of low grog-shops spring up, mainly **for the accommodation** of the crews **of merchant vessels of** all nations; a rougher or **worse lot of** men cannot be conceived. **Quickly, I am sorry** to say, all kinds of cheap bad **liquor spreads from these** treaty ports into the native villages near at hand; and from them, step by step, **far into the** interior, contaminating most fatally the unfortunate natives as it goes. In a wonderfully short time it is hard to find a spot where it has not reached. Hand in hand with foreign liquor travel foreign manners—drunkenness, **coarseness, and vulgarity.**

The refined and gentle manners of the natives soon disappear before this Western civilisation. It is most sad to relate this. As a matter of course immorality follows drunkenness and coarseness. The women change from their heretofore charming manners, and take to cursing and swearing to please the foreigner.

I have often trusted the Japanese with money and other valuables, **as a loan, or to** take temporary charge **of, and** I have never lost a farthing, or the equivalent in value to that amount; as for security, of course I had none. Western forerunners of civilisation teach these natives how to give bad weight for good; to say one thing and mean another; to promise payment and never pay; to charge treble the value of an article; and perhaps worse than all, we not only fall into their ways and customs regarding women, but far outstrip them in this particular species of immorality.

I have got a very long way from my subject, but in speaking of these delightful parts of Japan yet unvisited by the foreigner, I have been led on to explain how a new country may be, and is only too often, invaded by civilisation, and what the consequences are, at any rate for many years to come, to the country.

Having digressed, I may as well say a few words here about missionaries. First in every way comes the Roman Catholic. They are almost invariably well educated, self-sacrificing, patient, and persevering men. I have known them looked up to as the doctor, the friend for advice, the kind and considerate father of the whole village, to whom the old man or the child goes when in difficulties. Instances of their settling differences and stopping bloodshed between hostile villages (in China) I know of. In fact, by their general self-denial and thoughtfulness for their flocks, there is little to be wondered at in the way they ingratiate themselves amongst Eastern nations.[1] They live as the natives, and as a rule, I believe, remain for the rest of their days amongst those they are sent to convert. Their pay is exceedingly small. Protestant missionaries are, speaking generally, for of course there are bright exceptions, neither well educated nor gentlemen. I have often wondered where so many of this class of men come from. They are well paid, usually have their families with them, and live in the best houses to be got. They are constantly changing, often leaving the country before they have mastered the language of the natives they went there to convert; but as far as making converts they stand no chance with the Jesuits. It may be said the Roman Catholic form of religion is more taking. Granting this, still earnestness in such matters is everything, and whereas the Roman Catholic missionary always appears to have his whole heart in his work, the Protestant missionary certainly does not convey the same impression.

To return to the Kii coast. It will be many a day before Europeans find anything to attract them to this wild thinly-peopled locality. The great forests are full

[1] A friend, well acquainted with the American continent, tells me the same thing applies to the aborigines there.

of deer and wild boar; and many a charming day I have spent with my rifle and dogs in quest of these animals. As I have already said, there is only one species of deer found in the whole of Japan, *Cervus sika*. In the south the grass is coarse, rough-edged, and hard; consequently the deer are small, and usually very poor, seldom weighing over 100 lbs., and have stunted badly-shaped horns. I have shot numbers with only switch horns, and no brow antler. In the north, where the grass is long, soft, and succulent, the same deer are nearer 200 lbs. than 100 lbs., and have very fine antlers, always with four large points. I have never seen this varied, even by the smallest addition. The animal in the north is also fat, and excellent eating.

Four kinds of snipe are met with wherever swampy ground occurs. The most numerous of all is *Scolopax gallinago*, but it only appears in the winter. The solitary snipe, *S. solitaria*, is found but rarely. I do not think I shot half-a-dozen in as many years. There is no mistaking this species after having once seen it. To begin with, they are generally found in most unlikely places, as if the bird really searched out spots where no other snipe would dream of going. When flushed, their flight is quiet, straight, and quick, and generally one short note is uttered as they rise.

I used to think a great deal more of picking up one of these strange birds than half-a-dozen woodcock.

Gallinago australis I found occasionally. This is a noble snipe; in some ways they often reminded me of *solitaria*; I have seen them 6000 feet above the sea, on mountain peaks, and generally single birds. They are larger than the solitary bird, often weighing eight ounces. The painted snipe, *Rhynchœa bengalensis*, is common. The female of this species is beautifully marked, and larger than the male. They are very stupid, often objecting to rise at all, preferring to be picked up by the hand. They are dry and tasteless, and I seldom considered them worth a charge of powder and shot. Their chief food is beetles and rice, and the gizzard in consequence is of large size. I never saw the jack snipe, *S. gallinula*, anywhere in this part of Japan. Further north I have killed them. Pheasants are very plentiful, particularly the green bird, *Phasianus versicolor*. The beautiful copper species, *P. Sömmeringii*, although numerous, are much more difficult to see or find, owing to their keeping to the mountains and wild country; whereas the other bird is most abundant near the villages and cultivated ground. To mention all the birds that are found on the Kii coast would be too lengthy, so I will merely note a few more of the most interesting. The osprey (*Pandion haliaëtus*) breeds on the pinnacle rocks, and in the fork of large fir-trees. I have seen six nests within a quarter of a mile. The peregrine falcon likewise has its nest here. The sparrow-hawk, kestrel, kite (*Milvus melanotis*), buzzard, and one or two species of owl are common. A single species of sea-eagle I also met with. About this bird I was and am still rather puzzled. The mature bird has the tail white; I say so because in Korea I found this bird breeding when in this plumage. In the north of Japan I never found them breeding unless both tail and head were white. In the south I never once saw the bird with both tail and head white; and if I had not found it actually breeding on the islands off Korea with the tail only white, I should then have said the bird breeds in the north, and is merely a visitor in the south. Are these birds the same—the variety in plumage being due to locality—or are they a different species? I incline to their being distinct.

Sheep do not answer in the south, in fact cannot live there, owing to the coarse saw-toothed grass which alone flourishes in these parts. It appears to choke these animals. Deer manage, as I have previously mentioned, to find it sufficient for their wants, but not fattening. I have no doubt in the least that sheep would do well in the north or in Yesso, where the grasses are so very different, being succulent and nutritious. Both cattle and ponies do well.

I have spoken of the kindly feeling the Japanese invariably received us with, and an incident relating to another of Her Majesty's ships I will give, showing, as it does, how universal their goodness is. A midshipman died in the vessel when passing through the Inland Sea, and was buried on an island close to the village burial-ground. For years the villagers tended the grave, placing fresh flowers during the summer, and green boughs in the winter over the grave, in exactly the same manner as they did to their own graves near it. Off and on for years I visited the spot (the island being a favourite resort of mine), and always found the simple grave thus watched and cared for. Before leaving the country I publicly thanked these poor people, and represented this act of genuine kind-heartedness to their government through our minister at Yedo.

CHAPTER VII.

INSECTS.

It was always a matter of wonder to me when landing on an island without a habitation on it; without a living creature of any description to be seen; the only herbage a rank rough short grass and wild parsley; to find myself in a few moments covered with a species of tick, about one-sixteenth of an inch in diameter,— little, brown, active fellows, which came off the grass and the ground, and stuck pertinaciously to flannel clothing, or walked, for their activity hardly reached the act of running, all over one's body. As a rule, these little bloodsuckers appeared content with making an examination. At any rate, I was seldom attacked. Not so, however, with regard to the dogs. They were objects equally attractive—more so, I suppose, for at once these little flat shallow things stuck their combination of forceps and sucker-mouths into the dogs' skins, and soon, from being miserable starved-looking objects, became fine fat creatures, as large as a fair-sized bean. How they managed to swell to the size they did seemed extraordinary. If trodden on when in this state they went off with a report like a small pistol. Although the poor dogs were almost eaten up with these things, they never appeared to suffer from the bite. There was no after-inflammation, swelling, or irritation. In fact, I have no doubt the effect on their system was rather salutary than otherwise. Twice only did these ticks show any taste for myself, but on both occasions I felt the effects of the bite for at least a week. My men were also occasionally bitten, the result invariably being the same as in my own case, irritation and itching for seven or eight days. I concluded from this, that although the dog approaches nearer to man than any animal in intellect—which undoubtedly he does—yet in blood there must be a very considerable difference.

What did these ticks generally live on? These barren, rocky islets, as I have said, produced nothing in the way of animal life. Perhaps some diminutive species of insect may have afforded them an existence; but from their thirst for blood, and their wonderful capacity of stowing such a quantity, it appeared as if this alone was their proper food. There is a fly so like our common house species that I never could detect any difference except in their proboscis; it is a perfect little pest when fishing, or on a showery day. The house-fly's proboscis is soft, and has a broad or flanging end. The *Stomoxys calcitrans*—which is the name this little enemy to one's comfort rejoices in—has a hard, sharp-pointed proboscis, which pierces thick knickerbocker stockings with perfect ease, and inflicts a sharp sting on your leg into the bargain. I have often taken to the water, and stood up to my knees in that defensive armour to get rid of their pertinacious attacks. On a wet day they are particularly active, and from being unable to observe any difference between them and the harmless house-fly, one is obliged to wage a constant war against the innocent as well as against the wicked.

Wandering one afternoon through the fir woods, I came upon a large spider just commencing her web. I don't think I ever watched anything with greater pleasure. She evidently was a geometrical lady, by the way she commenced operations. First she crossed one or two lines from a strong high lily plant to some big bamboo-grass leaves about two feet off; then some more lower down, and a few across the corners. She seemed quite indifferent as to the shape enclosed by these outer lines; a circle, I suppose she knew, could be as easily inscribed in a triangle as in a square. These outer lines done, she hesitated a moment, evidently considering something, then immediately returned to the top line, and glued three or four extra ones along it. This, I suppose, was considered enough; for now, walking along to about the centre of the top line, she allowed herself to drop down by the thread she first attached to this spot, and then used as a means of reaching the bottom line; here she glued it. A little distance from this point she attached another line, and then walking along the main outer line, keeping the thread she was spinning clear by means of her hind foot, she, on reaching the proper distance, hauled the line well taut and glued it to the outer line. This now formed the second radius or spoke to the wheel. The other radii, to the number of about thirty, were spun and fastened in exactly the same manner. It was astonishing how quickly this part of her task was done, though occasionally she hove-to, as if considering some point.

Her outer work and radii being now completed, she commenced at the centre, and tested each line by pulling it with her feet. All appearing satisfactory, she glued six or seven concentric circles round the centre, about one-thirtieth of an inch apart, then a few more further apart. And now commenced the most wonderful part of her workmanship. I fear I cannot well describe it. The first concentric lines which she had just completed appeared to be mainly as strengthening stays to the spokes of her wheel. She then went to the circumference, or rather where she intended to form the outer line of her wheel. Here she fastened her thread to one of the radii, and walked down it towards the centre a sufficient distance to allow the thread that came from her to reach the next radius. This done, she stepped across to it and glued her thread at the same distance from the centre as the last, repeating this operation until she had completed the circle. Her circumference line was thus finished. Another, and another concentric line was, in exactly the same manner, passed round the radii, until she reached the first lines which she had spun close round her centre point. Her work was now finished, and taking up her station in the centre of her web, she awaited her prey. The wonderful accuracy she showed in judging the distance from one radius to another, as well as keeping an equal distance between the concentric lines, was very striking. I don't know how long I stood watching this very beautiful operation—not long, certainly, for the time she took making her net was much shorter than I could have imagined. The whole thing was most absorbing, and I was quite disappointed when her work was done.

There is a large yellow and black-coloured species of hornet which I have frequently seen, more than two inches long. They are most objectionable creatures—bad-tempered to a degree, attacking you without any provocation, in the most pertinacious manner. I knew of a nest by the side of a tiny trout-stream, which I frequently visited. A nice little pool lay just opposite or in front of the hornets' nest; but any trout that may have been there were quite safe from being disturbed. I invariably gave the locality a wide berth; but once I lingered, and was immediately stung on the hand by a creature like a small bird, which came straight at me from the hole in the bank where the nest was. On another occasion I sat down on a fallen tree to prepare my rod and line, and to my horror found I was actually sitting on a hornets' nest. To spring up and fly was the act of a moment: nevertheless I was stung. Both times I felt the effect of the stings for seven or eight days.

Centipedes, about six inches long, are by no means uncommon in the south of Japan. Waiting for deer once, I leant against a big fir-tree, and was enjoying the perfect stillness that reigned through the great woods. I had wandered away in thought to our own island in the far west, and was wondering when next I should see it, when I heard a sort of scratching on the bark of the tree close to my ear. Moving just sufficiently to see what was the cause, I found a centipede, quite six inches long, quietly walking up the stem. I was once bitten on my head by a small one, but suffered no serious inconvenience, although I felt it for some days.

Mosquitoes, in some localities, are great pests. The natives have curtains fitted to enclose the whole room, which is an excellent plan; and in some parts of the country, life would be a burden without them. These little brutes never were sufficiently fond of me to become a torment; but when reading or resting in the daytime, one was relieved from their constant buzzing sound if these large curtains were up, and at night they were a great comfort.

In the summer, the swamps in the east of Yesso are

infested with the common horse-fly to such an extent that it requires a considerable amount of determination to face these places, particularly towards evening. At that time of the day I have been nearly driven wild by them when waiting for deer to come to drink.

I suppose animal pests, in the shape of insects, act as stimuli up to a certain extent; at the same time, probably, it can be overdone. As before said, I certainly never observed that my dogs were the least the worse for the relays of ticks that they constantly picked up. Fat deer are equally attacked by ticks as those in poor condition. These animals have their favourite trees for rubbing themselves on, probably either the size or shape suits or fits the particular place generally attacked by the insect. Behind the ear and neck these blood-suckers appreciate more than the body. Wild boar never seem to be made food of by the same species of tick as deer are, but by one of the ugliest, coarsest, and largest insects of its genus I ever saw.

One of the most ingenious insects I know of is the ant-lion. The stratagems this curious-looking thing adopts to catch its prey are worth noting. I believe it belongs to a genus between the dragon-fly and the *Hemerobius*. It resembles a wood-louse, but is more triangular in form, the anterior part being wider than the posterior. It has six legs, and its mouth is fitted with a forceps, consisting of two in-curved jaws. It looks a most helpless creature, and as if totally unable to catch anything, yet its only food is the juices of other insects. Its pace is very slow, and, strange to say, it can only walk backwards. It has therefore to use artifice to catch its prey; all open efforts it could possibly bring into play would never provide it a dinner.

It forms a conical pit, two inches deep, in the soft sand, generally selecting a spot sheltered from the rain by an overhanging bank. In the bottom of the pit it buries itself, and awaits its prey. Very soon some unwary ant stumbles over the edge, and falls or rolls to the bottom, where it is at once seized by the ant-lion's forceps, and retained until all its blood is sucked out. Sometimes the ant escapes the deadly nippers, and struggles to regain the top of the pit, but the ant-lion is ready for such an emergency. Heaping loads of sand on its flat head, it jerks them over and above the poor ant, who, thus assailed, and being on a very crumbling wall of sand, soon comes down again; although I watched them very frequently, I never saw one escape the second time. As soon as the blood has all been sucked from the carcass, the remains are jerked out of the pit.

There is a very pretty species of "hyla," or tree-frog, in Japan. Being of a beautiful green colour when mature, they are then difficult to distinguish from the leaves they walk about on. Alder shrubs appear their favourite locality. Their delicate feet are fitted with little cushions at the end of their toes, which form a kind of sucker. They can squeeze the air out of these cushions, and then, by the pressure of the atmosphere, they adhere firmly to a leaf in any position, just as our house-fly walks on a window or ceiling. Although when mature they are green, when young they are brown, and at this time are carried about on their mothers' backs. I never heard this tree-frog give any note; possibly it does, but if so, it is at night. There is one very large species of toad, a lazy great awkward fellow, which lives in the rushes surrounding swamps.

I am unaware if there is more than one species of salamander in Nipon; the one I know of is found in the lakes in Kiusiu, and grows to a large size, being frequently three or four feet in length. Of ancient animals I can say nothing. An elephant's tooth was dug out of the thick clay at Yokoska, when the site for the dockyard at that place was being excavated. It is the only instance of the kind I know of.

CHAPTER VIII.

SHOOTING, ETC.

WANDERING one day in Yesso over the low slopes of country which stretched away from the hills to the sea, with here and there swamps and marshy ground, which alone broke the long rolling slopes of rank grass, I was in hopes of picking up a few of the large species of snipe, and a hare, or other small game. Some half-a-dozen snipe I had already bagged. As at any moment in this wild island, when a short distance from the few inhabitants, bear or deer may be met with, I always had a few bullets ready to slip down my old muzzle-loader, which up to eighty yards threw an **ounce-ball** very straight.

In the afternoon I came upon a deep ravine running round the base of an exceedingly rough hill-side. **A few** bleached, weather-beaten old trees stood out high over the coarse bamboo-grass. This kind of grass grows eight **or ten feet high, and affords the finest** cover possible for big game. Going down-hill I have often passed through its smooth stems with compara**tive ease, as it** always slopes that way, but to go up **hill is** quite impossible. Keeping along the edge of the ravine, and looking down into the great matted creepers and low scrubby thorn clumps, I could not help thinking **what** a place for an old **bear to take up** his quarters **in! A beautiful white-headed eagle, which I suppose** had been quietly **watching my movements** from the branches of one of the dead trees, now thought he would try a closer inspection, and sailed lazily down towards me, passing two or three times round my head, and then returning to the hill-side.

Just then a strange sound came from the grass on my left. I stopped and listened, wondering what it could be. In a second or two **it again occurred.** "A bear," I said to myself, and "close at hand;" and slipping a bullet down on the top of the snipe-shot, I cautiously approached in the direction the sound had come from. Once more it sounded much closer, and I felt more convinced of the animal's presence, but where can the creature be? I had gone only a few yards further when I came to a great hole in the earth. Ah! my friend, I thought, so you are at home, and probably two or three young ones as well. I now quietly retreated, drawing my second barrel, and loading that also with a bullet. At the same time I waved for my companion, who was a few hundred yards away to the left. He soon joined me, and I explained exactly where our bear was, for I now made quite certain of returning in triumph, with a fine skin as a trophy. As soon as he had also loaded with ball, we approached on tiptoe, both ready for a whole troop of bears. The sound now came from under our feet,—we were evidently just over his head,—and he was making for the entrance. I gave my companion a look, intended to imply "there he is, look out." We reached the hole, the grass round the edges of which was trodden down and worn. Our guns were at our shoulders, and the muzzles pointing where Bruin's head would appear. His ears did—two rough brown things—within eighteen inches of the muzzle of my gun. I waited for a little bit for his head to follow, and had time enough to calculate that, from the length of ear, and shaggy coat round them, the animal must be nearly two years old. I pulled the trigger, and for a few seconds the large hole was filled with smoke. As it cleared we both had our heads well over the edge peering anxiously in; and there lying, stretched on the ground perfectly dead, was—not a bear **but a wretched colt! I don't** think I **ever felt so taken** aback. The very last thing to expect to find underground was such an animal. How did it get there? The noise I had heard was evidently the poor thing neighing, which, coming from such a queer situation, appeared like the half-laugh half-growl of a bear. I suppose some mare had strayed away, and her poor little colt had fallen into this old bear's retreat.

While waiting for duck one evening by some open water which adjoined a large extent **of rice-fields, I was** amused watching **an otter as he** hunted up and down the pool. Sometimes he appeared to play, and forget for a time his evening meal. At last, on passing close to where I stood half concealed in the rushes, he got my wind, and raising his body half out of the water, he intently surveyed the strange and unusual sight of a man seemingly doing nothing, but looking intently in his direction. My retriever could not resist such temptation any longer, and springing into the water, **almost on the spot** where the otter was, swam about looking anxiously for the animal, which had dived long before the dog reached him. Presently there was a tremendous commotion, the dog growling and snapping at the water, and at the same time crying out with pain, making all the time as hard as he could for the bank. The otter had attacked him under water, and had it all his own way. I never saw "Pat" so glad to reach *terra firma* before; and I have no doubt if he could have had five minutes with his enemy on his own element, the result would have been very different.

The duck had now begun to come in, and for half-an-hour I shot almost as fast as I could load. Twilight in this, the south, part of Nipon is of short duration, but as you go further north and reach higher latitudes it lengthens out, and instead of only having half-an-hour or so of sufficient light to see, you have double that time.

In waiting for ducks I never took up my final position until I heard the first snipe utter his well-known note as he rose from the ground.[1] Teal generally are the first to come, then a few mallard in pairs, or small flocks of five or six; widgeon come later, almost always in flocks. It has over and over again struck me, that at a certain time of twilight, just as things

[1] Snipe always rise during twilight, and take an evening flight before feeding.

around are getting very indistinct, there is a sudden flash, a temporary return of light for a short time, which conveys a sort of feeling as if the day were struggling for a few moments to return. In shooting ducks at this time of the evening, or by moonlight, I always felt certain that anything in the shape of a bird I could see was sure to be within range. Everything appears smaller than the reality, and consequently further off. A white piece of paper round the muzzle of your gun assists very much. In the absence of paper I have used my pocket-handkerchief. Although I believe that in firing at birds on the wing you really stare with both eyes wider open than usual at the object, and the gun follows mechanically the direction of the sight, still, if waiting by water, and the birds light before you fire, then is the time that the white patch on your gun comes in to advantage.

One species of wood grouse I have shot in Yesso, I believe there is no other. It is never found in Japan proper,[1] although the Strait of Tsuga, between the two islands, is only ten miles across. Pheasants again never reach Yesso, although they are fairly plentiful on the opposite side. Blackcock and capercailzie would

---

[1] The expression "Japan proper" is used, as Yesso is, strictly speaking, a continuation of the Kuril Islands, and does not come under the old title of "Nipon."

both answer well in this country, though neither exist there. The immense masses of fir-wood, and the great tract of open hill covered with fern, young wood, and juniper, constitute just the country that would suit both or either. The common brake fern, *Pteris aquilina*, grows in prodigious masses, and so thick, strong, and compact, that I have come down the mountains by sliding over its surface. The great fronds all slope down hill, so that the surface if thick enough is quite smooth; and to sit on it and let yourself slide down is quite an easy process, but, as with the bamboo-grass, to work up hill over the same ground is perfectly impossible. It is in this dense kind of cover that wild boar delight, as a rule only coming out during the night. In a fine valley far north in Nambu, I determined one day to wait by moonlight in the rice-fields for whatever came, deer or boar. I left the ship soon after the moon had risen, and landing in a snug little cove, walked quarter of a mile up the valley to where a regular string of watch-huts were erected. My idea was to relieve one of the watchers for the night by taking his place.

I had, however, no sooner reached the nearest hut, and asked for admittance, than the inmate, who happened to be a female, set up an awful screeching, and although I tried all I could to quiet her and explain my object, she would neither cease nor be in any way pacified; so that I gave it up as a bad job, and started up one of the narrow branches of the valley that ran from the main one. Here I was more fortunate in finding a youth on the watch, who gladly accepted my proposal, and I have no doubt he slept the remainder of the night. Considering how the wind was, I took my station somewhat lower down than where the watch-hut was situated.

I don't think I had waited half-an-hour when I heard an animal passing down through the dry cover, evidently making for a favourite exit, still further down than where I stood. I could follow the creature perfectly, so still was the evening, and I heard it flounder out on to the narrow grassy path which ran round the edge of the rice.

It must have been a boar, for I could hear the brute sniffing the air quite distinctly. Presently back into the cover he plunged, and I could then follow for a long time the pattering and brushing of bushes as he retreated. About fifteen minutes after this, another animal passed down the cover, on the opposite side of the valley, and about thirty yards from where I stood. I again followed the beast down quite easily by ear, and saw a very large boar come out and sniff the air just as the first had done. This one detected no danger, and commenced at once to feed most busily on the rice. I could hear his great jaws closing on the all but ripe ears, as he munched his way to where I stood.

As the beast came out into the bright moonlight, he looked as big as a donkey. What a broadside to fire at! I thought. Taking a steady aim I fired, but what was my disgust to hear the cartridge go off like a squib! It turned out afterwards that I had loaded with a very old cartridge, and I have no doubt the powder was about strong enough to drive the bullet out of the gun and no more. The boar, of course, sprang into the cover, and made off. A fine stag came down soon afterwards, but I did not get a shot at him, and I soon returned on board, anything but satisfied with my luck.

The natives find it quite impossible to keep these animals from their fields. They fire off guns, keep rattles going, and sing and call out all night long from these watch-huts which they put up all over their cultivation. Still, boar appear to get used to anything, or slip in during some unlucky moment the tired watchman falls asleep or goes and has a chat with his next nocturnal neighbour.

The Japanese pony is a rough, hardy sort of animal,

not bad in the fore-hand, cat-hammed as a rule, big-headed, and nasty-tempered, standing generally about fourteen hands.

I was cantering along across the country one day in June, making for a river about twenty miles distant, where I knew sea-trout abounded. We had done over half the distance, and I was enjoying in my mind the delight of playing a fine big trout, with a light rod and line, when the horse of my Japanese interpreter rushed up from behind, and, seizing my leg above the knee, pulled me off my pony, and shook me just as a terrier would a rat. I never felt more utterly helpless. The native on the brute's back had not the presence of mind or nerve to haul violently on his reins, or hit the beast over the head, either of which operations would have probably lessened the nip the creature had. When he thought proper to let go, my leg was like a pulp. Fortunately for me the animal got such a good mouthful, otherwise he would probably have taken the piece out. As it was, I had to be carried back by some natives we luckily picked up, and was *hors de combat* for a month. The scars are still, and always will be, on my leg. Thus ended my fishing excursion, and I never afterwards had the opportunity or time to try my luck once more. The owner was most anxious to shoot the pony next day, but I begged the vicious brute's life; I trust, however, he never attempted a similar way of stopping a pleasant trip again.

My month's imprisonment on board was lightened and passed pleasantly,—thanks to the kindness and agreeable society of the English consul and his wife, and I shall ever remember with gratitude Mrs. Eusden's thoughtfulness and goodness.

HOME OF THE NIGOU.

CHAPTER IX.

SINGING-BIRDS AND FLOWERS, ETC.

In days gone by, the following was a familiar proverb:—" There is neither a bird that sings, a scented flower, nor a virgin, in Nipon."

I have previously said something about the songsters of these islands; and that, in my opinion, the lark stands alone and unrivalled.

Several species of birds have prolonged notes during the spring, but none can, I think, enter the list as real songsters. The blue rock-thrush has a short, peculiar little song, which the male utters while he darts off a rock, takes a short flight, and returns to the same spot again. When on board the *Sylvia* among the Goto Islands, I awoke one morning with a feeling or idea that I had heard the nightingale. I thought it was a dream, never having heard such a bird in Japan. Still it was so impressed on my mind, I asked the quartermaster, the man in charge of the deck between twelve and four o'clock, if he had heard any bird singing. "Yes, sir," he answered, "a bird commenced to sing about one o'clock, and kept on until daylight." Next night I was waiting anxiously to hear it myself, and sure enough, shortly after midnight, a bird commenced and continued at short intervals until morning broke. Afterwards I both saw it and heard it during the day-time. Its notes were short, spasmodic, and not melodious, so that only in a dream could I possibly have mistaken it for the nightingale. The only other bird I can mention, and this from hearsay, is a species of warbler which I had for some time in confinement. It is a handsome brown bird, as large as a nightingale, and, I was told, a good singer. During the time I had it, however, the bird never uttered a note. Canaries, amongst other things, have been introduced into the country, and retain their name. They are bred and reared to a large extent, and not only kept by the Japanese, but find a ready market amongst foreigners. A good bird and cage used to cost half a dollar, or if the cage had some extra ornamentation about it, a dollar would be the price.

The grasshopper warbler, *Calamodyta pragmitis*, I found in Yesso, but never remember seeing it further south. I do not mention this bird as classing it with the true songsters, but merely copy from my journal the fact of it occurring in the north and not in the south. One other bird I must mention is the hedge-sparrow, *Accentor modularis*. On looking one day for a pigeon I had fired at, I picked up one of these little birds, stunned, and unable to rise. It had no mark on it, and made an excellent specimen for my collection.

There are no other birds which, from my own experience, I can note as songsters. I often wondered at the scarcity of song-birds, and, in fact, of the paucity of small birds that are to be found in the country. For these species (small birds generally), Japan always appeared to me admirably adapted. At the same time I should add, that I have been struck with the absence of those insects which birds of this class are so fond of.

The largest variety of the feathered tribe is to be found amongst the ducks, or *Natatores*, the waders following.

Before saying anything about the scented flowers, I should like to mention a little incident which is still fresh on my mind.

I had followed one of the large Yesso bears for some distance through the open forest. This was easily done by the marks the heavy beast left amongst the leaves and grass, as well as from the big leaves of a bulbous plant which were left cut off from the stem on which he had been feeding. This particular lilium might well in the east of Yesso be called the "bear lily," from Bruin's great partiality to it. At last I came to a hill which was matted over with fallen trees, creepers, and very thick underwood. Here I confidently expected to find the animal, and proceeded as cautiously as possible. I had crawled under old moss-covered prostrate trees, twisted through fallen branches, parted the matted creepers aside, and was in the act of passing between two great trunks of timber, when, to my surprise, I saw—not a bear—but the most perfect gem of a primula[1] I ever beheld; of a delicate pink colour, clustering, on a stem eighteen inches high, with leaves of a fresh yellow-green tint, this lovely flower quite arrested my progress. Amongst the tangled damp moss, the matted creepers, and innumerable other wild lanky-looking plants, were a few square feet of uncovered mossy turf, and on this spot the single delicate-looking flower grew, as if planted by some fairy hand, and afterwards nourished and tended

---

[1] *Primula Japonica*, as I afterwards learnt.

with care. The sun's rays certainly never reached it. Perhaps I remained too long admiring and wondering why this plant grew here. At any rate, I never came up with the bear!

I must not leave Yesso without mentioning its lilies of the valley. I have walked through miles of these lovely flowers, which grow to perfection on the lower slopes of the hills, and just above the swampy tracts of country which surround Hakodadi bay. Here also I have walked by the side of hedges of honeysuckle, sweet as our own, but much smaller in the flower. Dark red burnet roses grow on the sandy hillocks along the shore, delicious in scent. Again, in the east, the wild rose flourishes. I was one day wandering about in the woods in the southern part of Yesso, in hopes of picking up a fat hind, when the most delicious scent appeared to spring from the ground. I looked around everywhere, but without being able to find the slightest clew to its origin. I then thought it came with the gentle summer air, which was just sufficient to stir the still leaves on the trees. I went straight to windward, the scent getting stronger every moment, and suddenly came upon a large magnolia-tree covered with blossom.

The lilies of Japan are fairly known in England. I say only fairly, as I do not think some of the rarer kinds have ever yet reached our shores. In the deepest shade, in the very densest covers, grows a lily, grand in proportion, beautiful in colour, and matchless in perfume. It is white, pure and simple, about three feet high, and by no means common. I have never found it except in the warm regions of the south, and, as I said before, only in the deepest shade. The other varieties of lilies are very numerous, and all less or more fragrant. In colour they are equally various. A species of water-lily is also found, pleasant to the eye as it is to the scent.

A large jasmine, the flower being about two and a half inches in diameter, is found in abundance all over the country, strong in a delicious fragrance. It is, I think, the same as is used in China for flavouring the teas of a particular brand.

The lotos plant is cultivated for the root, which is used as a vegetable. It has little flavour, and cannot in any way be compared to the potato as food. The flower is exceedingly handsome, and has a slight perfume.

I have now said enough to show that Japan is not by any means without the charm of scented flowers. In lilies alone it is most rich. Of scentless flowers there are abundance, commencing with the camellia trees (a shrub with us), but here I have measured the stem fourteen feet in circumference, and the tree forty feet in height. The flower of course is single, of a plain red or variegated with white. The azaleas are so prolific that they form the chief cover in many parts; when found growing together with fern, pheasants are pretty sure to be there also. Pink, orange, and mauve are the only three colours I ever saw. The colour seems to depend on the locality, as it is rare to find two plants of different colours together. Violets are nearly as common as in the south of England, but all scentless. Some of the campanulas are exceedingly pretty, and rich in colour, particularly a large blue one, which was always a great favourite of mine. The maple-tree is very much cultivated for its varied autumnal colourings. An old lady once showed me a tree, or rather what was left of it, on which she had grafted twenty-four kinds of maple at the same time. There were still left about six, and this on a very small portion of the tree. The Japanese are great adepts in the art of grafting, as well as in their peculiar dwarfing propensities. An oak, gnarled and ancient-looking, ten to twelve inches in height, a fir or maple of similar dimensions, is a favourite fancy amongst these people.

I have already alluded more than once to their

diminutive gardens, but I hope a more detailed description here will not be considered tedious. These gardens generally represent some particular scene, and the locality of some favourite temple is frequently chosen. The avenue leading to the shrine, the water, the trees, are exactly carried out, all alive and growing; the trees a few inches only in height, the running river of similar proportions. Men's figures, proportioned to the trees, are modelled and placed about, just as seen when visiting the temples, or whatever particular scenery the garden represents. Storks and deer, or wild duck, all most absurdly life-like, are also placed about, and the whole garden is kept in this state perpetually. The art of nipping back the proper shoots of these tiny dwarfed trees is thoroughly understood. My Japanese servant made one of these gardens for my cabin; it was about three feet long and two wide. It possessed a fine specimen of the *Pinus Massoniana*, several species of palm, an oak of grand proportions, a lake on which wild duck were always to be found, and fish of two or three species. Tortoises lived in the long grass by the margin of the lake. Beautiful ferns sprang from the lichen-covered rocks, and occasionally I found a lovely female quietly seated under the shade of the overhanging trees, evidently enjoying the tranquil scene across the lake. Next day a gentleman would arrive, and after much toil, had reached the summit of the largest and highest mountain, where he now rested, looking far across the country below. I had this garden for a long time on board, and it was a never-failing source of amusement and entertainment.

In my own garden in Gloucestershire I have plenty pretty button-shaped flowers, which we call chrysanthemums. In Japan this flower is grown in a very different way. On a single stalk, about four feet long, a single flower is allowed to remain, which in due time has become as large as a good-sized cabbage, or twenty to twenty-four inches in circumference. The long petals curl over each other, forming a charming great white ball. I have often been perfectly astonished at the size and beauty of the flowers. The sweet-scented daphne is in every Japanese garden, and very pleasant its odour is.

Fruit is both scarce and bad in this country; hardly any appears to come to perfection. I have shot numbers of pheasants in the peach-orchards, and have seen deer scampering about amongst the trees; but to find a single peach fit to eat was a difficult matter —nineteen out of twenty had a hungry insect in the centre. This grub attacks the fruit before it has commenced to ripen, and making straight for the then soft kernel, lodges there. Of course the fruit shrivels, ripens prematurely in a sort of way, and falls to the ground, much to the gratification of the copper pheasant.

Pears there are, beautiful to look at, well-sized, well grown, and exempt from the depredations of any insect; but nothing will induce them to ripen. The persimmon, or Kaki apple, *Diospyros Kaki*, stands almost alone as a fruit which does come to perfection. It is as large as a good-sized orange, oval, and has a very thin skin, which easily peels off a soft opaque pulp, not at all to be despised when just ripe. The tree is similar to our apple-tree, of moderate size, and grows much in the same way. This fruit is dried and preserved much as figs are, and, when thus dried, resembles the fig in appearance and taste. In the Kii peninsula alone have I seen oranges grown thoroughly and profitably. Plums, harder than horse-chestnuts, and equally tasteless, are appreciated by the natives, the horse-chestnut I found here being used as food. It is first soaked in water for some days, and then boiled and eaten. The Spanish chestnut grows as a shrub as well as a timber tree; the fruit is small, and not worth picking; it is, however, much relished by children and apes. The former roam about the hills searching for the nut, drive away the apes, and carry home quantities of fruit. The wild raspberry flourishes in some localities. It differs from both the American and European species, but is not at all bad in flavour. Strawberries also, in the wild state, I found, but only in one place, and that in the wilds of Yesso. Grapes are grown in some places, but they are miserable things. On the islands in the Inland Sea, I think, they would answer very well. The Japanese do not understand at all how to treat them; and I have found wild grapes infinitely better in flavour, and quite as large, as any I have seen that were cultivated. The ginger plant is successfully grown in the southern provinces. The leaf of this grass is strongly scented when crushed in the hand; the fragrance given out very much resembles the lemon grass, so common in Ceylon.

I cannot, I fear, answer for the last part of the proverb so easily or so certainly as that about birds and flowers. What I have said elsewhere about the fair sex of this beautiful country will probably convey the impression that a virtuous young woman, as we use the term, is uncommon. It is rather more than possible that this impression is correct; but with them continence is not virtue until after marriage,[1] and what in most countries is coarse and low, with these people is refined. The gentle, kind nature of the women has a great influence

[1] For the sole exception to this, see p. 192.

over the sterner sex. Like the women, the men are always courteous and kind amongst themselves, and also towards foreigners. In speaking thus generally of the Japanese, I refer more particularly to the poorer classes, the farmers and fishermen, and those who live by the sweat of their brow.

As a race the Japanese are certainly short. The men are well made, muscular, active, and strong, and their average height is, I should think, about five feet five inches. The women are diminutive, and I have often wondered that such small creatures should produce such a strong muscular race. The fair sex are womanlike in their figure from their waist upwards, but from there downwards they are more like badly made men, being narrow across the hips and thick about the joints. It is curious, also, that they have such ugly, flat, dumpy little feet, without any arch, whereas their first cousins the Chinese have the most perfect feet and hands of any race I ever saw. Like the men, the women are very muscular and strong, and capable of carrying enormous weights for great distances, and undergoing every degree of exposure to all kinds of weather. It may be said of them truly, "There is a great deal of good contained in a small parcel."

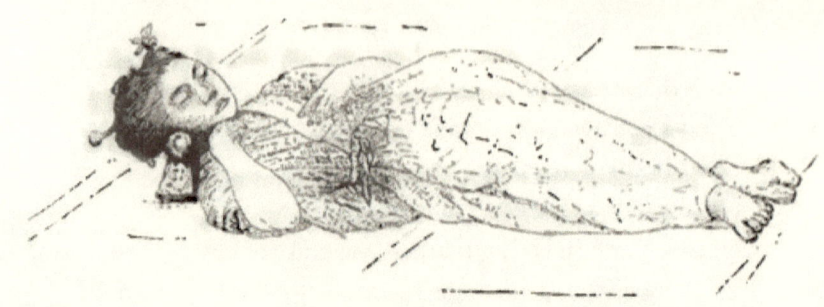

CHAPTER X.

JAPANESE CUSTOMS AND HABITS.

The Japanese are less given to romance than any people I have ever seen. The rather worn-out story of the forty Ronins approaches, if true, to the romantic. But the nearest thing to a little bit of true romance that ever came under my own observation was the following:—A Japanese girl of good family and position fell in love with a common coolie, and throwing aside all parental authority ran away with him. They crossed a good stretch of sea, and, reaching an island, set up their wigwam in this out-of-the-way place. The husband took to fishing for a livelihood, and for a time life was very pleasant to these two young things. But, alas! their blissful retreat was soon visited by the common enemy of mankind, and the young wife found herself a widow. Like all her sex, at first she was not to be consoled, but as time went on, and not a very long time either, she objected no longer to consolation, and a merry bright little widow she was. I cannot remember anything else in the way of romance that I ever even heard of during my many years in the country.

The marriage ceremony is very simple. The man having selected his future better-half, bargains with her parents for her person. The would-be bridegroom then invites his friends to a feast. Many presents are given on either side, and the marriage is complete.

Polygamy, of course, is lawful, but it is a luxury seldom taken advantage of. The strictness of conduct and fidelity of the Japanese wife is not copied or practised by the husband. He is an admirer of many women; and where women are so responsive to admiration, the addition of a second marriage knot is considered unnecessary.

In all their intercourse with each other the Japanese are most matter-of-fact. Their system of marrying is a stumbling-block to all romantic notions. It is a bargain between the parents, or between the man and the girl's parents, without any reference to her tastes, ideas, or wishes on the subject. Love or courtship is a very rare thing; how can it be otherwise where the fair sex are so frail, so easily won? Obedience is so innate in the woman, that she appears to have no opinion in the matter, but to please the man who says, "I will take you for my wife."

Truthfulness is not a matter of any moment amongst them; but they are just as likely to tell what is really the case as not. It depends very much on what subject the conversation may refer to, whether the information you desire is given truthfully or untruthfully. In comparison with our own poorer classes, I would feel far more dependence upon the word of a Japanese. They are more innocent in their untruthfulness—more childlike. They do not systematically lay themselves out to lie, to swear black is white with brazen effrontery, as our lower orders are so apt to do. Like their morality, truth is not looked upon in the same light as it is by Western civilisation. Untruthfulness is not being untruthful with them. There is no sin attached to it. It is strange how innocent it then becomes or seems. It is the custom to say what at the moment may appear the best thing to say, however contrary to the facts of the case it may be; however plain it is to both parties that it is diametrically opposite to the reality.

The kindness of these people is not confined to bipeds only. To their domestic animals they are particularly gentle and considerate. Cattle are used as beasts of burden and for agricultural purposes more than ponies. When it is easier to reach their fields by water than by pathway, the little black bullock or cow is taken there by boat. In the evening it is amusing to see one of these animals, on being unyoked from the plough, quietly walk straight down to the boat, lying in the water at the foot of the valley. If its master is rather long in following, it is sure to look anxiously up the valley and low, as much as to say, "Are you not coming? I want to get home." The plough used is most primitive and small, but quite sufficient for the purpose required, which is generally to turn over the wet muddy soil in the rice-fields. This instrument is carried down to the boat on the farmer's shoulders, who on his arrival holds the boat steady, and tells the wise little animal to get in, but until so ordered it never stirs. When once in the boat the creature stands perfectly still, and is in this way sculled home, often a considerable distance. The understanding between man and beast is very clear, and very pleasant to see.

These animals in older days led an easy life, and died of old age. To take life and to drink milk were two things contrary to Buddha's precepts. But of late years beef is very much appreciated, and Buddha's ideas of right and wrong are thrown aside. Consequently, well-conditioned kine are in demand, and their lives, at any rate, are of shorter duration. Although the Japanese are kind, considerate, and gentle in their intercourse amongst themselves, I do not believe they are people who have much feeling. Their kindness to their children is remarkable, but it is shown chiefly by allowing the little ones to have their own way, and by dressing them nicely. I have never once seen a mother caressing a baby or little child; and although the father or grandfather will take the whole family out to fly their kites, or play at other games, it always appeared to me that the men went as much to please themselves as the bairns. The system of letting out their daughters at an early age for a year or so, and receiving them back into their families, which has gone on from time immemorial, is against all ideas of love and tenderness; and, doubtless, I should think, is one of the chief causes of the absence of love which is so particularly apparent. They are a strange mixture. Girls are generally called after a flower, or something which has a pleasant meaning—honey, sweet, and so on; men, after rougher objects. The best Japanese man, all round, I ever knew, was the Governor of the wild eastern districts of Yesso,—a hard, energetic, active man, whose name, "Mat's Moto" (the pine-tree), always appeared most applicable to him. On my leaving Nemero, a settlement in the extreme east of Yesso, where he resided, he begged me to accept a little present—quite a small thing—consisting of a great relish, which he was sure I should find most excellent, most appetising; in fact, it was quite a delicacy. I wondered what this could be, what Nemero, a cold wild place, could possibly produce deserving such commendation. On his coming to say adieu, he brought this delicious morsel, which was nicely secured in a neat clean tub, and looked from the outside, though large, certainly as if it ought to contain something worth having. I thought it gave out rather a strong smell before it was opened; but on the top being taken off, those standing near were assailed with a most dreadful stench, something too awful,—need I say more than that it was whale's flesh in a putrid state! The Japanese are more enlightened now-a-days, and possibly appreciate less tasty viands; but whale's flesh in this condition was, in the days I am speaking of, considered a great delicacy. The tub and its contents went overboard the moment after the lid was removed, which, fortunately, was not till my friend had taken his departure.

A species of radish, or something between a radish and a turnip, is very much cultivated in Japan. When about eighteen inches long it is pulled, partially dried, and then salted in very wet brine. In this state it is immensely prized by the natives as an adjunct to every meal. Cut up in little pieces, and mixed with a small quantity of sauce, there is hardly anything **they appreciate more.** This vegetable, however, possesses one quality very objectionable to foreigners. Its smell when pickled is simply disgusting! My Japanese in the ship could not always resist the temptation of smuggling some of it on board, and stowing it away in the **most out-of-the-way corners.** This was against **orders,** and quite useless into the bargain, as the aroma it gave out at once indicated the presence of the forbidden fruit, and to the sea the delicacy was always at once committed.

My interpreter remarked to me one day, "You abuse our poor pickled relish, and call it disgusting, and all sorts **of names;** but what, may I ask, is your cheese? Is it not putrid milk? To us it is most objectionable." I declined to argue the point!

The Buddhist temples are everywhere, as a rule,

kept in the very best preservation, and the priests are most comfortably situated. The voluntary contributions which are collected at the shrines and temples are for the maintenance of the priests, and amount to considerable sums. They are supposed to adhere to celibacy, as being the rule of their order; but they by no means do so. Part of every temple is always set aside ready for the traveller or wanderer, and the charge for this most comfortable accommodation is very little indeed.

Visiting these temples for the purpose of propitiating the ruling spirit of Buddha is left almost entirely to the women. Men very seldom interfere in these matters, being quite satisfied with their wives and daughters doing so.

The centre of the Shinto religion is at Ise, in the province of Yamato. Here a temple of perfectly plain uncarved wood, of the *Cryptomeria japonica*, is erected to the invisible spirit. As before mentioned, no figure is ever used to represent Shinto, whose existence is everywhere, watching over the well-being of everything, but always in an unseen form.

The road leading to the temple passes through a row of houses on either side, where all kinds of mementos of the place can be bought and taken home by the pilgrims. At the end of this single street is a large gate, the entrance to the temple grounds. Just inside the gate a broad path leads to the river's bank, in the clear water of which every native dips his hands before going further into the grove of beautiful trees which surround the temple itself. Some of these trees are of grand proportions, particularly the camphor and *Cryptomeria elegans*. The latter reaches 150 feet in height and 30 feet in circumference.

The town of Yamato is a couple of miles distant from Ise; and judging from the number of tea-houses, and gaily-dressed young ladies, it would appear that visiting the Shinto shrine was never made a very serious undertaking, but rather as a holiday and pleasure time. At certain seasons streams of pilgrims from all parts of the country wend their way to Ise. Men take an interest in this as well as the women; and from the style and abundance of amusements that I have mentioned existed at Yamato, it was evident Ise and Shintoism was not the only inducement to take these frequent pilgrimages. The province of Owari, which is just to the northward of Yamato, is famous for its pretty girls, a good many of whom are to be found in the numerous tea-houses near Ise.

Music in this country is peculiar. One of their

most common instruments resembles a banjo. The sounds they manage to produce from this are more like a repetition of twangs than anything else, and a deal of patience is required to sit still and listen to it. At any great entertainment given by a prince or daimio this description of music, accompanied by singing, is always part of the ceremony.

Professional singing-girls are hired for the occasion. These girls are a regular institution of the country; and rather a strange circumstance regarding them, considering the general frailty of their sisterhood, is, they are invariably virtuous. If any of them happen to go astray, she is at once discharged from their community, and her place filled by a new one. Their style of singing is almost more discordant and trying than their style of music. All the notes are made to pass through their noses, and this imparts such a quantity of nasal sound, that when—often for absolute politeness' sake—I had to listen to this combination, the result was usually a bad headache.

It is curious that so many things are done in Japan just in the opposite way to what is invariably the custom elsewhere. For instance, in planing wood, they draw the instrument towards them, instead of, as we do, pushing it from us. The teeth of their saws slope in the contrary way to ours, so that they cut when being pulled to, and not when pushed from, the operator. A rider gets on his horse from the off (right) side instead of the near (left), as we do. Speaking of saws reminds me what excellent carpenters these people are. So smoothly do they work, that sandpaper is unnecessary and unknown, though in some cases the dried stem of the equisetum is used for very fine work, and answers admirably.

The women paint and powder themselves, to show that they are painted and powdered, not to deceive; there is no secrecy about it. Powder, rouge, and such articles, are not bought under feigned names, and put on secretly with closed doors, and as if no one ought to know that such a thing was done. A Japanese damsel sits by the open street, with her little cabinet of cosmetics, her glass, brushes, and other concomitants before her, chatting with the passers-by as she decorates herself. Many a time I have hove-to during a walk, and talked to these nut-brown girls, stripped to the waist, as they went through their toilet. One great aim, as showing especially good taste, is to leave two or three triangular patches of their skin unpowdered. These are always left on the back of the neck, running up into the powdered surface, and looking like dark cones.

Their bath system I have previously spoken about. Not only are their private and public baths so elaborate and complete, and such national institutions; but in their more ordinary ablutions they are equally particular. Winter and summer are alike as regards their predilection for water. Our own poorer classes generally have the greatest objection to look at water, whether it be summer or winter.

A young lady in Japan has her hair dressed and done up about once a week. The operation is long and expensive. It is kept in place by a quantity of paste; and not to disturb it during the night, the pillow is a small wooden stool with a cushion on it, on which the neck only rests, the hair being innocent of any *bonnet de nuit*. They have masses of black coarse hair, which, when well combed and brushed, and allowed to fall loose over the shoulders, looks very well. The children's heads are always shaved until they are about six years old. A little tuft is left on one side for a few months; it is then shaved off, and another little tuft allowed to grow. These queer little patches are ornamented with different-coloured bits of ribbon, and if not picturesque, are certainly quaint and peculiar to the Japanese.

In their little gardens, which I have also previously

mentioned, almost invariably stands a huge block of stone, with a hollow cut out in the top. This space is kept filled with fresh clean water. A small wooden scoop is also placed on the stone, with a towel beside it, so that on quitting the garden, you can, if disposed, dip out a little water, and wet and wipe your hands The idea is at least cleanly and nice.

Amongst their numerous games, that of **forfeits is one of** the most favourite. It is generally played by the girls. One mode of doing so is peculiar, and as **follows. A score or so** of damsels divide and sit facing each other, that is, they squat on the calves of their legs and heels,—the usual mode of sitting in Japan. Three or four singing girls attend with their instruments. **When all is ready, and** the laughing and joking ended, the instruments strike a few chords, and the game begins. The girls in one line challenge those on the opposite side to a round at guessing the number of fingers they are going to show. The whole number soon get into the regular swing of the game, and become quite excited. Every time one loses a forfeit she has to take part of her dress off;—first an arm appears, then a shoulder, and so on until everything is lost, and **she is** as nature clothed her. Of course the art is to pick out a weak adversary, and to hold out, and be the last to become so simply clad. When all are *in puris naturalibus* they get up, run away, dress, and return, and then go through different kinds of acting, comic and otherwise, some of which, introduced simply to please the vulgar taste of the foreigner, cannot be described.

Archery, amongst the men, used to be constantly practised. The target was eight or ten inches in diameter, with a two-inch bull's eye, and at thirty yards they made wonderful shooting. The arrow was pulled straight from the eye.

Their conjuring tricks have been too often shown in England, likewise their mode of performing on a slack-rope, to notice either here. In the woods I have come across youngsters practising away on the slack-rope between two trees. Both sexes, and at all ages, smoke. The fragrant plant grows all over Japan; the best, however, is in Kiusiu. It must have been introduced, as it is called "tobacco." Bread, for the same reason, is known by the natives as *du pain*.

There is nothing more refreshing when walking, and feeling tired and hot, than to come suddenly and unexpectedly on a habitation, far away, it may be, up the mountains; probably a poor charcoal-burner's wigwam. Wherever it may be, you are always welcome, and a small cup of tea and some millet cakes are at once placed before you, with apologies for the poor fare. This tea is most invigorating. I have over and over again been no less surprised than gratified at its refreshing properties. The tea this very poor class uses is rough and sun-dried, picked from their small gardens, or a few yards of clearing in some sheltered nook on the mountain side. Firing tea—drying it by artificial means—was introduced by the foreigner. Women and girls are employed for this work, and how they stand it I cannot tell. It has to be done in the summer, when the thermometer ranges between 75° and 85°; though this gives no idea of what the heat is within the firing-houses, which, having a hundred fires or more, are incomparably hotter. Those employed have to stoop over the hot iron pans, and keep stirring the tea with their hands. A very short time at this work is sufficient to make them fling their garments off their shoulders, and to appear bare to the waist. What with the steam from the tea, perspiration, and the dust that rises as the tea dries, they soon present an unpleasant spectacle. They work at this for nine hours a day, receiving ten cents (fivepence) as pay for that time. The operation may certainly have no bad effect on the fat ones, but, as a rule, I believe it is very injurious.

I know no people who so truly deserve to be called artistic as the Japanese. Most men and boys with a piece of stick, burnt at the end, will very quickly produce on a whitewashed wall or a board, a sketch of a plant or a figure, showing accuracy, spirit, and taste. In the grotesque line they are inimitable. This kind of line-sketching is taught at an early age. Their freedom, taste, and quickness of execution, is exactly opposite to their neighbours the Chinese. The nitchkies, or figures in ivory or wood, show wonderful humour. The Chinese have done all in their power to imitate these things, and with creditable success, but they are as much wanting in freedom and true artistic skill, as those they copy are full of it. Education, of course, has in the first instance a great deal to do with all such traits and differences.

Their system of education is excellent. In villages too small or poor to be able to support a regular schoolmaster, the priest takes his place, and one of the numerous rooms of the village temple is used as a schoolroom. When we put up in these temples the school sometimes had to be stopped, on account of insufficiency of room for all my party. The little scholars had no objection to these extra holidays. Neither, I think, had the priest, who invariably donned his best robe and visited his far-off parishioners.

The Japanese are from their early days given to fun, games, and merriment. To see a school-door open, and the **rush** of boisterous, **laughing** children that appear, does one good. The same incident in China is totally different; not a sound escapes the little urchins' lips. They go straight home, quietly, sedately, and as soberly as their grandmothers or grandfathers would; for laughing is strictly prohibited, and they are whipped if ever found doing so.

Toy-shops are in every village. Some of these toys are most ingenious. The dolls are true representations of the human form, even to the minutest particulars. Kite-flying is quite a national pastime. To watch the old grey-headed grandfather of a family taking a lot of little ones to fly their kites is most amusing. It is doubtful which child, the old or the young, **gets the** most excited.

All eastern nations are great fish-eaters, and the Japanese are no exception to this general rule. The sea adjoining their coasts abounds in excellent fish; the quality improves the further north you go, and as the temperature of the water decreases. They begin with the whale, as I have before mentioned. The tunny comes next in size. Quantities of this great coarse fish are caught on the Kii coast, and from thence sent to all the large towns, where it is exposed for sale, and looks as tempting as whale's flesh! Bonito are caught in great numbers, and eaten in many ways. The favourite method is by splitting the fish, and then cutting the back portions into two long slices, which are dried until they become as hard as mahogany, and of the same colour. In this state it is scraped and used as a flavouring, or addition to other dishes. Salmon, however, is the most universally used fish in the country.

The Japanese are fond of sport. One of their modes of catching wild duck—now almost obsolete—was rather amusing, and certainly novel to our ideas. In former days most of the Princes' and Daimios' castles were surrounded by splendidly laid out parks: the wild and the cultivated were both represented, and many a good day's shooting have I enjoyed amongst these forsaken and beautiful grounds. But about the ducks. Some portion of these park-like enclosures was often devoted to the sport of catching them. Narrow canals were cut in different directions; they turn and twist so that only short pieces of the water can be seen from any one part. Banks about six feet high were raised on each side of these little water-courses, covered with grass. The inside of these banks was arranged in steps, so that you could quickly mount to the top.

Wild duck were regularly fed in these canals, and from never being fired at or frightened by noises, they very soon took regularly to them. Towards evening the sportsman sallied out, armed with a large silken landing-net about two feet in diameter, mounted on a long, light bamboo pole, the whole thing being very light, so as to be handled and wielded quickly. Two or three attendants of course accompanied the sportsman to carry his game, when caught, and point out where the birds are, which was easily done by looking carefully through peep-holes. The exact position of a flock of ducks being marked, the now eager netter walked quickly but noiselessly along under cover of the grassy bank until he knew he had reached where the ducks were. Then suddenly springing to the top of the bank, he endeavoured, and generally successfully, to catch a bird in his net as they rose from the water. Quickness and decision were both necessary for this kind of sport. The object in having the canals so winding was to prevent the birds in one bend being disturbed by what was going on in the next one.

CHAPTER XI.

PAST AND PRESENT.

When I first saw Japan in 1855, the inhabitants were in a very different state from what they are at present. They themselves must be struck with astonishment, on looking back, at the extraordinary metamorphosis which they have gone through in the last few years. Two or three little incidents may be worth mentioning as showing how their Government then treated foreigners, and how we amongst those foreigners allowed ourselves to be treated. I was in a fifty-gun frigate, and as we sailed into Hakodadi harbour, at that time quite an insignificant Japanese town, the signal was made by the English admiral who was already there, not to salute his flag. We were also ordered not to fire the time immemorial blank musket at sunset, and **this simply because the Japanese objected to any foreigner firing guns on their waters. Another order was, that we were to receive on board a Japanese guard. A sentry was placed on each gangway,** and a Yakonin (officer) of **these queer people paraded the quarter-deck. The former** allowed no communication **with the shore; the latter was in** general charge **of H.M. ship and everybody** on board. **It must** have been a proud **moment,** or rather time, for this celestial. We midshipmen soon made friends with the Yakonin, who delighted in spending his evenings in our berth. I am afraid it must be owned that rum **or** other spirits, besides wine and beer, were all appreciated by our guest.

The authorities allowed us to get **water from a** small river far away from **the town, but** watched us most narrowly when we were so employed. No fresh provisions would they sell us, or otherwise allow any **communication on** shore. It may be easily imagined that any one in command of an English squadron who could submit to such ridiculous and humiliating **treatment,** was hardly the man to give a good account of an enemy. The absurd fiasco in respect to our search for the Russian ships in that year is too well known to be repeated here. The only chance our ships had of getting within range of Russian vessels during the whole war of 1854 to 1856 was lost.

Passing over several years to 1863, when, owing to a wilful lady, and an after-lunch expedition on horseback—we being entirely in the wrong and the Japanese in the right—we found ourselves involved in a war with one of the chief princes. The war commenced and ended by our squadron attacking about a mile of earth batteries, placed in front of the town or city of Kagosima. The first shot was fired by the Japanese, on which our ships, seven in number, went in within 300 yards of their guns. Steaming slowly round we passed in this manner, and in line, about half the extent of three batteries. How we fared is well known. Doubtless we thought our foes would be armed like the Chinese, and were considerably astonished to find seven-inch shell flying about our ears. In about an hour and a half we hauled out, or rather steamed out, of range. Our casualties were very heavy. On our getting out of the smoke one ship was found missing, and to our discomfort we saw she had got aground close under one of the batteries. The fact was, her captain thought a closer range than 300 yards would be more effective, and edging in shore rather too much had grounded. The ship I was in had to return to her assistance, and now singly we made a target for all the Japanese guns. To make matters worse, it was blowing half a typhoon at the time; and to keep our own ship off the mud, and at the same time to lay out hawsers and get hold of our friend in need, besides keeping a steady fire up with our 100-pound Armstrong gun, was no easy matter. It was done, however, and off came the *Racehorse*. Next day we one and all expected to go in again and finish up the other half mile of batteries; but the powers that guided us decided to return to Yokohama. We steamed out accordingly without firing a gun. The Japanese forts, particularly some situated on the very top of an island, and which looked down on our decks, blazed away as hard as they could. During the action on the previous day, every shell that passed over the earthen breast-works went rushing and crashing into the unfortunate city. This was perfectly unavoidable. The consequence was most disastrous to the inhabitants, for the place burnt for four nights and days at least. This one of our ships saw, having remained about the entrance of the gulf to watch what happened after the squadron's departure. The morning of the day on which we fought the action we had taken three steamers, which had been anchored further up the gulf, as hostages, or as an inducement to make the Prince of Satsuma accede to our demands. It had, however, the effect of opening his guns at us. The steamers were burnt. Before setting fire to the one we had in charge, I went on board, and landed all the crew on an island, except the captain and another official. These two were sitting quietly in the saloon: and on my asking them if they preferred to be landed as the men had been, or come on board the ship I was in, they consulted together in quite a matter-of-course tone whether they would not commit there and then the "happy despatch." It ended in their preferring to see a little more life, and we smuggled them on shore near Yokohama, where for several months they both remained hidden, their whereabouts only known to our consul. What became of the captain I never knew; but that he tried all he could during the time of the action off Kagosima to find his way to the magazine, intending to blow our ship up, I believe to be quite true. The other man became great in the counsels of his country, and on the change of Government, etc., he was appointed as Minister to England. I had a great deal to do with him some years afterwards, when he was Foreign Minister in Japan, and I was surveying the coasts. The result of our attack on Kagosima was to induce the Prince of Satsuma to grant our demands. He evidently was not aware how he had really driven us off.

At this time it was considered dangerous to go far from the town of Yokohama. Some people had been cut down by excited or drunken soldiers. At any rate, I never believed that the people generally were averse to us; and regularly once a week, I used to run down the coast in an open boat for fourteen miles or so, and enjoy a glorious ramble over the hills, bagging a few pheasants and snipe. Once when away in this manner it came on to blow hard from the north, and it was utterly impossible to return. I put up at a tea-house, and remained there three days, shooting the country round during the time. The wind still continuing obstinate, I decided to walk back, and leave everything with the landlady of the tea-house. Before the old lady would take charge, she made me make an exact list of every little thing in the boat, even to the nails in the carpenter's work-bag. On reaching Yokohama I found I was supposed to have been murdered. In a few days' time the boat arrived exactly as I had left it. I should be reluctant to leave a boat in the same manner anywhere on the coast of England, particularly if I did not wish to lose anything out of her. This tea-house I speak of was far away from the resorts of foreigners, and of course I had not the slightest chance of redress or recovery if I had lost everything. I have lent Japanese money at this same period, and have never lost a cent by so doing. If they were trusted, their honour was perfect.

Coming now to later years. In 1870 their great taste for foreign ways was particularly shown by their mania for Inverness capes, and the men cutting their hair as we do. European boots also were in great demand. English school-books of every description were now introduced; and I used to find the native schools far away from the foreign settlements, and in many cases where a foreigner had never been seen, teaching English. Frequently a little urchin at some out-of-the-way place would come confidently up to you, and, holding out a slate, say in English, "Please, sir, can you explain this?"—*this* being a sum. When passing over the mountain ranges hundreds of miles from the treaty ports, either making for some conspicuous peak to place my theodolite on, or perhaps shooting, I have come to some woodman's cottage, on the white-washed walls of which almost to a certainty, a lot of arithmetic sums, steamers, men in European costume, and other things would be drawn. A taste for rabbits followed; then one for pigs, and then dogs. I have known as much as forty-seven dollars given for a common black-and-white rabbit, and 500 for a wretched

European cur dog. The sporting men of Japan took to the latest breach-loaders, **giving** outrageous prices for them. I have known rich Japanese go into one of the large stores in Yokohama, where almost anything can be bought, and simply buy some of everything! **The price** was no object. No people, I should imagine, have **paid so heavily for wisdom as these.**

For **seven years I was working on their wild coasts** far away from the influence of the foreigner, and **generally** amongst the poorer class of natives. The kindness and real courtesy **I ever received and** met with during that time I shall never forget. I have lived with them on the mountains and in the plains, either putting up in a temple or in a cottage. Assistance of whatever kind required **was ever ready. To ask a labouring** man busy at work in his field to show the **way up some tangled mountain side was a very common occurrence.** He would at once leave his hoe, tie his loin-cloth on, and start immediately, frequently **for** the whole day. As for reward, it never seemed to enter their heads. One day when shooting I managed to double my ankle under, and sprain that joint so necessary for locomotion so badly I could only hobble a few yards and **then sit down.** A native, **working in his field, saw my vain** endeavours to get on, and donning his single robe came at once with many bows to the rescue, got me on his back, and trotted off a good mile to where I had left my boat. Placing me in the hands of my men, he turned and was off. Not having a penny in my pocket, I called to him, and begged him to come off to the ship with me. Not a bit of it, he positively refused. So I had him caught by two hulking blue-jackets and carried struggling into the boat. I half expected to see him jump overboard on our way off, but fortunately he remained quiet. Getting alongside I directed the Japanese official interpreter to explain to him I only wanted to make him some little present for his kindness, and begged him to come on board the ship. Nothing, however, would induce him to leave the boat, so, giving a dollar to the little man, I sent him back. His wonder and gratitude at receiving such a large piece of silver was unbounded. I don't think he left off bowing his acknowledgments until the boat reached the shore. Then turning round, when on *terra firma*, to the crew who had pulled him there, he again made a low bow and disappeared. The nearest European settlement was more than 100 miles distant, and I believe we were the first and probably the last foreigners he ever saw.

The complete change in the system of government

that took place a few years ago did not add to the comfort, happiness, or well-being of the poorer classes, the small farmer, or the great mass of fishermen. Formerly, although the numerous princes were really absolute in their own territory, yet they were not harsh on their people. Taxing was in kind, and regulated by the amount of crop. Now it is fixed, and in money. For example, as to the amount. A small cluster of houses I knew, situated on a wild mountain side, and numbering twenty men and three women—a very unusual proportion of the sexes amongst the Japanese,—paid forty dollars a year. Few more extraordinary things of the kind have ever happened than the sudden change in the constitution which took place in this country. It was certainly very like taking a plunge in the dark. It is equally wonderful how well it has answered. The great nobles whose dignities had been handed down to them from unknown generations at once gave up everything—their territories, their position, their unbounded power, their wealth, and consented to become pensioners, many of them taking to semi-detached European houses about the skirts of Yedo, and there living contentedly, dressing in European clothes, driving pony carriages about the streets, smoking wretchedly cheap cigars, and giving croquet parties and five o'clock tea. Some of the ladies took also to the European dress, but happily for themselves the Empress wisely stuck to the picturesque native costume, which suits their square short figures exactly, whereas the other utterly disfigures them.

The Prince of Kii—whose family is one of three from which the Mikado was always chosen—invited the English minister to pay him a visit at his castle, situated near the western shore of his province, and fortunately I was able to take the party. On arriving at the port nearest his capital, we were at once visited by officials, who invited the whole party on shore. Here we found the Prince's sea-side residence prepared and fitted up for our reception. The floors of all the rooms were covered with purple blankets, the passages with scarlet. Beds, washing-stands, chairs, tables, and even tooth-brushes were provided. Deer, sheep, and cattle were hanging up in a spacious larder. He had sent to Kobe and bought all the champagne in the place. He had also sent to Osaka and procured a noted cook, a Frenchman, from one of the hotels. Refreshment of every description was provided,—the servants numerous and attentive. A company of lancers was stationed in the establishment, as a combination of guard and compliment. The gardens round this charming place were laid out in **true** Japanese fashion: small ponds, cascades, **tiny** hills, with plains intervening, diminutive forests, as well as flowers, and domestic gardening. Next day at noon we visited the Prince at **his castle, a** great massive building, three miles off, surrounded with a moat and fortifications. **The reception** was most cordial **and kind.** We all dined **with** him that evening, and were regaled sumptuously. The Princess, who had never seen a foreigner, sat at table, in compliment to our minister's wife. Her behaviour was most perfect, entirely free from curiosity or stiffness, and just as if she had been accustomed to similar entertainments all her life. After dinner the Prince asked his guests what they would like to do next day. Some placing themselves in his hands were **taken out to see** curious old **ruins,** fourteen miles away. The whole road had been cleaned and swept for the occasion, and every native who was seen went down on his knees as the cavalcade passed.

My choice—which **was** also that of our consul—was to shoot. "Then," said our host, "you shall go to my preserve." About noon next day half a dozen lancers escorted us some miles further into **the extensive** plain which surrounds the city. Here we entered an artificially made and laid out wood, and, following a beautiful road which wound through it, suddenly came upon a delightful cottage. Smooth grass sloped from the broad verandah down to a lake fifty yards off. This was covered with wild duck, and here we were politely requested to amuse ourselves, but as for shooting the almost tame birds, I could not think of such a thing. Discarding the cover, which was cut through in many ways by canals and paths, and appeared alive with bitterns and pigeons, I struck away into the rice-fields, trusting to find geese and snipe. In a couple of hours I returned with my two coolies laden with white-fronted geese and other birds. A most enjoyable lunch was ready. Over a pipe afterwards, my companion, who had remained about the preserves in preference to trying the open plains, confided to me that he felt ashamed of himself.

"Why?" I inquired.

"The fact is," he said, "after you left, I watched the duck on the lake for half an hour. I went down and fed them with bread. They came up to my very feet in hundreds. There were mallard, widgeon, teal, shoveller, and others I don't know. The Japanese attendant kept urging me to shoot, but I had not the heart. However, at last I thought I would put them up and then have a bang at them. I got my gun and began to call. They only came nearer. I took stones and pelted them. We both did, my coolie and myself. It was no use; the ducks only laughed at us; they would not get up. I got desperate and blazed away my first barrel right **into the middle of** them, pulling the second trigger as they rose, for **now** they got up in earnest, thousands of them."

"Well," I said, "how many did you kill; **a dozen** or two?"

"Not a single bird! can you believe **it?**"

We were entertained for four or five days longer in the most thoughtful and charming manner.

No people could be kinder, or more polite, amongst themselves than the Japanese. Two coolies—the lowest class of society—on meeting, never fail to go through the usual custom in the country of bowing several times, and asking after each other's health, then that of their families, and so on. Little children act towards each other in just the same way, or if an old grey-headed man meets a little girl six years old, the same ceremony is gone through. Two musumees coming across each other bow and go through the most engaging and pretty way of saying good-morning. The bath system in Japan has often been commented on. When foreign institutions were being introduced faster than they could possibly take root, I was much amused one day to observe a notice on the doors of the bath houses, that "for the future the house would be open for men on certain days, and for women the remainder of the week."

"What new arrangement is this?" I asked my Japanese companion.

"We wish to adopt," he answered, "the European mode of having men's days and women's days, and not all together, as we always have done."

"Do you think it will answer?" I remarked.

"No," he answered.

And he was quite right; the idea could not be carried out, and the old general system very soon came into vogue again. In passing through villages, I have often found the street dotted over with girls bathing themselves in little tubs, and they do not hesitate to talk to you as if quite unconscious of being undressed. A pleasant "How do you do?" "Where have you been for a walk?" "Is it not a lovely evening?" and so on, was usually their simple and smiling greeting. After a short time I never thought of these creatures as being naked, and I believe such would always become the case if anything was started, however outrageous we might at first consider it. Entire disregard of covering is by no means a mark of immodesty when met with in a primitive, matter-of-fact way, as it is here. Modesty, as we understand it, is unknown in Nipon, particularly as referring to the more private habits of the genus *homo*. Virtue also, as we apply the word regarding the morality of unmarried women, is equally unknown amongst them. A girl in Japan is a piece of goods, for pleasure or use, as the case may be; and irregularity is thought of much in the same light as having a cup of tea. This is no detriment to their marrying, which they do at an early age, and become the most strict and faithful wives and mothers,—an example in this way to their own sex generally, and particularly to highly cultivated civilized nations. It might be supposed that in consequence of such general freedom amongst the younger women, their manners would be coarse and rude. Such is not the case. No people that I have ever seen have, all round, such charming manners as the Japanese. Their women, young and old, are always nice. I have often said every woman is a lady and every man a gentleman. The gentle kindness and pretty ways of the musumees have a charm which is simply captivating, and although our notion of modesty is thrown aside, there is no such thing as vulgarity. This word is, in fact, never applicable to the Japanese, except when expressions, words, or manners are used to imitate foreigners. The semi-civilized, uncouth, no-nation sort of beings that merchant ships are usually manned by, bring an amount of vice and badness with them, which is terribly detrimental to aborigines everywhere. The foreign merchants who first appear on the scene, at any lately-opened country or port, are by no means the best specimens of their class. In fact, the foreigner in these cases, who is necessarily a European, shows a wonderful aptitude to take to the very habits and customs of the natives, which are so preached about and condemned by the missionary.

The Japanese are a happy race ; they take life easily and lightly ; fun, amusement, and frolic, are constantly going on. Picnics are in great vogue. I have often had boat-loads of whole families come great distances to see the ship and picnic on board. On such occasions the children were never left behind, and it was quite amusing to see these holiday-takers, got up, as they always were, in their best. The young ladies of the party delighted in seeing themselves in a large mirror in my cabin. I remember an old doctor and artist, who constantly came off, accompanied by a very pretty daughter, who, while her father showed his sketches, used to sing song after song, and drink tea.

At places where numbers of people either pass through or resort to on holidays, fair-days, or as pilgrims, when *en route* to some favourite or noted shrine, the number of tea-houses is very great. Putting up at these resting-places is exceedingly pleasant during the summer.

Japanese fare is rather light for western constitutions; but many of their dishes are exceedingly good, and with a little addition in the way of tinned meat, I found I could get on very well. As a rule these people retire early, and are up with the first streaks of light. Sometimes I have known the whole village assemble after working hours, and spend almost the whole night talking and tea-drinking. The children on these occasions of festivity are placed on **the matted flooring, and** covered over with their quilted sleeping-garments, **a** mosquito-curtain being hung up round them.

Quarrelling does not often occur; it is quite the exception. When they do quarrel, however, it is rather serious, knives being used at once.

The attention and care the Buddhists take of their burial-places might well serve as an example to us. Beside the grave is always a small saucer filled with rice, and a joint of bamboo or other vessel to hold **water.** Flowers in the summer, and green boughs or sprigs of fir, or other evergreens, are also invariably placed by the small stone which marks the resting-place of their friends. The rice and water is for the spirit of the departed when it returns to the earth, which it is supposed frequently to do; the flowers are to give it pleasure, and to show it is still remembered by those left behind.

The Buddhist funerals are conducted in a very simple manner. A square box of white pine wood contains the remains to be deposited in the earth. A few women and girls, dressed in yellow, or having some portion of their dress in that colour, attend. It is carried to the Buddhist temple, and placed in a small building outside, where a priest goes through a set form of prayer over it, which lasts ten minutes, after which it is carried to the grave, and dropped into it, covered over, a bamboo stuck on the top, and home all the party goes. I have never seen tears shed at a funeral. In fact, such marks of feeling are very rare under any circumstances. Women during the night often sing a certain song, particularly on the water, after the death of a relative. It has a queer, wild, plaintive effect.

The feast of lanterns, one of the Buddhist time-honoured customs, takes place in August, at the full moon. The graves of all their relatives are lighted by different-coloured paper lanterns; rice and fruit are at the same time placed by the graves, and after dark, or rather after the sun has set, thousands of people, all in their holiday clothes, visit the resting-places of their departed friends and relatives. At midnight little straw-made junks, after their own models, are sent out on the water. Each junk has a lighted lantern placed within her straw sides, also a little rice and fruit, tea or saki. The meaning of this latter part of the ceremony is, that the spirits of those lost at sea are now supposed to return to the surface. Their friends despatch a little offering in case the spirit should feel hungry, and become unsettled in its watery abode. When the lanterns are all lighted, ranging over the hills, as they do at Nagasaki, in hundreds of thousands, the effect is exceedingly pretty; and those in the junks, looking like hundreds of great fire-flies crossing the water, dancing about over the tiny waves, have a quaint, weird appearance; the whole scene filling the mind with strange reflections on the various views taken by different races throughout all ages with respect to the spirits of the departed, all of which, however, show a belief in a future state of some kind.

The Shinto sects burn their dead. At some places they have buildings erected for the purpose, with earthen fire-places in the centre. The body is just placed across the clay fire-place, and attended to by an old man with a long stick, who keeps poking it into its place, as it gradually disappears by this slow, grilling process. No bad odour arises during the operation.

The population of Japan is put down at over 30,000,000. Judging from my own experience, I should say this must be far too high a figure. A single example will go far to prove the justice of my view. Yedo, or Tokio as it is now called, used to be put down at over 2,000,000 inhabitants, but on counting heads it turned out only 800,000. There are immense tracts of the country uninhabited, and likely to be so, being nothing but a succession of ranges of mountains. The plains, and those parts of the country which can be utilised, most certainly are thickly peopled.

With the poorer classes the mortality amongst the children must be great. Not that the parents are careless, indifferent, or unfeeling to their little ones, and consequently neglect them; far from it,—they are exceedingly gentle and kind to them; but owing to the woman being almost as much a labourer as the man, the children have to take care of themselves and each other from a very early age.

Although the bath arrangements are so good, and it

is the regular custom of the country for the coolie to have his hot bath every evening, yet they don't **wash** their clothes. The winter clothing is all put away in boxes during the summer; and although small-pox is never absent from the larger towns, still when winter comes round, and their garments for that season are **brought again into use, small-pox is sure to increase.** The loss of infantile life from this scourge was excessive **before** they took eagerly to vaccination. Even to the present day it is looked on as a fatality, and no precautions are taken against its spreading. I have over and over again met mothers in the streets carrying a child one mass of small-pox.

Neither lunatic asylums nor poor-houses exist in Japan. Idiots and deformed people **are very rarely seen.** During the number of years I have spent in the **country I never saw one** of the former, and but very few of the latter. I presume, not knowing for certain, that both descriptions of unfortunates are quietly put out of the way.

Heart disease is common, which is not to be wondered at; **for** although both sexes are brought up to endure hardship, exposure, and heavy work, particularly in carrying great weights, still there is no doubt that they very much tax and strain their endurance and strength.

I have already noticed the weights that the young girls and little children carry home from the woods. At low tide women and girls collect small fish, crabs, and certain kinds of sea-weed, which get left, as the tide recedes, in holes and pools amongst the rocks. A piece of cloth of thin cotton material is all they have on, and I have seen them at work in this way for hours, their half-bare backs exposed to the direct rays of a sun sufficiently fierce to knock over any stranger. They begin this sort of life so early it becomes half nature. The very small girls take care of the house and babies whilst the mother is working in the field. In fact, before the parents leave, the baby or babies (there are always several in a Japanese house) are strapped on the backs of their younger sisters, who go about their duties of house-caring and nursing in the most methodical and attentive way.

Although the Japanese are affectionate, and particularly so regarding their children, they never kiss. There is no such word in the Japanese language. Infanticide, nevertheless, is not uncommon. When shooting along the shores of the Inland Sea, I have frequently come across small infants tied up in straw bags or matting, washed up on the sand. I believe this crime, however, is seldom, if ever, committed by married people, but is always the sequel of youthful indiscretion.

The people who inhabit the villages along the coast invariably combine farming and fishing as a livelihood. In these situations a great deal of the field work is done by the women. These fields are generally about ten or twenty yards square. The plains and smaller valleys **are all, however** flat and level they may be, cut up into little patches of the above size. A raised pathway, eight or ten inches wide, divides one piece of ground from another. At the head of every valley are almost invariably several huge reservoirs of water; and all these valleys have a stream of water, either small or large, running down them. The reservoirs are constructed by building a huge bank across **from one** side of the steep hills to the other. Further down again a similar bank is thrown across. These great tanks are more like small natural lakes than artificially constructed water-holders.

Many a lovely mandarin duck have I bagged from these places. Boar and deer are also extremely partial to the hill slopes and alder thickets that generally surround these far-off reservoirs. Very frequently the higher ones are buried in the thick wood, miles from cultivation. These are very seldom tapped, an exceptionally bad drought must take place before that becomes necessary. I wonder something of the kind has never been tried in India.

Generally the houses are only one story, built of wood, plaster, and tiled or thatched. The size of the flooring is determined and measured by so many mats, the mat being six feet long by three wide, made on a frame of wood two inches thick, and filled in with straw, so that it forms when on the ground a nice cool covering, neither soft nor hard. The divisions between the rooms are made to slide, so that the whole house can be opened to give free ventilation, with the wind from any quarter. As the sides of these lightly-made houses are also made to open at pleasure by sliding, as the inner partitions do, it follows that when everything is thrown open, little but the flooring and roof is left. In the summer this description of residence is charming, but in the winter the cold is intense. If it were not then for their great quilted robes and coverings, in which you quite disappear, there would be no comfort at all. There are no fire-places. Charcoal is used and burnt in brass pans, vases, etc., but to receive any comfort or warmth from these things you must sit on them!

The common domestic cock in these regions crows

with wonderful regularity at twelve at night, two, and four. In China they are equally valuable, and even more **used for the purpose** of time-keeping. Every fishing-junk carries a bird in a small cage, hung over the high-peaked stern, for this purpose alone.

I had hove-to for lunch one day on a lovely white sandy beach in the Inland Sea, not thirty yards long, bound in by fir woods. Strolling a little way up the small valley I found a charming grassy **spot, and here I remained** an hour. Two natives had approached, and, respectfully remaining some twenty yards off, watched the wonderful sight of a foreigner eating. No European had ever been there. **One of my** men presented the elder of the two Japanese with an empty preserved-meat tin, which we had just flung from us. It was a wonderful thing, evidently. How they examined it! **How they** both thanked us, then spoke earnestly together for a few minutes, and away ran the younger, returning in a very short time with a live cock, which the older man took from him, and with many bows and apologies begged me to accept the bird, as a return for the handsome present of an empty meat-tin. This cock was, I doubt not, almost the most valuable thing the poor kind-hearted native possessed. They are the only time-piece the poorer class of Japanese have, and are, besides, generally great pets. Of course I did not deprive the small farmer of his fowl, his only clock, and his children's pet.

The poorest individual in the country lives in luxury compared to our humble classes. Their wants are few, and those few easily obtained. In the summer clothing is all but unnecessary; and during the winter fuel is cheap and plentiful. One of the great secrets of their well-being is the absence of drunkenness: tea is their main drink. The native spirit, called "saki," is, of course, drunk by the people, but in quite a different way from what the poorer classes in England do, *i.e.* in moderation.

Speaking of saki reminds me of an occasion when I was staying in a Buddhist temple, situated on the top of a mountain (Asama Yama)—in fact, there were seven temples clustered together. The old chief priest invited me to visit him. He lived at one end of the temple; and here I found him surrounded with books of every description, histories, geographies, and astronomical works predominating. Before his open-sided rooms was a lovely miniature garden, with a pond of clear fresh water, where an enormous tame carp lazily enjoyed life, coming constantly to the old priest's feet for bits of biscuit, sugar-plums, and rice. This priest of the mountains was a most keen talker on physical geography and history. The amount of information the old man possessed was wonderful. He gave me the Japanese theory of a great flood—the Flood—as follows:—" 2200 years ago Japan was covered with water, and every living thing was drowned. Heaven then opened, and a male and female of the human race were dropped on the highest mountain, as the water receded. Japan was again repeopled." My host was an inveterate saki drinker, and went through the operation in the most matter-of-fact way. He drank it hot and sweetened, and I am bound to say I found it exceedingly nice taken in this way. As soon as he could drink no more, he lay down and slept the effects off. In about an hour he seemed to rouse up as fresh as a lark, and turn to his books at once, and hot saki at the same time. This process went on all day long, the younger priests performing the necessary religious routine. I must in justice say that my friend's partiality for strong waters was exceptional, the Japanese generally being, as I have before remarked, very temperate. Notwithstanding his constant and sudden collapsing, I found him a most entertaining host, and spent the wet days, when confined to the temple, most agreeably. Deer barked all day long in the thick wood which abutted against one side of the enclosure. A tame white heron walked about the garden in front of my verandah, and a lovely half-wild kingfisher kept coming and going to and fro, diving after the small fish in the pond, then watching me most intently from a rock half-a-dozen yards off. I have no doubt the beautiful little bird wondered at the strange-looking biped.

I have already spoken about the two national religions—Buddhism and Shintoism. My remarks were more properly applicable to olden days, for since all prohibition of Christianity or any other belief has been removed, there is very little religion of any kind. The upper classes despise their old ideas, and don't feel sure about the new ones. Many different sects of missionaries have entered the field, but none with any success excepting the Roman Catholics. These have received very little encouragement, but still, in my opinion, Protestantism has little chance against them. The Christians I found in considerable numbers on the different western islands, were *all* from the old stock, from those who were persecuted generations ago, the relics of former times. When the early Christians, some three hundred years ago, became so numerous, the followers of Buddha feared the consequences, and sad to relate, a European people were induced to assist them in the persecution and attempt at extirpation. Still, strange to say, although hemmed in and cut down, seemingly almost to a man, the seed had become so rooted that it sprung up again and again. Whenever and wherever this occurred, extinction was the order of the **Government; until our own** good advice was so far listened to, that the wretched native Christians, though they were no longer killed, were scattered over the kingdom. A family, for instance, was known to be believers in the forbidden doctrine; immediately the father was sent to one place, the mother to another, and the children somewhere else. Strange it never struck the ruling powers that this was in reality the very best plan they could adopt to propagate and spread the belief they so much dreaded. The times, however, are changed, and liberty of conscience is now the order of **the** day. I hardly think it is generally known **that** when these people were simply insane after European ideas a very few years ago, amongst other wonderful notions and plans either at once introduced or thought of, changing their religion by Government decree was **one**. A committee of a few intelligent men were to be selected to proceed to France and England to observe and report which religion, Roman Catholicism or Protestantism, worked the best. Whichever did, was to be adopted. I have not the slightest doubt this could then have been done, but again we stepped in with advice which was listened to, and this extraordinary idea was given up. It would not have been more wonderful than many changes which were brought about at the time, successfully and entirely.

Why, it may be asked, has Protestantism so little chance against Romanism? I think there are many reasons why it is so. In the first place, it is less showy, less appealing to the senses, less made of it, and is more secret. Its forms are not so open: it belongs more to the closet than the church. There is no mistaking the Roman priest, he dresses like no other foreigner; the Protestant dresses as any ordinary stranger. But there is another reason why the Protestant's chances are small. His whole conception of missionary work does not give him the same chances of winning the hearts of the natives, for he does not in the same way make himself one of them; he is well paid, lives in a good house, changes his situation when he pleases, and, as before said, tries another part of the world when tired of one locality. The Romish priest, be he Jesuit or not, is in nine cases out of ten an educated gentleman. He has given up everything—land, home, and family, for the sole purpose of propagating his faith. His very beginning is earnest, and this at once strikes home to the native. He not only is the priest whose duty it is to spread certain views of religion, but he is the friend, and often physician as well, of the poor. His life, his mode of carrying on his duty—for duty it certainly must be to them—is all earnestness from beginning to end. He has no dreams of promotion or advancement. He generally has said a long farewell to relatives and friends, and does not look forward to meeting them again, until he does so in heaven. He expects—nay, intends—to die among his converts, and to do God's work is his sole reason for trying to keep alive at all. That there have been Protestant missionaries, self-sacrificing and earnest men, I will not deny; but in my experience I have not found that earnestness which alone can carry success with it, was ever the leading characteristic of our Protestant missionaries. Some men might go so far as to say that they fail to see that we have any right to introduce missionaries into these countries; but this is a subject on which I decline to enter here. I have never observed that natives become kinder, gentler, more truthful or honest, or more sober. Drunkenness and civilisation—of course I do not mean Christianity—in these cases run side by side. The introduction of civilisation is accompanied by the former; and as for honesty, the main aim of the white man is to extract as much from native innocence and ignorance as he possibly can.

How often has not the so-styled savage said to me, "You come to us and say we are very wicked, we are doing wrong, and are sure to go to a place you call hell, and at the same time you take to our customs, and live just as we do in many of the ways you say we are so wrong in; this is very strange. How can we believe you are in earnest?"

JAPAN.

CHAPTER XII.

KOREA.

In 1855 our squadron cruised up the coast of Tartary, searching for the Russian ships, which were not to be found, though I think they might have been if we had been more in earnest. At any rate, several magnificent bays and harbours were entered and looked into; subsequently a few of our vessels found the Russians, or some of them, in Castries Bay. The result is not worth mentioning. My object in referring to a circumstance so devoid of spirit in ourselves, is to show that at that time we were cruising in Chinese waters, off a portion of that kingdom. Since then the Russians, by treaty, have procured the whole of this coast, as far south as the forty-second parallel of latitude. Amongst the grand bays and harbours which stud this coast-line, there is not one which remains open during the winter. The most southern, Vladivostock, is only free from ice by the beginning of April. Saghalien, which island now belongs *in toto* to Russia by treaty, is devoid of a harbour altogether. The Japanese were induced to exchange a few wretched, barren rocks, the continuation of the Kuril Islands, for the south portion of Saghalien, which, although without a harbour, possesses abundance of coal; virtually, therefore, the Russians are without an open harbour in the East, that is to say, a harbour that can be entered at any time during the winter. This is, of course, a very great drawback, and they are naturally anxious to possess a good port further south. Why they stopped short in their southern encroachments on the borders of Korea I don't know; but I think they showed less cunning than usual in so doing, and certainly less than their neighbours, particularly ourselves, would have done. At the time they got possession of Tartary, Korea was to the world all but a *terra incognita* —Japan had not come forward. Our interest did not reach beyond Shanghai. The Russians at this time ought to have crossed the Korean boundary, and, at any rate, gone as far south as necessary to embrace a good port.

After visiting the Tartary coast we came south; the vessel I was in touching at Chosan, in Korea, on our way to Nagasaki. A little incident which happened will show the extreme objection the officials at that time had to have any communication with foreigners. I had been laid up with a **bullet** through my leg for **some weeks, and my messmates** were anxious to get something fresh in the shape of vegetables for me. A few had landed and persuaded a native **to** sell a chicken; before they left the beach, however, an official arrived, and had the seller of the fowl immediately flung on the ground, and bastinadoed.

Of late years it has been pretty well understood that Russia has cast longing eyes on Korea. **We knew** as little about the country as our neighbours. **On a** few different occasions during the present **century, a ship** had been sent to examine the southern coasts; but one and all had met with opposition, insult, and downright refusal to allow any surveying work to be done, or, in fact, any communication with the shore. Such was the state of affairs in 1878, when I—being in command of **H.M.S.** *Sylvia* surveying the coasts of Japan—was sent across to do what I could in the way of examining the coast. I pointed out before leaving **the** almost certainty of my meeting with or receiving exactly the same treatment as my predecessors. There was no reason to expect otherwise. The Americans and French had both attempted to open communication with the capital. Neither had succeeded, owing mainly to the insufficiency of force; but bad management had also something to do with their failure. It was not only an undignified attempt to get the thin edge of the wedge entered, but it was certain to fail. However, I was sent, and made for Chosan,[1] where, twenty-three years before, I had first touched these shores. We anchored about noon, and no official coming on board, landed to stretch my legs on the island, which, crossing the entrance of the bay, forms the excellent harbour of the above name. In less than a couple of hours I returned with three pheasants, a hog-deer, one snipe, and a small boar. Starting early next morning, and following the coast to the south-west, about noon I found we had entered a magnificent basin. The chart showed nothing, neither land nor sea. Continuing a southerly course, all the time in an even depth of about twelve fathoms, we at last reached a sugar-loafed island, which appeared to be situated at the southern end of the basin. Here we anchored, about twelve miles from the northern entrance of the bay. Landing immediately, the peak was arrived at without molestation, and I

[1] The Japanese call it Fu-san-ki.

SOUTH ENTRANCE TO SYLVIA BASIN KOREA.

discovered there was another entrance to the southward.

Very soon after returning on board, the chief official of the district came off. He was accompanied by numerous personal attendants, two of whom never left his elbow, but always on his moving held his arms. About 200 soldiers constituted the old man's guard. After the usual ceremonies were gone through, he begged me to tell him what I wanted by coming to **Korea**, and to this particular place, and **expressed** repeated hopes I would go away. I tried to get him to understand my object was perfectly friendly, and that my wish to land unmolested, and make some observations from the peak of the island, was entirely harmless. The poor old man then explained most **emphatically** that his head would answer for such proceedings. **The law of the** land, and which he had to maintain, or lose **his life, was** that "**no foreigner was to land** in his **district.**" I could not help feeling that this argument was unanswerable. All I could say was, that I must obey my orders, **as he** his; my repeated assurances that I had no evil intentions, but merely wished to examine the locality, only added to his fears and perplexity. I did land, **of** course, and with instruments, surrounded **by** rifles, obtained the observations I required. The natives, although they thronged round howling and hooting, were too discreet to commit themselves more seriously. It was obvious that work done in this way was a mistake, a great loss of time, and necessarily incomplete. I could not take all the observations myself, but had to send officers to different spots and localities. They were all young men, who might at any moment, under the above circumstances, lose their tempers, or consider it time to check the natives by more forcible means than remaining passive. If blows had once been struck, our difficulties would immediately have increased tenfold.

Next morning I sent several of my boats to sound and examine in different directions. One did not return in the evening, and as morning dawned there were still no signs of her. I therefore got the steam cutter ready, and started for the south entrance of the basin, the particular part I had directed the officer in charge of the boat to examine. When I reached the narrow channel which led into the open sea, I found each shore lined with soldiers; I suppose there were five or six hundred. A score of boats or so were pulling up in my direction. Each boat had a motley lot of soldiers on board, twenty-five to thirty, who got most unnecessarily excited over the appearance of the steam cutter, threatening by signs to send us all to the happy hunting-grounds. I concluded at once that my unfortunate missing boat, with its crew of six men and an officer, had been caught by some means, probably when they hove-to in the middle of the day for their usual hour's rest. If such were the case, I knew any attack on our part, unless thorough and sudden, would merely seal my men's fate and probable torture. This consideration alone, I may say, induced me to submit to being aimed at within half-a-dozen yards by dozens of these rascals. Such a variety of weapons that were presented at our devoted heads would have made a very fair collection in themselves,—old rifles, matchlocks, flint and steel instruments, jingalls, and crossbows. These latter articles were really curious. Underneath the stock was a large box, with a handle on one side, which the owner kept turning fiercely round as he aimed. Steaming quietly through them, I returned to the ship, intending to go back to Chosan, and demand the restoration of my men. When in the act of getting under weigh, my missing boat returned from the opposite direction, having, as it turned out, been chased when approaching the narrows by a number of boats filled with soldiers. A rattling breeze was blowing at the time, and she had dashed through them, and out into the open sea. All night long they pulled up the coast of the large island, which forms the outer boundary to the basin, and had by the time the ship was reached gone over eighty-four miles.

I returned to Japan, and reported my reception by the Koreans, stating I could carry on the work only by using force. Some months elapsed, during which time I continued work in Japan, then again went to Korea, being ordered this time to visit the south-west end or corner, far from the place of my previous *contretemps*.

The south-west corner of the Korean peninsula is bounded by a labyrinth of islands, extending at least forty-five miles off the mainland. Here the inhabitants consist mainly of fishermen living in small villages, and being so far away from officials they were less opposed to us. At the same time each village had a headman, who always requested me to go from their waters. Their orders were to allow no foreigners to land. "We," they said, "have no objection to communicate with you and allow you to land, but our Government objects to it, and we must obey orders." After being among these outer islands for about three weeks, a few junks with officials arrived from the mainland; and now the old bother had to be gone through again. All my work was done under arms, and I never felt certain that the boats' crews would return without coming to blows. I took as much of the shore work as possible; and never, I think, was my patience more sorely tested, a mob of these gaunt, dirty, white-robed beings always followed us to the peaks, or wherever I went, howling and gesticulating, and sometimes pelting us with stones. One day, when on shore, I met quite a *rara avis*, in the shape of a polite old man, who insisted on my having some of his tobacco. On this same island, amongst some stunted firs, I invariably saw an enormous number of magpies, seemingly the same as our own, except perhaps that these birds were rather smaller.

I had an excellent opportunity once of examining a native's house. It was built on a small island, no other house being near, and like all others, whether in villages or isolated, had an artificially raised and levelled yard round it. This yard is always surrounded by a high wall, as if to screen, which it does, the movements of the owners from their next neighbour's observation. The house was twenty feet by eight, and six feet high in the centre, but only four where the roof rested on the walls, which were very thick, made of mud, and whitewashed over. It was divided into three compartments, each quite separated from the other, and each having an entrance from the outside, which served both as door and window. One end was the kitchen, with several fire-places, and jars of water ranged round. The other end was a store-room, in which rice and millet-seed, besides dried fish and some corn, was stored in earthen jars. The centre compartment was the sleeping-place. A little way from the dwelling-house stood the cow-shed and outhouse, and here also was another store of rice and grain. Their winter-padded clothing was all out airing on the bushes, under cover of which bushes the inhabitants evidently were hiding. Brass spoons formed part of their very few utensils. The use of spoons amongst these people, if general, is curious, as both Chinese and Japanese stick to the chopstick.

Neither temple nor shrine of any description did I see, with the single exception at Port-Hamilton, where a small Buddhist temple of old and dilapidated appearance stood just outside one of the villages. A priest from the mainland occasionally came over and visited this place. The headman of one of the villages told me they thought our object in visiting and staying about amongst their barren islands, muddy water, and inhospitable shores, was simply and only to seize and carry off their women, and probably kill the men! Usually when the ship anchored near a settlement, or I landed for observations, the women were to be seen scampering away up the mountains like scared deer. I never got very near any of the fair sex, but the little I did see was quite sufficient. Amongst themselves these people are rude, coarse, and uncouth. They have no salutation, except buffeting each other; no mark or sign of respect to their headmen or officials; and altogether are a dirty, uninteresting lot. Occasionally I allowed some on board. When their headmen or officials were visiting the ship, and, sailor-like, some of the blue-jackets were sure to give them a pipe, tobacco, or something, their neighbours would immediately snatch at it and endeavour to get possession of the article, and a struggle and blows would at once ensue, the weakest losing the day, unless the donor came to the rescue. I spent a month or more at the Mackau Islands, a group some fifty miles from the mainland, and otherwise isolated from the great mass of islands off the south-west corner of Korea. Here the inhabitants were less antagonistic to foreigners, but I put this down to their distance from officials. The chief resident left in an open boat two days after I arrived, to report the foreign ship to his Government, and had not returned when I left. On two occasions only were we made marks of for stone-shying. One native used to steal off after dark and beg for biscuit, a little cloth, and as much rum as possible. In exchange for cloth, he gave me half-a-dozen books, one of which, being a history of Korea, is of interest, but unfortunately I only got a single volume. Their mode of burial is more like the Chinese system than the Japanese, their graves being anywhere about the hillsides, and usually detached. I came to the conclusion, from the scarcity of the graves, that it was only the most wealthy whose burial-places were marked by a green mound, and sometimes a few fir-trees planted round.

The great rarity of animal life is most remarkable, but is probably owing to there being very little cover or shelter on the islands for birds or beasts. Seals were very plentiful, and otters almost equally so. Rats alone appeared to flourish on shore. What they live on I never could determine. On every rock and island, equally on the uninhabited as on the others, these creatures abounded. My dogs used to go perfectly wild with excitement on landing, and of those they killed, half at least were piebald. Although the people were abominably dirty, I never saw one with any of the commonest skin diseases. Considering that their immediate neighbours, the Chinese and Japanese, are so subject to cutaneous ailments, the fact that none was observable amongst the Koreans seems strange. They are a taller people than either of the two nations mentioned; but on comparing them with the marines on board, they at once appeared short. Seeing them on the hill crests, or lounging about outside their houses, they look big gaunt figures; but this evidently is mainly on account of their style of dress, very loose white bags for trousers, and jacket equally so. This costume, topped by their high black hats made of horse hair, gives them a tall appearance. Their cattle, though small, were of very pretty form, and universally red in colour. The pony of the country is not much to look at; their tails are always kept long, the hair being used to make the peculiar Korean hat.

Crichton harbour is safe and good, and large enough to hold the fleets of the world. It is formed by a group of islands of the same name five miles off the mainland. Port Hamilton, about twenty miles from the nearest point of the continent, and thirty-five from the north-east end of Quelpaert Island, is a harbour of the very best description, easy of access, perfectly protected, and of regular depth; it could hardly be improved upon; its capacity is sufficient to hold the largest fleet of any nation; and its position most commanding. In the present state of affairs in the East, this admirable harbour ought to be jealously watched. It is unlikely that Korea will much longer remain the unknown country it at present is. And I should think, almost equally unlikely that it will remain intact much longer. The Russians appeared to hesitate about advancing at the very moment they might have advanced almost with impunity. This short-sightedness, however, may, and no doubt will, be retrieved some day. It appears to me absurd to suppose that having the interest, and this continually increasing, in these quarters, they will rest satisfied without having a good port open to navigation all the year round. In fact, no nation would, if situated as they are, and one could not blame them. Again it is time that the Korean coast should be—if not opened —well surveyed and known to the world at large, and particularly to us, who have more at stake than others, in the way of merchant shipping passing to and fro along their coasts, which abound with excellent shelter and anchorage, as yet not only unknown, but shut to the public. At present a vessel seeking shelter anywhere in Korean waters is almost sure to be attacked by the natives. We should insist at least on the coast being surveyed, and that our shipping should find protection if obliged to come to an anchor. This might be done as the Japanese did in 1877, by sending over half-a-dozen men-of-war and a few troops as a guard to the minister plenipotentiary, whose demands were, roundly, that the Japanese were to be allowed to survey the coast, that three ports were to be open, and that a mail service between the two countries should be established. All this was done at once. And I found, wherever I went in Korea, my Japanese servants were looked upon in a most friendly manner, the officials always making them presents, and asking at once, on coming on board, "Have you any Japanese with you?" There was no bloodshed, or anything approaching it, when the people from the country of the Rising Sun crossed over, and quietly but firmly insisted on their demands. I should imagine that an isolated harbour, such as Port-Hamilton, is not exactly what would suit the Russians. They ought, and must have, one on the mainland, a continuation in fact of their at present extensive coast line, including a port or ports, as the case may be. Port-Hamilton ought, in anticipation of such an event, to be taken possession of by ourselves.

The Goto Islands, forty miles west of Nagasaki, are wild and rugged in the extreme. They are very thinly peopled. Most of the islands are cut into by creeks and bays; some of the creeks are of great length, turning and twisting into the heart of the islands. Very little cultivation is tried owing to the hilly formation of the land. Wild boar, deer, and pheasants abound. It was to these islands that the Christians fled for safety when, years ago, they were, as before mentioned, so persecuted on the mainland; and here I found them still living in small villages amongst the hills. Periodically they cross over to Nagasaki for a supply of books, which are always ready for them at the priest's house. They are all Roman Catholics, and wear a charm suspended round their necks, which, of course, marks them at once from their fellow-countrymen, and points them out as believers in the once much-persecuted religion. I never heard that the persecution extended to these out-of-the-way islands, and should say that it did not. Considering the little value of this group of wild rock-bound and weather-beaten islands, and how little even now the Government considers them, it seems almost certain that here a safe retreat was found. All these Christians, I have said, were from the old stock—from the seed that great man Francis Xavier sowed in the sixteenth century. The Roman Catholic missionaries have told me themselves that, as far as making converts, their success was all but *nil*. They frankly acknowledged that what Chris-

THE GOTO ISLES, FROM HIRA SIMA

tianity was found at present in Japan was not of their planting, but from the teaching of their great predecessor, who spent nearly two years in the country—I suppose about the years 1550-51. I could see no difference in the habits of these people from their fellow-countrymen who were followers of Buddha or Shinto, but my own Japanese seemed to think they did differ very considerably. I never, however, got him to explain why, except that "they only had one wife." This, in his opinion, evidently constituted a very remarkable trait in their character. The Japanese who work in the coal-mine at Takashima, just off Nagasaki, are also Christians. At Ojika there appeared a mixture of the two races—Korean and Japanese; the natives being taller and coarse, and unpleasing in features and expression, which at once reminded me of Korea. Their cattle, also, were generally *red*, whereas the Japanese animal is almost always black.

The following tradition of them was related to me by one of the chief inhabitants:—Many years ago these islands were as much Korean as Japanese, both nations meeting and mixing. Five hundred years since, an island existed far out at sea, but during a terrible earthquake it had sunk below the surface of the water, and now there was a shoal at this spot, where the fishermen of Ojika frequently resorted for trawling and other modes of fishing;—a jar which he showed me had been brought up in one of the trawls not long since. It was an old earthenware vessel, covered with barnacles and other shell-fish. On asking the Japanese for a fisherman to point out the spot, a man was at once sent. The first day proved unsuccessful, but on the second I found the shoal, with exactly the depth of water on it that they had said, namely, eighteen feet.

It was among these islands that I heard the Japanese nightingale; it usually commenced singing about twelve at night, and continued doing so until morning. I have also heard them during the day. Their note is more peculiar than melodious, rather short and spasmodic, and their plumage is a dull slate-brown colour. I shot a goat-sucker, I suppose *Caprimulgus Asiaticus*, which bird I do not think I saw in any other part of Japan. About the end of April great numbers of albatross and shearwater appeared to arrive; whimbrel and snipe made their appearance, and cormorants were breeding on the cliffs of the out-lying rocks and islets. A large species of swift is common on the northern island; one I shot was twenty inches and a half from tip to tip. Another kind, resembling our own bird, I got specimens of; it has a white patch across the lower part of the back. Its throat, also, is white, with longitudinal black streaks, and all the black plumage has each feather tipped with white. By the 14th of May the wheat was being cut, and the rice fields being prepared.

The north end of Nosaki Sima, one of the northern islands of the group, was, when I could find time, a favourite resort of mine. The island rose from the sea very abruptly for 1000 feet, ending in a ridge, then fell as steeply to the water on the other side. It was thickly wooded on one side, gigantic camellia trees forming the principal cover. The ground underneath was open, covered only with the common brake-fern, *Pteris aquilina*. The opposite side was matted over with shrubs, creepers, and ferns. Here deer enjoyed life unmolested, and were in consequence very plentiful. On the unwooded side great pinnacle rocks sprang from the hill, far above the cover of shrubs, etc. A pair of ospreys had their nest on the flat top of one of these great boulders, and from the ridge above I could see right into it, and watch the old birds feeding their young. I sent one of my men to scramble up to the nest, in case an egg remained unhatched; but on his reaching half-way up the rock, and when clinging to the ivy which shrouded it, the old birds made such a fuss, dashing down close to his head, and screaming so angrily, that he beat a hasty retreat, much to my amusement. A couple of eagles were always hovering about the peak, or along the rocks off the shore. They were immature birds, which had probably crossed over from Korea.

The Japanese who inhabit the Goto Islands are very poor. They live, like all the others, chiefly on fish and rice, but seem to have less of it, and their lives are harder than those on the mainland. In fact, they appear very much neglected and unthought of by the Government. I had some difficulty in finding accommodation for a surveying party, which I intended leaving on one of the islands. At last a fair lady turned up, who had a house she would let, though very reluctantly; she never appeared herself, but transacted the business through a friend. The house was shown to me by her servant, a nice-looking musumee. On my returning in a month or so, the young widow[1] not only had got over her antipathy to the foreigners, but looked on them in a most friendly way, coming on board, and appearing by no means anxious to part with her tenants. Her little domestic was as sorry to lose the society of the blue-jackets as her mistress was that of the officers.

[1] The one referred to, p. 184.

The whole of the locality of the Goto Islands is very boisterous. It appears always to blow hard from whatever direction the wind may happen to come. Calm or moderate weather was quite the exception.

KOREA HOUSE VISITED.

CHAPTER XIII.

EXTRACTS FROM JOURNAL.

January 1st, 1875, *at Kobe.*—A lovely, bright morning; numbers of seagulls busily picking up what they can find floating astern. They look like flakes of white snow, as they hover about close to; both the herring-gull and black-headed are here. The sun is not yet over the horizon, 7 A.M., thermometer 36°.

4th.—How these people keep up the New Year! The streets were full yesterday of men, women, and children, but by far the greater part were girls, dressed in their best, painted and powdered to a great extent.

They were one and all playing at battledore and shuttlecock, or ball.

5th.—At Sozu Sima, forty miles or so from Kobe, one of my favourite shooting-quarters. Bagged a fine hind, in capital condition, killing her dead at 250 yards Express,[1] standing.

6th.—Went to the peak, 2500 feet; the view was very beautiful. Freezing hard up there; my moustache immediately became as hard as a board. I was right glad to dip underneath the crest, and enjoy the warm sun. One of my men, carrying my gun, loaded with No. 6, knocked over a hind. He got by some means within half-a-dozen yards of the beast without being seen.

8th.—Thermometer 30°. I see some exceedingly good and handsome dark granite here and there, along the foot of the cliffs, and great giant sort of nine-pins, which rise 100 feet in height, all round the amphitheatre-shaped formation of agglomerate breccia which runs round the head of the bay for some miles.

13th.—Thermometer 37°. Cloudy, and inclined to rain.

18th.—Thermometer 37°. Very cold. Ran back to Akashi, near Kobe, to examine the tides, which here are very erratic. I was five hours making good one

[1] That is, with my "Express" rifle.

mile towards my destination, steaming as hard as I could, about nine knots. Fortunately the current does not always run like this. Quantities of duck everywhere, mostly mallard. So far as the winter has gone, I think it has been decidedly milder than last. Last summer was exceptionally wet.

19*th*.—Thermometer 31°. Went to a favourite old shooting ground, Tango Sango. Everything was just as I left it two years ago—in fact, as I first saw it five years ago; but the geese, which used to abound in such quantities, have quite forsaken the locality. In looking across the country formerly, it appeared as if the fields were covered by a gigantic cobweb; now the Japanese don't find it necessary to erect the long poles in the centre, with straw-roping drawn from the top to the tiny bank surrounding each field, to scare away the birds. The ground was quite white with last night's frost.

26*th*.—At Kobe again. The hills all white with snow this morning. I can only make out three species of seagull in the bay. Went over the hills behind the settlement, but it snowed too heavily to see anything.

27*th*.—Thermometer 29°. Quantities of snow on the high ground.

31*st*.—Thermometer 31°. Took a long walk over the hills behind the Moon temple. The fir-trees are most beautiful in their white silvery covering.

February 6th.—Gave Bruin a dose of strychnine, poor thing; for eight minutes there was no result, then she suddenly lay down, stretched her limbs out, and was dead. The other day she infringed on her liberty. She was never allowed to go below the upper deck; she was quite well aware of this prohibition, and never attempted to trespass on forbidden ground but once. It was Sunday afternoon, when the ship was particularly quiet, and Miss Bruin evidently thought now was her chance to satisfy a curiosity she had long felt, of having a peep below. Down the companion-ladder she noiselessly but quickly went, straight into my cabin. The quartermaster on watch soon missed her ladyship, and finding where she was, rushed to me, reporting, "The bear is in your cabin, sir." I thought of all my glass and crockery, my dressing-table with all its nicknacks, and Bruin's horrible inquisitiveness; no monkey I knew was more addicted to curiosity, and none half so apt to do so much mischief in a few moments, as my big rough pet of a bear. Down I ran to my cabin, expecting I hardly knew what, and there sat Bruin quietly on the locker close to my dressing-table, looking the picture of wickedness. How well she knew she had no business there, her expression was simply too ludicrous. Speaking very kindly, I got between her and my treasures, and sat down.

The first lieutenant came also to the rescue, and got on her other side, and there we three sat. Neither Holland nor I dared use strong measures to expel Miss Bruin, who watched us both very narrowly, as much as to say, "I know all about it, but I am not going yet." I called the quartermaster and made him take my place, then getting a large lump of sugar, enticed Bruin to the foot of the ladder. Making room for her to pass, I gave her the sugar, and the next moment she went up the ladder like a shot, giving a loud call of half anger, half pain, knowing well I meant to help her up with a good kick behind, long before my boot reached her hide.

February 7th.—Thermometer 20°, the lowest we have yet registered. It was bitterly keen over the higher ground, particularly during the gusts of wind, as they passed down the valleys. Saw nothing but one ape: these animals make a curious foot or hand print in the snow.

9th.—Killed a fine deer. The mountains are perfectly white, it having snowed all yesterday afternoon.

18th.—The icicles are most beautiful along the path by the stream which runs up amongst the hills behind the waterfall.

28th.—Thermometer 37°. Rain.

March 1*st.*—A most beautiful morning. Spring is coming fast. The warm sun has had considerable effect on the snow, which has disappeared a great deal. Shot a stag; saw three woodcock, and several pheasants. A little of this spring weather, and no more woodcock will be seen.

3*d.*—Thermometer 46°. A great change in the temperature.

4*th.*—A heavy fall of snow last night. Shot a very old stag.

9*th.*—Spring has decidedly come. Birds pairing, and the larks singing merrily. I can see no difference between this bird and our own *Alauda arvensis*. Their habits are exactly the same, and the bird itself appears in every respect identical, yet, if I mistake not, it is called *A. japonicus*. I think some people are much too ready to make distinct species. Making new species of birds varying in plumage, or a little in size, is a mistake.

20*th.*—Snow again last night on the hills. They are all white. Down here it fell as rain.

21*st.*—Mallard and teal are still about, but the widgeon have left for the northward. The provision shops are now full of game, particularly hares and pheasants. The cock birds are easily found by their constant crowing. The Japanese huntsmen know this, and, lying concealed, imitate the call of the female, shoot the cocks with a small single bullet.

27th.—Violets are out on all the banks; so is the cuckoo plant. Birds are paired, and in some cases building. I found two pair of ospreys on Isumi island, each pair busily at work on their nests, which were within eighty yards of each other, on two old fir-trees. By the size of the nests, they, I should imagine, had done duty before. The young fronds of the ferns are shooting, and the shrubs have a fresh green flush over them. The blue rock-thrush is extremely active and merry, flying from rock to rock, uttering his interesting but rather spasmodic note. At other times of the year he is comparatively a dull bird.

30th.—Saw three woodcock.

31st.—To-day when walking over the rough mountains on the south of Awadji Island, I found the bay-tree, or rather shrub, in abundance—the first time I have seen it out here, also a new kind of sweet daphne.

April 8th.—Blowing a gale. Left Kobe for Oosima, the most southern point of the Kii peninsula; wild raspberries and cherries in blossom, cormorants and mallard still about,—both breed in the neighbourhood. Wheat is well in the ear; beans and peas in full blossom.

9*th.*—Went on to Awasi Bay. A button-hook which I lost here last October was returned to me to-day. A poor woman found it and kept it safely until I turned up again. Rather different from what one would find in England, where finders of other people's property either keep it or destroy it.

11*th.*—Found an osprey's nest and three eggs.

12*th.*—I came upon a large crested seal fishing about some rocks; what a curious animal it is! This one was by no means frightened at the boat as we pulled close up to it. I believe it is only the male that has the curious top-knot to his head. This one must have been quite twelve feet long, of a yellowish colour, head and shoulders darker, hinder fins very large and black. It is amusing to watch an osprey on her nest in a fir-tree which is growing on a small rocky islet, close to the ship.

15*th.*—Blowing hard from the south, and raining. Wolves are very common here—Taskara Ura, Kii coast. No large wood or timber about; dense fern, shrubs, and rank grass constitute the cover. The people are of the very poorest class, the country being far too mountainous, rugged, and rough, for anybody but charcoal-burners, and a few fishermen, and very small farmers. Wild boar and deer are very numerous. As

I walked, or rather struggled up a mountain to make a surveying station at the peak, deer kept constantly barking at us, but only now and then did we see them.

20th, Matoya.—A calm bright day, pheasants crowing on every hill or mound. Shearwaters very numerous along the rocky shore; I wish I could find where these birds breed, for breed they evidently do, not far off.

21st.—Lots of snipe now here, teal and mallard; the latter are in small flocks of drakes. Green peas to-day for the first time, picked from the fields. How kind these people are! When asked if they will sell some pease, "Oh, no, pray take what you like, they are not worth selling;" and at these truly native places I believe half my vegetables are got in this way. My servant, a native, goes on shore, enjoys his walk, makes love to the prettiest girl he meets, asks a cottager if he will kindly sell him a lettuce, and is begged to take what he wants; cucumbers, vegetable marrows, peas, beans, melons, and so on, are all to be had, as a rule, for less than the asking.

26th.—Put up for a week in a delightful Buddhist temple. Busy surveying all day. Found a buttercup; the flower I should say is the same as our own species. Four different-coloured azaleas here; they are now in perfect blossom.

May 7th, Toba.—Came up here two days ago. Yesterday on a small island I came upon a heronry, consisting of a mixture of the white and the blue bird. Most beautiful they looked mixed together on the trees, as many as eight or ten nests in one tree. The trees they built in were nearly all camellias, which were in blossom, and about forty feet in height.

11th.—Hundreds of boats are now employed collecting a certain kind of seaweed, which is used for manuring their rice-fields.

12th.—The rocks about here are generally a rotten sandstone mixed with steatite. I had to go up to Ominato, a town some miles in Awari Gulf. A large river, which runs down from the mountains backing the plain, is full of timber being floated down for shipment. It is all small, and pine wood. I came upon one huge kiarki tree (the native elm), thirty feet in circumference. The plain which runs up from Ominato, all along the west side of the gulf, is exceedingly rich, and beautifully cultivated; a very different style of country from the other side of the southern mountain ranges on the Kii coast. Barley and wheat were both grown on this plain.

13th.—The evenings are hot, but by midnight the temperature is delicious and refreshing. The number of osprey nests I find astonishes me; scarcely a pinnacle, rock, or well-forked big fir-tree is without a nest.

June 7th.—Have been to Yokohama and back to Toba, anchoring at Omae Saki *en route*. Here I found quantities of large turtle, but failed to catch any. In sounding near that point preparatory to getting a cast with the dredge, I got two hundred fathoms, and then a successful haul of the dredge. The next cast, to my no little astonishment, was just over 1000 fathoms, and close to here were only fifty fathoms. I brought the bottom up each time, so there was no mistake about it. I never came across such a sudden dip before or since.

8th.—Both barley and wheat are being cut, quite ripe; and the young rice is transplanted. In certain localities a great deal of lime is used on the rice-fields, besides seaweed, shrubs, grass, and sprigs of all kinds; it is trodden into the soft and well irrigated rice-fields by women.

9th.—The temperature has lately ranged between 78° and 68°. Found that interesting seagull, *Larus crassirostris*, breeding on Kami Sima, an island at the entrance of Awari Gulf.

14th.—Saw a brown *Corvus japonicus*, with a white streak in each wing.

19th.—At Matoya again. Great numbers of women diving for seaweed. The pheasants are just beginning to moult. That delicious large jessamine is now out in blossom; I believe it is the *Olea fragrans*.

21st.—In sounding down to Katzura, on the Kii coast, I dipped the dredge over in 460 fathoms, and brought up a perfect specimen of a spider-crab, which turned out to be a new species.

I had now finished the work connected with the Kii coast, and left for Kobe and Nagasaki, and then returned to Simonosaki, the western entrance of the Inland Sea.

July 19*th.*—Simonosaki. Temperature 85° in the shade, 115° in the sun—oppressively hot and sultry. It is astonishing how the native children and babies stand the sun with their little bare heads.

25th.—Swifts flying about all night long.

30th.—At Yayo Sima, in the Inland Sea, a large island, thickly populated by the most unhappy class of Japanese I ever saw. It struck me as being an unhealthy island, the natives all look so sickly.

August 7*th. Simonosaki.*—The rice-fields have now a peculiar smell, resembling that of a mouse-trap in which a number of those troublesome little animals have been caught.

21st.—Heavy thunder-storms are of frequent occurrence. Sandpipers are beginning to make their appearance. Quantities of melons are grown about here in the fields; some of them excellent. The young pheasants are in capital condition for shooting; they are almost as large as the old ones, and quite plump. They are hatched earlier than in England, and owing to the greater regularity and warmth of the weather during spring and summer, shoot up quicker.

26th.—A few grey plover appeared to-day, turnstones and knots, and last night I heard curlew flying overhead. These birds appearing indicate summer is nearly gone.

30th.—Thermometer 75°. Very heavy rain.

September 1st.—Thermometer 77°. Rain. At low tide scores of women and girls turn out on the rocks to pick up seaweed, crabs, and small fish which have been left in the little pools. Their chief, if not only garment, is usually a large straw hat. How they stand the sun on their backs is a marvel,—being brought up to it from their babyhood, I suppose, in time their heads and skin become naturally thick. I should like to know if the skull of a Japanese is thicker than ours. Temperature quite low to-day to what we have lately had, the thermometer not having been as low as 77° for many a long day.

2d.—It feels cold; thermometer 70°. Shot a few pheasants.

6th.—Seagulls begin to appear, mostly young birds. The old cock pheasants have got their young feathers well forward, whereas the hens have not begun to cast their old ones.

9th.—The late heavy rains have made a great difference in the crops. The rice is well in the ear, and swelling fast.

11th.—A beautiful, bell-shaped blue flower is now out all over the hills. Two young pheasants I shot weighed four pounds.

19th.—Thermometer 65°; deliciously cool.

23d.—Crossed over to Tsu Sima *en route* to Korea. Shot a perfect specimen of the large scarlet kingfisher, *Alcedo coromanda major*, and some pheasants, which here are the China bird and not the Japanese. Very little indeed of the island, or rather islands, is cultivated. Rice, sweet potatoes, and some millet, are almost the only kinds of grain and roots to be seen. The islands are very mountainous, and overgrown with timber, chiefly fir. A magnificent basin cuts into the west side, which runs away in endless creeks, and smaller bays, marvellous harbours, and landlocked nooks. One and all have the drawback of having such deep water, and I had great difficulty in finding a single bank with twelve fathoms on it, twenty and more being the general depth. Picked up three or four couple of snipe, and saw some teal.

24th.—*Mackau* group, off the south-west coast of Korea. I got six books from a Korean last night; he paddled quietly alongside after dark; his great idea seemed to be rum; I gave him some cloth for the books, and a little rum, over which he smacked his lips, and chuckled. Shot a Japanese teal, and saw two golden plover. A few days since I saw some Korean women in their fields; they didn't know I was so near; but I had come up by myself from the beach, to the sharp ridge which overlooked them, and lying well concealed amongst the rocks, I watched them with my telescope. They were big women; but they appear larger than they really are, on account of the enormous baggy trousers they wear, and which are always white. Besides these baggy breeches, they wear a short jacket, buttoned in front. The few Korean females I have been near are, without exception, the very ugliest of their sex I have ever seen in any part of the world.

To-day, when using the theodolite, two inquisitive crows (*Corvus japonicus* without doubt) came to see what I was doing. First they carefully examined the instrument box, which was on the ground about five yards off; finding nothing of much interest within, they then walked a little nearer and watched me most attentively. They were perfectly fearless; coolly walking up to my men, who were lying about on the grass, and looked into their faces, much to Jack's amusement.

A heron has appeared, and a kingfisher (*Alcedo ispida*). What a widely distributed bird this is! I feel sure that the eagle about here is different from the Yesso bird. They are now breeding, and have the white tail only; I take it, therefore, they are mature birds. The Yesso bird I never saw breeding without both white head and tail. This Korean bird closely resembles our fishing eagle, *A. albicilla*.

24*th*.—Crichton harbour. What a grand safe harbour, sufficient to hold the fleets of the world! Here is a place for advancing Russia to take possession of; being well off the mainland would add in some respects to its value. The islands which form this excellent harbour seem to have few inhabitants on them.

26*th*.—Put into Nama Ura, in Nakadori Island, one of the Goto group. Shot five pheasants.

October 1*st*.—Tried an island five miles off for deer; bagged two. I missed a stag in a most unaccountable way.

8*th*.—Thermometer as low as 59°. The rice is being

cut (Simonosaki). Made a very fair bag over my old ground—pheasant and snipe. Otters are very numerous about here. This place seems to be very flourishing from the large numbers of junks that start both west and east. It is the chief rice port of the whole of Nagato. I often see these great unwieldy craft backing through the straits most cleverly, when a good breeze blows against the eastern tide; they keep perfect command of their vessels in this way, lowering or hoisting the one great sail according to the wind, all the time being carried through by the strong current, which is also acting on their enormous rudder. These vessels are steered with the greatest nicety. The people in the town are always asking me " when Simonosaki is to be opened to the world." The telegraph, which runs through the entire country from north to south, passes by here, and, if need be, I can telegraph to any part of the globe. What a difference a few years has made in this country!

10*th.*—Shot a beautiful species of dark pigeon, called *Columba janthina*. The shores of the islands about the entrance to the straits are generally rocky, of a dark red sandstone. Ducks are arriving. I have seen some widgeon. The natives are hard at work on their rice, which is half cut. An excellent crop.

16th.—Thermometer 58°. The Japanese grow about here a small plant resembling in leaf the acacia, which they use as a substitute for tea. The persimmon trees are laden with beautiful ripe fruit. The wax **tree**, *Myrica cerifera*, is now of a lovely red, russet, and bright yellow colour.

25th.—Range of thermometer in the last twenty-four hours: maximum, 74°; minimum, 63°.

28th.—Steamed through the Inland Sea to Hirosima. **In** days gone by this beautiful island was kept as a **deer** preserve by some prince. Since, however, foreigners appeared on the scene, he, like most others, had all the deer killed off. When I say all, that is hardly correct, for there are deer on the island now, and many a good day's work have I had **after** them.

The weather lately has been uniformly fine. Hirosima is chiefly made up of decomposed granite; and here, and elsewhere when such is the case, I notice the streams and springs are always milky, but otherwise good in flavour.

November 1st.—Thermometer 51°. The coldest day as yet. I heard a deer calling yesterday evening.

4th.—Awadshi Island. The wild boar here are absurdly plentiful.

12*th.*—The rutting season is, I think, now over. Thermometer 55°.

15*th.*—Hot and sultry. Thermometer: minimum, 57°; maximum, 72°. Rain. Returned to Kobe.

17*th.*—The black-headed gull appeared to-day in complete winter plumage. Bullfinches very abundant on the hills. I can see no difference between this bird and our own, except in the amount of red being less in the Japanese bird, which only extends as far as the throat, and not to the breast: but in habits, note, and size they seem to be identical.

21*st.*—Thermometer 46°. At the Moon temple, where I have been for three days, there was ice this morning. Height above the sea, 2500 feet. It is a most charming place, and there are plenty of deer in the wood which surrounds the temple. Shot a good stag to-day. I had left the temple, meaning to shoot my way home. I knew every likely cover and the whole country well. As I was walking along the sharp ridge of a very steep line of hills, I saw two hinds and a stag on the opposite side of the valley. They appeared to move very quietly, and not as if they had been frightened. So, retracing my steps for half a mile, I went down the centre of the valley, and sent my man and dog round to where I first saw the deer. I reached somewhere beyond where they had disappeared without seeing or hearing anything. A rustling in the long grass fifty yards up the hill-side made me halt, and standing perfectly still, I again heard it; at the same moment the stag's horns showed like two dried sticks, and judging where his shoulders ought to be, I fired. With a few desperate plunges the fine beast came crashing down the hill-side, and fell dead within five yards of where I stood. His horns were very poor, but the deer was one of the largest I ever shot in the south of **Japan.**

29*th.*—Bamboo clumps and plantations are always fenced in. I believe it is **to protect** the young shoots from boars. The shoot, when twelve to eighteen inches long, is a most excellent vegetable. **The tea-plant is in flower.**

30*th.*—Thermometer: maximum, 63°; minimum, 44°.

December 1*st.*—Matoya. **The** women still at work diving for seaweed; temperature of water 66°. The wind is sharp and keen. How they stand it appears extraordinary.

7*th.*—Extremely cold on the mountain peaks, but quite warm in the sheltered valleys.

Came round to Toba. How this lovely place, with its grand old castle, and magnificent trees dotted about the gardens and grounds of the castle, has been spoiled! New Japan! since the Government changed, the trees have been cut down, and turned into money; and the Daimio is pensioned, and lives in a semi-detached villa in Yedo,—Tokio, as it is now called. How well I remember this place when I first visited it, and how I thought it the very prettiest spot I had ever seen in the country. The way also this Daimio entertained me; his officers and retainers in their picturesque dresses, and wearing their two swords. It is sad to think of this old chieftain as he now is, dressed in badly-fitting European clothes, giving croquet-parties and five o'clock tea to foreigners at Tokio, and instead of the two-sworded, clean, polite retainers, the town has a number of policemen, and a man they call the Mayor in charge of it, the former dressed in a sort of German costume, with yellow bands round their ugly flat caps, who consider foreigners beings to be particularly looked after.

I sometimes doubt the accuracy of my tide-watcher's statements, his figures are rather too correct to please me.

8th.—I find the tent on shore, where the two men noting the tides reside, is a rendezvous for the fair sex after dark. Must relieve them, and send others. Shot two deer, one a stag with switch horns; he gave me a grand run of two hours before I got him.

EXTRACTS FROM JOURNAL. 277

9th.—I see the mountains inland are quite white this morning. Thermometer down to 38°.

13th.—Finished the tides, and left for Yokohama. Thermometer 43°, cool, fresh, and bright.

19th.—Ice in all the valleys. Thermometer 30°.

Christmas Day.—Very clear. I saw Fusi Yama last night by moonlight forty-five miles off in a bee line. The upper half of this gigantic cone is quite white.

31st.—What perfectly enjoyable weather we have had lately! Thermometer averaging—maximum 55° minimum 36°.

LARUS CRASSIROSTRIS.

CHAPTER XIV.

CRUISING AFTER PIRATES.

ALTHOUGH my first acquaintance with China was in 1855, I mean to relate a few piratical incidents of a later date, and afterwards, perhaps, return to that year, and the war which immediately followed.

In 1864 the coasts of China, and particularly the southern parts, were infested with pirates. I commanded a gunboat, whose particular duty was to keep them in check. The Gulf of Tonquin, the island of Hainan, and the coast from thence up to Macao was

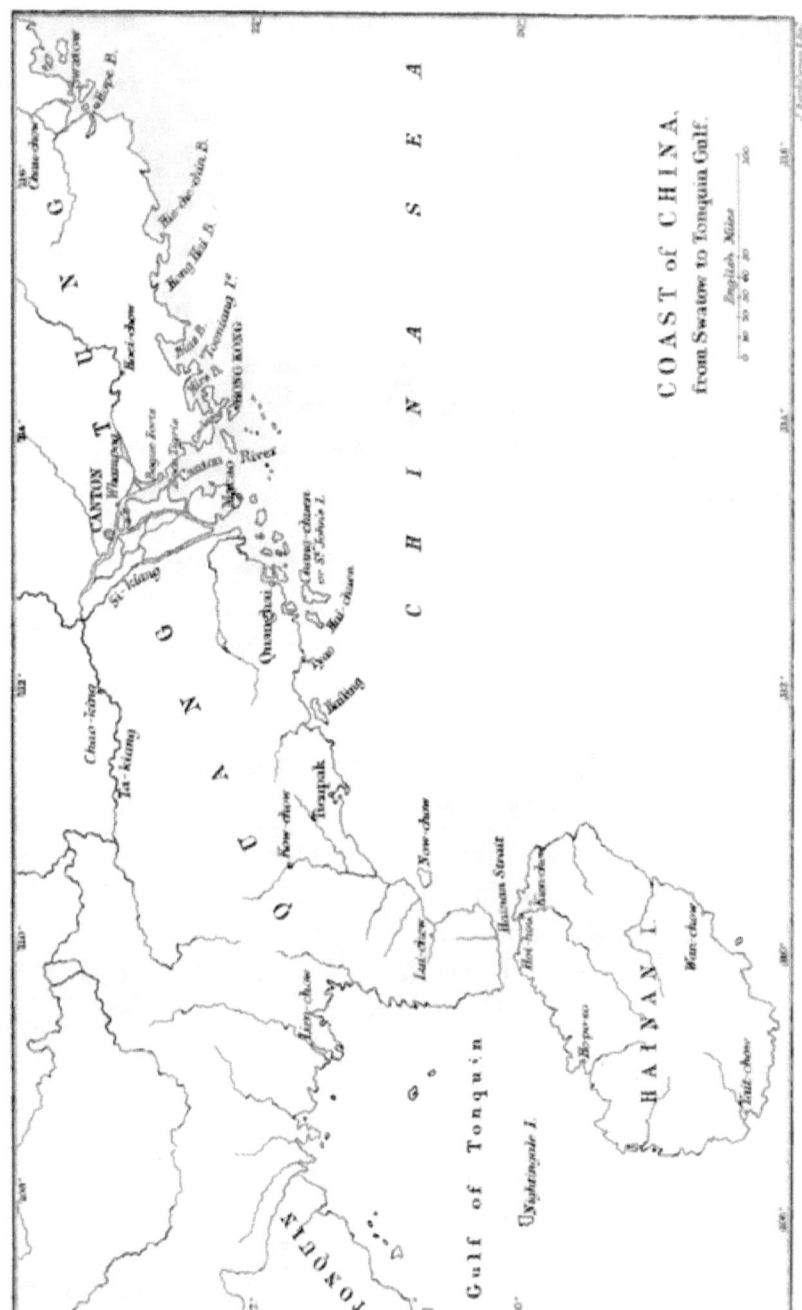

unknown and unvisited except by myself, or an occasional other gunboat. There was no commerce, neither port nor town existing of sufficient size to excite trade, excepting perhaps Hoihou, the chief town of Hainan. The anchorage there, however, is very bad, being merely a roadstead, and to get to it numerous dangerous shoals have to be passed. Islands and shoal water stretch a long way out from the main coast line, forming at all times innumerable safe retreats. Rough sketches of the coast have been taken at different times, but to this day it remains unsurveyed.

The island of Hainan is 300 miles round, and the length of the other coasts which I have mentioned would amount to, roundly, 400 miles. The whole of this considerable extent of coast was, in the days I am speaking of, entirely at the disposal of these lawless Chinamen.

I was lying at my anchorage in Hong-Kong harbour one day; a fine large opium junk, armed to the teeth with a dozen 12 to 18 pounder guns on board, and a crew of about forty-five men lay close to me.

In the afternoon a number of passengers went on board her. These people intended taking advantage of the security afforded by such a vessel—supposed security would perhaps be more applicable. At any rate, when an opium junk was about to proceed up the coast, owing to the strength of her crew and armament, applications for passages were sure to be made.

She was bound for Swatow, a port 180 miles to the northward, and towards dusk she got under weigh. As she reached the outer roads of Hong-Kong, or a few miles from the Lymoon Pass, it fell calm, and she anchored. This was about nine o'clock. A few hours afterwards, probably about midnight, a large junk quietly ran alongside, a number of men jumped on board, and before the passengers and crew could show any resistance, they were entirely in the power of a band of pirates. The crew and passengers were at once secured under hatches, and the junk got under weigh and steered for the back or south side of the island of Hong-Kong.

Soon after daylight, one by one of these unfortunate beings, men and women, as they came up from below, had their hands tied behind them, their feet tied together, and were then flung overboard, a single exception being made out of the eighty-three on board. This was a boy about twelve years old. He was spared, being small enough to make their tea and prepare their opium pipes, etc. The pirates then took the junk, which had a most valuable cargo of opium, a description of plunder these gentlemen particularly appreciate, being easily turned into money, and made for a favourite harbour a little to the north of Macao. Here they divided their spoil, burnt the junk, and dispersed. This plan was frequently adopted to elude pursuit. Seven went to Macao, and from thence took their passage by the usual passenger steamer to Hong-Kong. The poor little urchin whom they had spared, but whose father had been drowned, was allotted to one of these seven.

Before the steamer reached her destination, the Captain noticed the boy, who appeared to be in much distress, and being a kind-hearted man (peace to his ashes!) asked what ailed him. On hearing the story I have just related, instead of running the steamer alongside the jetty at Hong-Kong, as was usual, he anchored in mid-stream, hailed the police-boat to come alongside, drew up the hundred odd Chinese passengers, and with the boy's assistance picked the seven men from amongst them. They were taken possession of by the police and locked up.

The previous evening, one of the eighty-two unfortunates who had been flung overboard arrived at Hong-Kong, and gave the same account as the boy did. This man's fate was evidently not drowning. It appeared when he found himself in the water, and going quickly to the bottom, he managed with a desperate effort to free his hands by slipping them through the lashing, and then bringing himself to the surface he soon got his feet free. Chinamen as a rule swim like fish, and fortunately for this one, he was no exception. He reached the nearest island safely, and from thence to Hong-Kong in a fishing-boat must have been a pleasant journey after the short but peculiar one he had just gone through. His account had been received previous to the boy's; both agreed, and in consequence I was sent out to examine, and, if possible, capture some of the other pirates. Of course it was useless; no trace whatever could be obtained.

The seven men were tried and condemned at Hong-Kong, and one morning I had the satisfaction of seeing them all hanged. I think a more cold-blooded affair could hardly be imagined than the above wholesale drowning of eighty-two fellow-countrymen.

I was cruising up the coast one day, merely on the look-out, having no definite information to go on, when, on passing a small island, two fishermen paddled off in a sanpan.

"Have got pilong," one immediately said.

"Where?" I asked.

"Can makee see," he replied, and on looking in the direction he pointed, I saw two small junks making the best of their way to sea. There was no wind, so I steamed quietly on, knowing they could not escape. **About a** dozen other smaller junks now put off, and opened fire at the two larger ones. Guns, jingalls, and other explosive instruments were **discharged** indiscriminately. As **I ran alongside the** nearest of the **two junks,** this fusilade ceased, and I soon had both **junks secured.** The crews I took on board the gun-boat, and steamed in and anchored off the town. The Mandarin, the governor of the place, at **once came off,** when the following conversation took place between **us.** First thanking me for my opportune appearance and capture of the two pirate junks, with their crews intact, numbering, all told, to twenty-one, he said—

"These two junks have given me a great deal **of** trouble for four days; they have **blockaded** the place; neither a fishing or trading junk has been able to get out."

"Do you mean to say," I answered, "that these two miserable junks, with twenty-one men between them, and mounting one two-pounder gun, have actually shut your port up for that time?"

"**Yes,**" he said. "We are, my people are, very frightened of pilongs."

"Have you no troops?" I remarked; "your personal staff seems to consist of at least fifty."

"Oh yes," he replied; "I have 800 soldiers on shore!"

RETURNING TO HONG-KONG WITH THREE PIRATES, 2ND MARCH 1864

There were something like a hundred junks of all sizes, some large enough to have run over the pirates without feeling the shock.

"Why did you not put some of your brave men in the fishing-junks and capture these pirates?"

"Ah, you English are very brave," he replied; "my men are very easily frightened."

Well, I thought to myself, that seems pretty certain.

"How many inhabitants are there in the town?" I asked.

"More than 4000," was the answer.

"I think," I said, "if I were a Chinaman, I would turn pirate at once. They must lead very jolly independent lives."

"Yes, they do," answered this blue-buttoned warrior; "the only things they fear are English gunboats."

A score or so of fishing junks had assembled round. The crews, consisting of quite as many women as men, were making a fearful clamour, talking over the last four days, and their sleepless nights; and now their relief had come, and their dreaded enemies were captured.

"Give us the pirates," they cried; the women particularly bawled for their possession.

"What do they mean," I asked my Mandarin friend, "by demanding these pirates to be handed over to their tender mercies?"

"Oh, they only want to drown them," he replied.

Just at this moment the poor Mandarin, who had evidently for some time been longing to reach *terra firma* again, had to be seized by two of his officials, and hurried to the ship's side, when his head was held well over the water, much to the amusement of his surrounding countrymen. A splash and an immense uproar at the same moment took place. The unhappy Mandarin recovered as if he had been electrified, and roared out sundry orders, which increased the confusion tenfold. It was a most laughable sight. The crews belonging to the fishing-junks, and the two or three score of soldiers and other officials rushing about with sticks, oars, and anything they could grasp, all giving directions at the same moment. The Mandarin was nowhere; he might just as well have gone on feeding the fishes; his directions were utterly lost in the general uproar and confusion. Two of the pirates had managed to slip from their guard, and took a header overboard; but they had no chance of escape, there were too many small craft about, and they were soon retaken. But to bring this story to an end. I handed over junks and pirates to the Mandarin. In twos, well secured, they were then placed in different junks, under a strong guard, and taken on shore. I bade my friend good-bye, and went on my journey up the coast. These twenty pirates were sent to Canton, tried, condemned, and executed.

The Chinese mode of decapitation is simple and expeditious; a short account of it may not be amiss here. A dozen or more of the condemned are taken to the execution ground, which at Canton is a small open space within the city. They are made to kneel down, their hands are then secured behind them, and the executioner goes along the line and arranges their heads and necks. I remember one poor wretch who shrunk up whenever the executioner approached, drawing his head into his shoulders, as if the very touch or nearness of the man was too much for him. The executioner tried to explain how much easier it would be for him to take his head off cleanly and neatly if he kept it well out, and thereupon gave it a good pull, and bared the unfortunate wretch's neck once more. Going to one end of the line he walks along, at each step with one blow severing a head from the body. The implement used is a sort of heavy half-sword half-butcher's cleaver, and is used with both hands.

I had been a couple of days cruising along the eastern coast, anchoring at night, and examining during the day-time the numerous creeks, bays, and hiding-places, but without success of any kind. Towards evening of the second day I reached a favourite creek, which, bending back from the head of a deep bay, twenty miles from the open sea, expanded into an inland basin, with innumerable smaller creeks and passages, twisting and turning about amongst the hills in all directions. It was a grand place for pirates. By having men stationed on the peaks of the hills, signals were easily passed along very quickly to their junks inside, which warning generally was in time to allow them to escape by some of the interminable creeks.

Soon after anchoring I went on shore to see the missionary priest, a Roman Catholic and a Jesuit. I never met or heard of a Protestant missionary taking up his quarters in such situations as I am now speaking of, viz., amongst the poorer villagers far away from the open or treaty ports, where half the people live by piracy and robbery, in petty ways as well as in a more wholesale manner. A few words about this little man. He was an Italian of very good family, and had received an excellent education. Chinese he spoke like a native, besides six other languages as perfectly.

He was a botanist, and full of intelligence on most subjects. Although he resided at this particular spot, his district was extensive, running inland about fifty miles, and to a greater distance along the coast. He had built a small chapel and school; how he managed this out of a monthly pittance of eight dollars was always a mystery to me. I believe, however, he made pilgrimages to Hong-Kong, and there, by his energy and charm of manner, managed to raise occasional help by subscriptions. Fifteen native children he entirely supported. He was the doctor, the friend, the counsellor of the village, and on more occasions than one had he, by his influence and the respect in which he was held in the surrounding district, not only kept the peace, but made villagers who had turned out against each other on some petty quarrel return home in friendship. His influence for good was very great; considering the people he was amongst, it was marvellous. His small, thin, delicate figure looked as if his life hung on a very slender thread.

"I suppose you are looking after pirates?" he remarked, as we walked up from the beach to his house. "A few days ago I had to cross the bay, and I feel sure there was a large piratical craft at anchor under one of the rocky points; they are a bad lot about here, I fear;

but you won't, I know, ask me anything I do not voluntarily tell you about these things. Poor people, they have hard times of it."

"Why do you call them poor?" I asked.

"Because those who do not live by piracy are squeezed by those who do, and squeezed into the bargain by the Mandarins."

"No wonder they don't become rich," I said; "but I must tell you about a neighbour of yours, who now is rather a friend of mine, although he is an arrant rogue, and the head of a pirate gang. I find him, however, very useful sometimes; but I will tell you how I made his acquaintance. A fishing vessel belonging to Hong-Kong was attacked by a couple of pirate craft, and of course taken. I suppose they thought no ransom would be forthcoming for such poor people."

"Yes, I fear that is the way they work their mischief," answered my companion.

"The pirates quietly sailed away with his junk and all his property, having first landed the owner and his family. The fisherman reached Hong-Kong, gave information, and I, as usual, was sent out to recover, if possible, the junk, etc. Step by step I traced the pirates until I ran them to earth at Kato; here a good deal of the stolen property was found stowed away in the house belonging to the headman of the village, and it

required a deal of perseverance before he would part with it; but after sending a twenty-four pound shot through the roof of his house, he thought better of his sins."

"It was time he did," laughingly rejoined Voluntari.

"He keeps fifteen junks employed robbing his own countrymen chiefly, but foreigners as well when a good opportunity to do so occurs. Since my first little episode with this worthy I have frequently called on him, and although, of course, I gain no news about his own craft, he has no objection to give information relating to the movements of his neighbours, or rather one of his neighbours, who happens to be a fellow-piratical chief. It was only about three weeks ago I took two large junks which I should never have found except through this unneighbourly rascal."

"I have heard of him," answered the priest, "and I fear he is a great rogue. The most wealthy men in many of these out-of-the-way villages live chiefly by piracy and plunder."

I decided to remain about the locality for a day or two longer, and early next morning got the gun-boat into a small bay, so narrow, and so perfectly hidden, that she had only just room to swing round her anchor, and until you came over the low hills which surrounded the spot, nothing of the little craft could be seen.

About three miles off I knew pheasants and partridges were to be found, and crossing the piece of water which intervened, I beat all the likely cover along the edges of the millet and maize fields. Toward midday I had bagged a few brace of each, some quail, and half-a-dozen snipe, and the sun being by this time warm enough to make a drink refreshing, I made for the village at the foot of the highest range in the neighbourhood, hoping to get some good water, or perhaps tea. As I reached the place, to my surprise it appeared deserted; not a human being, neither pig nor yelping cur, being visible. But as soon as I got amongst the houses, a face, then a head appeared, at an open casement; then another, until any number of heads popped out.

"Lofu! lofu!" (tiger! tiger!) they cried.

"Where?" I said, thinking of the No. 6 shot with which my gun was loaded.

"He come down just now, and walk through the village; he very hungry."

"I daresay he is," I answered, "but I don't see him; where did he go?" That, however, no one knew; probably picking up a pig, he had returned to the thick impenetrable cover, or the mountain-side.

Quietly walking down to the nearest village during

the day-time certainly appeared a very cool proceeding, but I was assured this was by no means an unusual incident, and that generally a pig or calf disappeared. The inhabitants themselves, when it so happened, drove their animals into their houses, shut themselves in, and remained perfectly quiet until the tiger thought proper to walk **away. Sometimes they send to Canton** for professional huntsmen, who generally manage to bag **one or two of** these troublesome beasts in **a year.** Either finding the remains of the animal that has been **carried** off, or, if that cannot be done, setting a bait, they then fix a cross-bow some yards from the trail by which the tiger will probably come, a string being led from the trigger of the cross-bow across his path, and pressing against this string **as he quietly passes along,** he lets loose his own death-warrant, **in the shape of a poisoned arrow,** discharged with all the force that a bamboo bow twenty feet long is capable of giving. I have seen some very beautiful and fine skins taken from these tigers in the south.

Returning to the gun-boat, soon after leaving the village with its inhabitants in a happier state of mind that when I entered it, I found a couple of **Chinamen** on board, who had brought word that some large pirate junks were at anchor a **few** miles away, in quite a different creek, and entirely hidden and separated from where the gun-boat then was by a mass of mountains. We were under weigh in ten minutes, steaming for the spot indicated. The course, however, led past my pirate friend's residence, and as we reached the village, a sanpan pulled vigorously off with a couple of men in her. On seeing them approach I stowed the first informers away, to ascertain, without their seeing each other, the news that these men evidently wished to give. They, too, had information in substance much the same as the first gentlemen.

I did not quite like this eagerness to show me where the said pirates were, but of course without disclosing my doubts, and keeping the informers out of sight of each other, on we went. The creek was reached; it was about half a mile wide, and very shallow at the extreme end,—the gun-boat, in fact, could not get within a mile of the bottom of it,—so I anchored, and started with my two boats, taking about twenty men with me. As we pulled along the south side, within fifty yards of the shore, I noticed several men running along amongst the trees, which here grew thickly up the hill-side, and as they were all making for the head of the creek, as we were, I conjectured that those I saw thus hurrying on were bent on picking up odds and ends of spoil from the junks, which I now felt sure we should very soon find. My boat had got a couple of hundred yards ahead of the other, fortunately, and had just opened out the mastheads of a fine large junk hidden behind a low point covered with thick bushes and trees. "I have you, my friend," I inwardly **said.** At that moment, a flash, a report, and a shower of grape passed over our heads, ploughing up the water like hail on the other side of the boat. It passed through my mind instantly that I had been caught napping in a cleverly devised trap. Pulling short round, three strokes landed the boat in front of the battery, not five yards from their guns; another discharge, which certainly ought to have sent us all into **the** middle of next week, and the next moment we were amongst the pirates. Every **bush and** tree appeared to have a **rascal behind it** blazing away with a jingall; one fellow's eye I caught sight of along his barrel, and feeling at the moment rather vicious, pulled the trigger of my short rifle at him, but a wretched snap was the only result. However, he missed his object as well. The scuffle was soon over, the pirates being driven from their battery and junk into the thick surrounding woods and cover, where I did not care to follow them. The battery and junk now took my attention. The former was armed with 18-pounder carronades, one of which had evidently been loaded to the muzzle, the discharge having capsized it backwards. By allowing us to approach so near before opening fire they had missed their mark; if we had only been a hundred yards instead of fifty, I don't think many would have escaped. As it was, our luck had been extraordinary: not a man was touched either by jingall or gun.

On one occasion a fine clipper tea-ship, when on her way down the China Sea, got becalmed near the southeast part of Hainan. In a very short time fifteen junks appeared on the scene, and with the assistance of large sculls were soon within range, and opened fire. Fortunately for the vessel a light breeze sprang up, and with her lofty spars and quantity of light canvas she soon drew ahead out of range, and escaped closer quarters.

On the information reaching Hong-Kong I was ordered out to see if anything could be done towards capturing some of these junks. It was a lovely evening when we left, moonless but starlit, and as we steamed quietly through the shipping, and reached the open water to the west of the island, one could not help feeling how peaceful and quiet everything was. Keeping on during the night, we passed through the labyrinth of islands that extends nearly thirty miles to the south-west, and at daylight had reached the first of those that stud the south coast, directly west of the Canton river. A single junk was in sight, well inshore, and some miles ahead; but as it was quite calm the course I was steering would bring me within half a mile of her. Her great batwing-like sails flapped as the long swell lifted and rolled her from side to side, and on looking through the telescope I saw several neat round holes through her mat sails. I thought it strange, moreover, for an honest junk to be alone in that locality, knowing well that they usually went in small fleets for self-protection.

Deciding to have a better look at her, I altered course; but before the little gun-boat's head was round, a boat from the junk had been launched, a dozen men had jumped into her, and were pulling for the shore as hard as possible.

I first caught the sanpan, and then towing the junk to a favourite anchorage, burnt her; we then proceeded down the coast with the twenty-four pirates on board, whom I handed over to the Governor of the nearest province. Three exceptions I made—one because the rogue had once actually belonged to the *Opossum*, the gun-boat I commanded; another, because he was quite a youth, and had been to England; and the third because he was only fourteen years old, and I thought at that age he might learn a new trade, although he had been seven years with the pirates. To shorten a long story, this junk had, about three months before, been taken by pirates, when in company with a small fleet of Hong-Kong trading junks. After killing the crew, the pirates had kept her. They had then been so fortunate in their depredations that their own companions had attacked them; but, being a good sailer, the junk outstripped her envious friends, and when we hove in sight was all but at her journey's end, Macao, where her crew would have divided 20,000 dollars, and dispersed.

As we steamed up to her I observed the rascals flinging things overboard, but little dreamed they were bags of dollars, which were thus reduced to something less than half the number mentioned when I got on board.

The prisoners were forwarded to Canton. Six or seven, however, managed to escape on the way. The remainder were tried, condemned, and executed. On their trial they swore that those who escaped bribed the Mandarin to allow them to do so; and that had they themselves only possessed, or been able to raise money, as their more fortunate companions had done, they also would have been allowed to take to their heels. The authorities, at any rate, believed these wretched men, and the Mandarin, a first-class, red-buttoned individual, was recalled from his station, degraded, and sent into retirement. Altogether it was a queer piece of justice. **In time I managed to get the** unfortunate man reinstated, so far as his rank went, but he was never again given the governorship of the **province.**

On leaving Quanghai I kept on to the west, intending to reach Tienpak, where I thought I might hear some news regarding the Hainan pirates.

Tienpak was a queer place to get to, situated five miles up a narrow creek, scarcely fifty yards wide, which at low water led through flat sands, but **at high** tide the whole immense extent of sand was covered with three or four feet of water. After the military Mandarin had been on board I returned his visit on shore, and found him comfortably settled in a temporary residence on the outskirts of the town. He had collected all the prettiest girls of the place to wait and attend upon him during his short stay at this rough village. None of these people had ever seen a European before, and their curiosity in consequence was greatly excited by my arrival.

One girl, as she handed me a cup of tea, begged to be allowed to touch my whiskers,—such articles being scarce, if not wholly wanting, amongst her own countrymen.

I jokingly asked them, "Who would like to live on board the gun-boat?" and next morning, rather to my consternation, half-a-dozen of these fair ones came off, got up in all their best robes and cosmetics. The rough but honest old Mandarin accompanied his harem. It was amusing to see these girls, who, I fear, really thought half of them might be chosen to remain on board, trying to make themselves useful at once, by dusting and arranging the different articles in my cabin.

But adieu we bade them, and started for Hainan,—Mandarin, two war-junks, and gun-boat.

A hundred miles west of Tienpak, I found a narrow entrance leading through some low sandhills into a spacious basin, which, on steaming across it, proved to be ten miles in width. No signs of junks were to be seen; but finding the mouth of a large river emptying itself into the north-west corner of the basin, I followed its course seven or eight miles up, passing several earth-batteries on either bank in that distance. Here we came across a large junk loading with oil, and from the crew ascertained that a couple of days before a fleet of pirates had been in the bay. This was bad luck, but there was nothing for it except the chance of finding them about Nowchow, an island just to the north of Hainan. Thither therefore we went, but the birds had flown from here also, probably for the southern parts of Hainan. It was rather more than provoking, considering that ten to one these were some of the very fellows who had attacked the clipper ship. However, better luck next time, I thought, as I turned the gunboat's head towards Hong-Kong. Our coal was getting very short, and we had only enough, and barely that, to take us back. We anchored for a couple of days *en route*, at a favourite snug bay, and landing early the following morning with my gun and setter, I soon picked up some snipe, a few teal, and several quail. In crossing a soft muddy patch in the marsh I came upon the print of a tiger's track, perfectly fresh. Probably the beast, after hunting about the skirts of the villages in the valley, had crossed the swamp on his way to the mountains. The four toes measured exactly seven inches across. Partridges, as the day advanced, began to utter their curious wild note, as they answered one another from almost every hillock along the lower ranges. Turning homewards, I soon added a brace or two to my bag, and felt well satisfied with my forenoon's sport and walk as I reached the beach. Almost as I stepped on the clear sand, a bullet whizzed past my head, and went with a thud into the bank a few feet off. The report had hardly done reverberating amongst the hills, before my telescope picked out the enemy, some 300 yards off on a grassy mound, and not a little to my astonishment, the enemy was one of my own marines. It appeared that during my absence a small pirate craft had turned up amongst the bushes which line the creek, and that I was taken for one of the crew by those who were hunting them up. During the night the quartermaster on watch believed he heard the tiger. I slept, however, too soundly after my week's work to be easily disturbed, and I don't know whether the man was dreaming or not. I have no doubt, if I had time, I might have got him, by watching at night with a calf or pig for a bait; as it was, I returned next day to Hong-Kong to find another piratical report waiting for me.

CHAPTER XV.

SHOOTING IN CHINA.

Sport in the north of China is so well known that it is hardly worth while remarking on it. At the present time it is necessary to go a long way for the best shooting; but in former years, when Shanghai was less than half the size it now is, most wonderfully varied sport was to be had within thirty miles or less of that port. I started one evening with a friend or two, in a Chinese covered boat, which are excellent things for shooting trips, and during the night we were sculled or sailed along very quietly, and at no great pace, up what is known as the Sou-chow Creek. It was a beautiful, clear, moonlight night, and although cold and frosty, it was very pleasant on the outer deck of the junk. The Chinamen working at the huge scull hardly ever uttered a sound, but worked away steadily, now and then relieving each other during the night. Occasionally a downward boat passed, when a few words would pass between the two craft, otherwise we glided over the still water of the creek in an easy, sleepy way, most conducive to a good night's rest. At daybreak the following morning we awoke to find our vessel made fast to a pole stuck into the bank.

The banks of the creek here were high, and could not be seen over from the deck of our junk. A henpheasant flew across from one side to the other, just as I emerged from below, flushing a second bird as she passed the bank. "No doubt about pheasants being here," I thought. After an excellent breakfast, we started, each taking a man to carry our game; but after going together in line for some short distance, I struck away at right angles by myself. The whole country was as flat as a pancake; a small blue hill rose far away in the distance, and this was the only variety of any description that was to be seen, that in any way changed the perfect sameness of the level country.

Grass about up to one's knees, small clumps of bamboo, ruined villages, and patches where cultivation once existed, constituted the general features of the whole face of the land for many more miles than I got over during the day. Deep creeks or canals intersected in all directions this perfect level. These were a considerable bother to **get across, and** made it difficult to find your game if it dropped on the opposite side. Many times, on knocking **over a** bird, and going to pick it **up,** I found a deep, broad, impassable piece of water between my dead pheasant and myself; so level was it, and such a sameness existed over the whole place, that when thus actually within a few yards of the edge of one of these troublesome creeks you did not know it.

The way we kept in view our floating wigwam was **by** hoisting a good large flag at her mast-head, which, waving above the banks, pointed out her position,—otherwise to get totally adrift as to direction, or which way to go when wishing to return, was not only easy, but a certainty. I walked in a circle through this grass, and on coming to a bamboo patch got to one side of it, and putting my man in on the other, had it walked through, tapping with a stick the bare stems of the graceful plant as he did so. Pheasants in streams came out, twenty or thirty, one after the other, and amongst the grass they got up, just as fast as I pleased to load. I am speaking of muzzle-loading days. Teal and duck every now and then rose at my feet from the creeks, as I came suddenly on to the banks. Snipe in any number rose from every swampy or damp patch, however diminutive. Stupid hares who appeared most anxious to be shot, by the half-curious, half-silly way they hopped about close to me; and as for quail, they were perpetually rising under my very toes. The quantity of game was simply extraordinary, and I very soon found, if I did not turn round and look for the junk, I should have more game than we could possibly carry. When within a couple of hundred yards of the craft, a flock of teal rose from a small pool of water; a straggler fell to my right barrel, and although I again picked out a single bird, three others managed to pass within his line, and four fell to the left. This was really like the last straw to the camel's back, as, besides a bag, my man—a strong blue-jacket—had a bamboo across his shoulders, with a dozen pheasants at each end of it, and as these birds average nearly three pounds a piece—the cock-birds weighing quite that weight, and the hens two and a half—his load was a good one. It was early in the forenoon when I returned; my companions soon joined me, and, slipping from our stake in the bank, we moved a few miles further up the creek during lunch, and again in the afternoon had another turn at the birds, the result of which was much the same as that in the forenoon.

In one of the numerous creeks I came upon some Chinamen busily employed fishing with cormorants. They had three sanpans, each being paddled along at short intervals from one another. In the first boat **were** about three dozen cormorants perched on the gunwale, all the birds sitting bolt upright close together, looking like rows of black wooden figures, so quiet did they remain; presently the man in charge, in the first boat, gave the order, and overboard the birds went, each taking the neatest header possible. The boats now were paddled very slowly. The cormorants soon began to appear, and as they came to the surface with fish in their mouths, **whichever boat they** happened to be nearest put out an oar, on to which they at once got, and were swung into the sanpan; there they disgorged their fish, and then perched on the gunwale for a short time before again going into the water. I said disgorged; but it is hardly that, as the birds have an ivory ring round their necks, which is passed over the head and rests on the shoulder, and prevents the fish from getting beyond the throat. The throat, when a large fish is caught, or several smaller ones, appears distended to a great extent,—in fact a large fish only partially disappears; he is swallowed head first, but leaves half his body and tail outside, which waggles about in the most uncomfortable-looking manner. These birds were under the most perfect control; they seemed to understand their duties most thoroughly, and to expect no reward. I never saw any given them, and in fact they seemed to work away as a matter of business. I don't know, but imagine that very small fish would pass through the ring, and that in this manner they received an occasional relish and fillip to proceed with their work. The water, unfortunately, is by no means clear in these creeks, and the birds' movements when at work could not be followed; but it was a most interesting sight, which I would willingly have come all the distance to see without the consideration of the shooting. I had once before seen a couple of these birds belonging to a gentleman in Yorkshire, trained, and fishing in a clear stream in Scotland, but he had not the complete command over them that these Chinese professional fishermen had; his birds, I remember, occasionally came out on the bank, and the wrong bank, and there disgorged their fish, or getting on a stone in mid-stream, would do the same, and the lucky trout would swim away, and no doubt have a venturous story to tell his fellow-trout; but the Chinese birds never attempted to reach the bank; they were evidently too well up to their business to forget their duty in this way.

Great quantities of game are now netted by the natives in these northern parts of China; the demand is sufficient to make it **well worth** their while doing so, and **not only is** the game thus caught sent to other parts of China, but a great deal is sent over to Japan, where, in Kobe and Yokohama, the markets during the winter months are quite swamped by it; so much so, that before I left the latter country, the Japanese had almost given up supplying the shops and market with their own country's game, being unable to do so at the price they can supply China game at. It is always a sort of admitted fact, or understanding, that game, if killed by being shot, **was infinitely more tasty and delicate than if** caught in traps or **nets.** I cannot own to ever having detected the slightest difference myself, and I am quite certain that I could not possibly tell one from the other, except of course by observing shot-holes, or finding the shot itself. However, most of the buyers of China game objected to netted birds; the Chinese suppliers soon found this out, but as soon decided on a remedy, which was simple, and had the decided effect. Before bringing the birds to the market, they tied a great bundle of them up together, snipe, pheasants, hares, geese, and duck indiscriminately, and with an old musket, or gun of any description, loaded with some handfuls of shot and slugs, fired several rounds into the birds. I remember an instance of an epicure, when in the act of eating a snipe, telling his companion the bird had been shot.

"I don't doubt it, I assure you."

"But why, what's the matter?" exclaimed the other man, on observing his friend making the most dreadful face, as if in great pain.

"O my tooth, my tooth! I believe I have broken it. Look here!" he added, pulling a piece of iron from his mouth which looked as if it had been cut off the end of a bar. "Those abominable Chinamen! why, the bird was shot after it was dead, the rascals, and I gave that piece of iron a crunch enough to break my jaw, much more my tooth."

I remember a gallant admiral, long since gone to the happy hunting-grounds, going out shooting not far from Shanghai; his secretary and some one else accompanied him. Presently one of the small hog-deer was started, and several shots were fired in its direction, some of which took effect, and wounded the animal. Of course the admiral's shot *must* have hit it! Away rushed the secretary to capture the struggling creature; but just as he stretches out to grasp it, the deer shakes itself together, gets on its legs, and makes off. It can hardly run. And now ensues a most exciting race. The secretary strains every nerve to catch it, and appears just on the point of doing so several times, **when the wretched animal makes an effort, and struggles on again.** Round **and round** they go, through paddy-fields they flounder, **out again on the** grass, again into the sloppy mud and water, which is sent flying in all directions, **and** only appears to add to the excitement. **The admiral** gallantly roars encouragement to his secretary, who renews his energies. Off they go again, the admiral stamping and perspiring with excitement, his running days having long since been expended. Everything has an end, and the poor secretary looked much **as if** his was coming. The deer being kept on the move, gained temporary life. This is **always the case, whereas if a mortally wounded deer is left alone, it will soon lie** down to die. The secretary was pumped and **done** for; they regained the grassy ground, and the unfortunate animal struggled ahead, and was seen no more. The mud-spattered and completely done-up secretary returned. The admiral swore.

"Why didn't you catch it?" he exclaimed.

"I tried," was all his **poor right-hand man could** utter. What he afterwards said **was more like: "I'll see the admiral somewhere before I'll run after any** more of his deer; and, confound him! I don't believe his shot ever went within yards of it."

Sport in the south of China is quite different, and very moderate in comparison. Snipe alone are abundant. This bird appears quite indifferent to climate. As early as August I used to get very fair snipe-shooting up the Canton river; but the rice being then uncut, it was both difficult to find them before and after they were knocked over. I used to get a boat-girl to retrieve for me, and very well she did it.

I remember one day shooting with a friend about this time of the year,[1] and near Canton, when a Chinaman made his appearance suddenly, and told me I had shot him. He certainly had three No. 6 shot under his skin, from which he bled freely. I felt morally certain I had not done it, and told him so. He politely refused to take this in.

"However," I said, "depend upon it, that was the gentleman," pointing to my friend, a couple of hundred yards off, "who shot you. Try if you cannot persuade him so."

"Oh!" said the Chinaman, "I have been to him, and he said it must be you."

"Very well," I said, "so let it be."

[1] August.

A dollar made **him perfectly happy, and quite** willing to be again peppered.

There **was an old** Chinaman at Canton who regularly lived by his gun, a long, single-barrelled implement of perfectly unknown make. He shot his snipe from the *hip*, and **not from the shoulder. Of course,** where they **were so plentiful,** he could afford to pick his bird. Still, it showed how practice and a good eye could knock over these birds in a **very unusual** manner. This thorough old sportsman very often bagged a woodcock, a rare bird in these parts of China, and although he was offered a fabulous price if he would take an Englishman to the place, he stuck to his occasional woodcock in preference to a small fortune. I admired him for it. I now and then picked up **one** of these birds in some of the out-of-the-way places **I** visited when in search of **pirates, but the occurrence** was so rare it deserved to be noted. Pheasants in one or two places were not uncommon. Quail were everywhere. The little orange-legged partridge is very common, and is a most quarrelsome, pugnacious bird. Never but once have I flushed two together; they **appear** always alone, whether male or female. Before rain they get on the open hillocks or big blocks of stones, and utter their curious wild cry, which sounds most suitable to the barren hill-sides. Towards sunset also they do this, and keep answering each other far and near until dusk.

During the winter months, very fair shooting could be had up the Canton river. Duck and geese at that time were to be found all the way up from the Bogue Forts to Canton, the former often in great quantities. I used frequently to make excursions to these grounds with a friend at this time of the year, and exceedingly jolly times we had. Rather a large party wishing to go once, R—, another friend, and myself went away during the afternoon in R—'s yacht; the rest were to follow, and intended taking a good round to look for some hog-deer on an island. We reached our destination early in the evening, and after a good dinner, a pipe, and a yarn, we prepared for any emergency in the shape of pirates, by loading a little swivel-gun on deck, our rifles, guns, and so on. I had brought two of my gun-boat's crew to assist in the yacht and keep watch; they would also be very different fellows from the usual Chinese crew in a row. We were all sound asleep, and enjoying the fresh clear air, after the more confined and used-up atmosphere of Hong-Kong, when about one in the morning the man on watch called me, saying a large junk was standing into **the bay. I was up in a moment**, and after seeing there was no mistake about it, roused my companions.

"What is it?" inquired R—.

"I have no idea," I said; "I never knew a trading or fishing-junk come in here before."

"Ten to one it's a **pirate**. What's to be done?" said R—.

"We can't run," I answered, "for he is too close to **us**. I'll let drive at him, which will, at any rate, bring forth his intentions."

The junk was now about forty yards off, standing right for us. I fired a rifle-bullet through his sail, just clear of the deck. Not a sound came back in return. **Another minute or two and he would be over us.** This silence to our very decided challenge proved him beyond doubt to our minds **a pirate**. "Blaze away the gun, the rascal means mischief!" was shouted, when clear and distinct from the bows of the junk came, "*Gipsy*, ahoy!" We all on board that renowned craft looked at each other; it was our friends whom we were on the very point of receiving so warmly. It never occurred to us at the moment that they **might** have shortened their run, which they did, and thus reached the rendezvous long before we dreamt they could. It was some time before we got over the chaff about this little event and the cordial way of receiving our friends!

When wading through the rice-fields looking for snipe one autumn afternoon, I was surprised to come across a Chinaman standing on the side or dry bank of the field, with a fishing-rod in his hand, and a fine line leading from the end of his bamboo into the rice-field. What can he be fishing for there, I thought; some very diminutive fish, as nothing a couple of inches long could swim in the few inches of water that covered the muddy soil; the rice also stood quite two feet high. I had not long to wait to have my curiosity satisfied. A bite, a jerk, and out came a frog, and looking into his basket I found he had more than a dozen there already. These Chinamen are funny fellows I thought, but after all, if he was bent on *fishing* for frogs, or rather on catching frogs, I daresay he did so in this manner quite as quickly, and certainly far more cleanly, than going into the paddy after them. Canton frogs are by no means to be despised, and I have eaten an excellent curry made from their hind legs.

In speaking of shooting in the south, I must not omit the small pigeon, which is plentiful in most of the cultivated valleys. They afforded me many an evening's really good shooting, by ascertaining their usual flight as they left the millet-fields for their roosting quarters. I have often had an hour's sharp work, where a really straight gun is necessary; and they are excellent eating, which adds very considerably to the pleasure of bagging them. Snakes are often started **when wading** through the rice-fields, and one kind, which is almost perfectly black, I have seen ten feet long. I believe they are harmless, but a fellow of that size gliding past your legs is not agreeable.

Chinamen resemble their neighbours the Japanese in one thing at any rate; they never waste manure of any kind, that which is chiefly prized being from their own houses or tubs outside their doors. This is collected in great pits in the fields, and covered over with a thin coating of mud, which hardens in the sun, and acts as the crust to a pie. It preserves the precious article underneath from the sun and rain, both of which deteriorate the strength of this most potent manure that is so grievously wasted in our own country.

In January 1876 the gun-boat was laid up for a week for the purpose of being repaired, and I had gone up the Canton river with three companions to have some snipe-shooting. A good junk was hired at

Whampoa, and away we sailed for well-known ground a few miles further up the river. R— was again of the party, and we landed together, the other two taking another beat. The rice had been cut some time, and the fields were in capital condition for snipe. It was unnecessary to go through the muddy slush; all we had to do was to walk round the narrow divisions between the fields, and send a coolie whom we had with us in to pick up the birds. Favourite patches are always to be found amongst these paddy stubble plots, for although the cultivation may *extend* for miles, yet the divisions of what I have called fields are very small, a quarter of an acre or sometimes half an acre being about their size. The narrow bank or division is raised, and about a foot or eighteen inches wide. Along one of these tiny banks we were walking; R— was first, and having all the shooting. Snipe were rising in ones, twos, and half dozens. My friend had not lately had much practice, and found the birds rather crooked in their flight; at last a paddy bird (a white egret) rose, and this he knocked over. Off he darted to secure the bird, which had fallen some twenty yards from the bank. A smooth tempting piece of mud came in his way, and before I could call out to him he was on it. The next moment the crust had broken and poor R— was struggling in the contents underneath. A good deal must be left to the imagination. Suffice it to say, after being extricated the coolie stripped him of his large overall gaiters, which fortunately he had on, and picking out a slushy wet bit of paddy, R— was rubbed well over with this, and we then hurried back to the junk, where abundance of soap and water was expended, and the damaged nether garments were tied to a rope's-end and flung into the river, where they floated astern, and were made fast when about thirty yards off. With sundry glasses of sherry we talked over our morning's shooting, and now that the disagreeable effects of R—'s false step had been rectified, we laughed most heartily. For my own part, I had been retaining the inclination so long, I felt almost ill from the effects. R—'s face as he emerged from the hole was indescribably ludicrous; it is imprinted on my mind to this day. One thing we agreed upon, our companions must be kept in the dark on the subject, otherwise R— would be awfully chaffed on returning to Hong-Kong. Lunch-time brought our friends back, each with a moderate bag of snipe and a few teal. They had no sooner arrived than R— and I fancied a certain too well-known effluvium had returned, which we firmly believed was concentrated in the garments towing well astern. We both involuntarily looked anxiously in that direction to see if the Chinaman had hauled them in. No, they were safe enough. I ventured a remark—

"What a queer smell there is; don't you find it so?"

Our two friends looked at one another; R— and I did the same.

"The fact is," one of them exclaimed, "we both got into those abominable manure pits, which are covered over with a coating of mud,—regular traps,—and we have been standing in the river for the last hour, but it seems impossible to get rid of the disgusting mess."

R— and I on hearing this almost roared with laughter.

"What on earth are you laughing at? I don't think it so amusing. If you had been in as well, I don't think you would find it funny," remarked one of them.

"Why, look astern," said R—, "those are my breeches etc., made fast to that rope's-end; I went in myself."

On hearing which, the absurdity of nearly the whole party being so easily trapped, was too much for our companions' gravity, and in a hearty laugh they forgot their troubles.

CHAPTER XVI.

MORE CRUISING AFTER PIRATES.

In 1875 an English brigantine bound for the northward had been attacked about 100 miles from Hong-Kong; the captain and a boy were killed, but the rest of the crew, having taken to the top, and remained there while the pirates ransacked the vessel, were otherwise unmolested. As soon as the coast was clear, they descended from their airy refuge, and in a day or two brought the vessel safely back to port. Whilst we were coaling to go in search of these rascals, another case occurred, information being brought that a large fishing-junk belonging to Hong-Kong, with the owner and his family on board, had been boarded by pirates when fishing just outside the island, and his three daughters carried off for ransom. The owner himself had been launched adrift in a sanpan, and directed by his considerate countrymen to collect 500 dollars as the price of his daughters' release; if not paid in a short time, the girls would be, never more, of any trouble to him or any one else. The senior officer had arrived while I was still in port, and being entirely ignorant of all matters connected with piracy, he very much doubted my being able to do any good in searching for the culprits in either of the two cases, and especially in the release of the damsels. In answer to his doubts, I said, in the latter case I should probably succeed, but not in the first, the time elapsed being too long. Towards dusk I left, so as to reach a cluster of islands called Tooni-ang, thirty miles east of Hong-Kong, and a very favourite rendezvous for pirates, towards daylight. In the channel between the islands were coves and nooks where junks could stow away very snugly, and the approach being open at either end, they could easily slip away on danger appearing from any direction. I reached the spot before the sun had thought of throwing light over the high peak of the largest island. Gradually, however, the morning grey cool feel of the approaching day stole over the scene, and as it did I kept quietly creeping in, until I reached the very centre of the passage.

Presently, close under the rocks, a **junk was seen**, moving cautiously in the shadow of the cliffs towards **the further entrance. Early as I was, they were equally on the** *qui vive*, **and the whole crew managed** to escape to the shore before I caught **the junk. This** proved to be the very pirate craft which had captured the girls; so far so good, I thought. Now, to trace these unhappy fair ones. A deep bay lay immediately abreast of Tooni-ang, at the head of which, and faced by shoal water and a long flat island, a town with **about** a thousand inhabitants lay almost **entirely concealed by a** prominent woody point, and **the island mentioned. I knew this to be** a den of thieves, and from what the father of the girls had gathered, and otherwise conjectured during his interview with the pirates, it appeared more than probable that to this place the prisoners had been taken. When passing a cove, **a** junk hove in sight, inshore, and on my bearing **down** for her, **was** run on shore, and a dozen men or so skedaddled and made off into the bushes as hard as they could. This was my friend the fisherman's own **craft; he nearly stood on his** head with joy. I don't believe he thought half as much of his girls as his junk. The one cost money, the other made it, I suppose he might have said. She was easily rescued from her sandy bed and taken in tow. The guns (all fishing-junks used to be well armed) had been taken out of her, but with a little searching they were found buried in the sand close to. Without further incidents I reached the head of the bay, anchored off the village, and at once demanded the three girls. This request, however, was met with blank looks of astonishment, and professions of utter ignorance regarding them. "The three headmen of the village must then return with me to the gun-boat," I said. These worthies made all the delay, excuses, and difficulties they could, but ultimately appeared robed in silk, accompanied by a couple of blue-jackets, who escorted them to the boat, and then on board. This sort of proceeding was more native police work than an English man-of-war's; but if such ideas had been stuck to, and I had simply confined myself to the open sea, and to my bare orders, which were to that effect, the gun-boat might just as well have been returned into store, for all the good towards the suppression of piracy that she could have done; and many scores more lives would have been lost, and vessels taken, than was actually the case.

I now made great preparations to hang these three silk-robed gentlemen, passing a rope from each masthead, arranging the most elaborate knots, and so on, taking care that they should see and understand what was going on. Their expressions were curious to watch; one, in particular, tried to treat it as a good joke, but with the most evident inward uncertainty. The other two appeared stolid, but very grave. All now being ready, one was taken to each mast, and the rope passed carefully over their heads. The effect of the ominous-looking noose touching their skin was as if their faculties had received an electric shock. They suddenly remembered "the girls were there; I should have them at once if only I would spare their lives." The gentleman that laughed at the preparations was so overcome by the excess of his feelings that he fainted, but came to in a few moments on a little salt water being judiciously applied. Directions were sent to their subordinates in the village, and in a very short time the girls appeared on the beach, escorted by a crowd of men and women: the three rascals were quickly exchanged for the kidnapped fair ones, who were fed with tea and jam, and wrapped up in a sail for the night, and I started on my return to Hong-Kong. It would have been a good lesson, and certainly not an undeserved one, if these celestials had been hanged instead of only frightened. There was no doubt, however, that they firmly believed their last hour had come, otherwise they would never have disclosed their guilt.

For a couple of months I was employed entirely on the coast east of Hong-Kong, during which time we took a number of junks, some prisoners, and released others kept to ransom. The coast between Macao and Hainan I purposely left alone.

The China New Year was approaching (February), a great time with all Chinamen—a general holiday—a feast time—a time that business is thrown aside, and revelry and dissipation are alone thought of. Even the pirates cannot resist the temptation of general laxity, and as a rule return to some rendezvous or stronghold for at least three days. Another custom, and a very good one, connected with their New Year is, that every Chinaman pays his debts; it is a point of honour with them to do so; an item in the general routine of a Chinaman's life we might well imitate. Relying on this general slackness, I had decided to cruise down the west coast during their holiday-time, hoping to make a good bag. The day before the commencement of their New Year, 1876, I visited some Chinese merchants, and talked over the state of trade, piracy, etc., but none had any news such as I wanted. As I was in the act of getting under weigh, one of these same men came quietly on board, **and in a** mysterious manner **whispered**—" Better look see Puckshui."

" The very place I am going to," I answered.

An hour before, when surrounded by his fellow-merchants, **he knew nothing; evidently there was no** safety in **numbers to his mind.**

Next morning at daybreak I was on my ground. Two islands with a shallow passage between them, and an entrance at either end, situated about midway between the mainland and the outer line of islands, formed a remarkably good and safe retreat for lawless characters. As I rounded the point, and opened the channel and anchorage, no **less than fifteen junks** appeared, **drawn up in line so as to cover the centre of the channel with their guns.** Knowing the place well, I went full speed through the soft mud on the north side, and **by doing so kept all** the junks end on instead of broadside, as they would have been if I had taken the mid-channel course they expected. With our guns out, and loaded, the little gun-boat rushed into the middle of **them.** This was too much for their nerves, however well they may have **been strung up** before; they entirely gave way at such close quarters, **and** without a shot being fired on either side, overboard they went, and made a hasty and undignified retreat on shore. I now anchored. They then manned the guns in their battery, situated immediately abreast of the gun-boat, and in front of the town. Before, however, they fired, I sent a big shot in their direction, which cleared them out.

As we had steamed in, we passed a large salt junk, whose crew appeared dancing about the deck like lunatics. They were certainly in the wildest state of joy at being released from captivity. They mustered twenty-seven in all, and were soon well on their way to Hong-Kong. Little had they expected, an hour before, to get off without paying the heavy ransom demanded.

I decided to take the battery and utterly destroy the place. Taking all my crew except three, not of course counting the Chinese part of it, I landed at a point a little way down, to avoid some swampy ground abreast their guns. We could also land here under good shelter, and afterwards approach within 200 yards without being seen; this we did, and then had a good look at the formidable army of men drawn up in front of the village. There could not have been less than 300, but there might have been 500. Two or three, who walked up and down in front of the rest, kept opera-glasses steadily at work, and watched us narrowly. Not a woman was to be seen, which looked as if they meant business. I knew our eight-inch gun was keenly alive to our movements, and ready to send forth a very effectual messenger if needed. Forming in single file, we opened into view over a small hillock, and went at them at a steady trot. A minute they stood as if irresolute, then wavered, turned round and ran, as if a whole regiment with fixed bayonets were at their heels; instead of only twenty blue-jackets and marines, which constituted the whole of my force. The only creature we caught was a stray young female, and how she got adrift from the rest of her sex, who were evidently stowed away in the hills, I cannot tell. The battery we simply walked into from behind, and the whole affair was at an end, except the destruction of the village, which was soon accomplished by burning it to the ground. During the time that the preceding events were taking place, a couple of junks had been blown up, and with them three of my men, but fortunately they had come down again, damaged considerably, but not altogether expended. The gunner was one; he was three months in the hospital, and then returned to duty, but wonderfully changed for the better in appearance. A marine was a year ill; the other case was not so serious.

There was, of course, no possibility of bringing the pirates to bay, and nothing was left to be done but to return on board. I was just about ordering the men to fall in, when, on looking down the creek, to my no little astonishment, a whole fleet of junks appeared steering in. The Chinese interpreter immediately pronounced them to be pirates. Pleasant, I thought; why, they will take the gun-boat long before we can get on board. My telescope, however, revealed that they were all the same class of craft, a thing never the case in a fleet of piratical junks; Mandarins I felt sure, from their uniformity and number of flags flying. However, to make things certain, I got quickly down to the boats, and pulled out for the headmost craft, hailing her as I came near as to her friendliness or otherwise. This proved the commander-in-chief's junk, whom I requested to come on board the gun-boat, and returned myself to receive him. I shall never forget the man's face as he reached the deck.

"I am so glad to see you," he said; "twice have I been here, and each time have been beaten off; the pirates were far too strong for me. I should never have come in now if I had not seen a gun-boat in the place."

"What force have you?" I asked.

"I have forty-four junks, each with eight or ten guns on board, and 1600 troops, besides the junks' crews," he replied.

All I thought I did not utter; but telling him to take charge of the junks, the forty-seven guns, and the remains of the town, as I must be off, and also to make what report he liked, I bade him good-bye, and made for Macao as fast as I could. From there I sent my injured men across to Hong-Kong, and started immediately again for the westward. As I left the gallant Mandarin and his war-junks, and before I got clear of the passage between the islands, he had opened fire, but at what I could not see. I heard some time afterwards that the pirates returned directly the gun-boat was out of sight, and drove the warriors from their island, who then retreated as fast as a fair wind would take them.[1]

[1] I was much amused when I returned to England, at a penny illustrated newspaper which had been sent to my address, soon after this piratical affair had taken place. Amidst any amount of smoke and fire, men mounted on ardent steeds are represented galloping about in all directions, armed with long spears, shields, and battle-axes,—these are the pirates. Other men, with helmets on, and clothed in complete armour, are closely engaged with these mounted warriors; some are in the act of springing on shore from numerous boats, which are just discernible amidst the fire, smoke, and confusion,—these represent the gallant British tars, the *Opossum's* crew. It must have been a fertile imagination that got all this together, to show what piracy in China was like!

Leaving Macao, and steaming about thirty miles to the west of Puckshui, I turned sharply to the right, and towards the mainland, which was separated from the chain of islands by ten or twelve miles of shallow water, with only here and there a passage across it. The water being invariably muddy, it was very difficult to follow these narrow, deep lines of soundings, and such I found it this time; for after getting something like half-way across towards the coast-line, the gun-boat grounded, and all the pulling we could accumulate on the anchor laid out for the purpose had no effect; fortunately it was very nearly low-water, and the tide would soon make. The aspect of the heavens suddenly changed from bright sunshine to a mass of heavy and gloomy-looking clouds, the wind rose quickly, and a shower and squall approached from the eastward, and quite shut out the land. The muddy water was soon lashed into excitement with the increasing wind, and looking all round the general impression was gloom and unpleasantness.

At this moment a junk emerged from the heavy rain, and came booming on with her great sails full before the breeze. That it must be the craft that we were after I felt almost certain, and to stop him I was determined. Pitching a big shot across his bows for

the purpose had no effect. Another, still nearer, was equally unnoticed. In another minute the big gun would not bear; the junk would have passed, might rake the gun-boat as she lay helplessly in the mud, and go flying away before the half gale with perfect impunity.

"Fire into her" was the order. But, fortunately for the junk, before the trigger was pulled, down came his great sail, and in less than five minutes she had rounded to and anchored close to us. Almost at the same moment the rising tide floated the gun-boat, and, dropping into the deeper water, I went immediately on board the junk, where I found no less than forty-three men. In small parties they were sent to the gun-boat, and secured for the night. Next day we arrived at the nearest Mandarin station, and were by no means sorry to hand junk and crew over to his tender mercies. This was the very craft I was in search of, and, being captured on the eve of departure, prevented mischief being done during her intended cruise. She was armed and strong enough to take any merchant ship that might be met with during calm weather. The gun-boat looked quite a diminutive affair when alongside of her, and she had eight big guns on board, besides all kinds and descriptions of small arms. After this I was not sorry to return to Hong-Kong for a few days' rest.

This western part of the Quang-tung province, the coast of which I have so often referred to, is to this day a *terra incognita* to Europeans.

The part I chiefly had occasion to visit appeared inhabited by two tribes, the Hacka's and Punti's, who by no means lived at peace with one another,—quite the contrary. They were always fighting or cutting each other's throats on a small scale, as well as by more wholesale operations. I had on one occasion to follow a lorcha and a couple of junks up a sluggish river which ran through this country, and the amount of fighting we passed through was absurd. Neither party molested us in any way, although, if so disposed, they might have made it very disagreeable, the width of the river being only at most sixty yards, and the banks here and there well bushed over. Dead bodies in scores floated down, or were grounded on the banks. The hills on either side of the river were quite decorated with the flags of the contending parties; but it must be understood that these emblems of warfare in a Chinese army, or in a tribal squabble, invariably are almost as plentiful as the men themselves. The three pirate crafts were captured and destroyed.

It was not always plain sailing amongst these islands, which studded the coast for at least 100 miles west of

MORE CRUISING AFTER PIRATES.

the Canton river; for notwithstanding the numerous good anchorages that existed, it was ticklish work occasionally during the typhoon months, which were nearly half the year, or from June to October.

These disagreeable visitors had always, during this season, to be considered. Luckily, with a good barometer, their approach could generally be foretold by twenty-four hours, and sometimes by double that time. In June 1875, for instance, I knew that a typhoon was brewing up, and in consequence got into a snug anchorage beforehand. The place I was in was perfectly safe; being land-locked on all sides, no swell could even enter, and I knew that the wind alone was what I need think of.

Towards evening it was blowing very hard from the eastward, and still increasing; by midnight the force of the wind during the gusts was simply terrific. I had everything well secured long before it commenced; the boats were lashed and relashed, so that they might be blown to pieces, but they could not possibly be entirely taken away. Soon afterwards I went to get some rest and shelter in my cabin, leaving the boatswain in charge on deck. At one in the morning he called me, and reported the gun-boat to be drifting on the rocks, adding—

"I never saw it blow like this before, sir, in the thirty years I have been at sea."

"What are you doing on deck?" I asked.

"Steaming ahead as hard as we can, sir, to ease the anchors and cables, which are veered to the clinch."

"Very well," I replied; "you had better turn the hands up; I shall be on deck in a moment."

On reaching the gangway, I could just see through the thick vapour and driving sea the black rocks about thirty yards astern; and going to the engine-room, I gave orders to go ahead as fast as possible, and again returned to the gun-boat's side, and, holding on, sat down to watch the poor little craft drifting quietly but surely to the angry-looking shore. I knew that, the water being smooth, all hands were perfectly safe, as far as their lives went, and that the only thing that could happen would be the gun-boat's driving against the rocks, and probably knocking a hole in her bottom. It certainly did blow; and I thought if the weather-beaten old boatswain had ever seen much more wind, he would probably have been taken clean off the face of the earth. I had been about half-an-hour thus musing and watching the rocks getting gradually more distinct. I could see the clefts, and almost trace their jagged outline, and was wondering what the result would be, what amount of damage would be done to the gun-boat, and how I should manage to get back to Hong-Kong, a hundred and fifty miles off, when suddenly I **saw the** little vessel was moving up to her anchors. I immediately stopped the engines, and in less than ten minutes from that time it **was perfectly calm.** Both anchors were at once **weighed, and steaming** out to the centre of the bay, I let them both go to the westward, veering nearly all my cable out, and keeping steam up ready to move the engines at any moment. **The wind** had left off at east north-east. In an hour or so a sound like steam being blown out of a boiler was heard to the westward, and immediately afterwards the gun-boat was struck by a furious **gust from that direction,** from which quarter it blew for some hours as hard as ever, the barometer all the time going up. **The centre was, however, past, and towards noon I was able to get under** weigh and proceed on my journey.

The word "Typhoon" is of Chinese derivation, and means "mother of winds,"—a very good and significant designation. **Typhoon,** cyclone, and hurricane are **all synonymous for circular storms or** gales of wind, which, **in my** opinion, have **all the same origin,** and all the same purpose to fulfil,—the restoration of the **atmospheric** equilibrium, which has become disturbed.

Y

Doubtless electricity has a great deal to answer for in connection with these great atmospheric disturbances, if not wholly and entirely responsible for them. For my own part, I believe typhoons, cyclones, etc., to be *purely* electrical phenomena.

I have mentioned the barometer as being a never-failing guide. I consider it, in fact, the greatest friend a sailor has, though in these days of steam it is not sufficiently considered. A steamer, for instance, cuts across, goes through or passes the storm's course; she is independent of the wind, and, consequently, changes in the weather are less watched and attended to.

I often tried to ascertain how the great fleets of fishing junks, which everywhere along the Chinese coast are found working away diligently at all seasons and in all weathers, knew the approach of a typhoon; for know it I always felt sure they did, first from the fact that so few are lost during the passage of these storms; and secondly, because I had frequently seen them getting to safe harbours well before the typhoon had commenced.

One answer was always returned to my queries on this point, and no other; and this was, that the water always got thick on the approach of a storm. When anchored at some of the out-of-the-way small ports on the coasts, often full of merchant junks, besides numerous fishing craft and others, the masters or owners of the former, particularly if trading with Hong-Kong or some of the open ports, frequently came on board the gun-boat to ask me, "What that thing makie talkie to-day?" "that thing" being my barometer, in which they showed the greatest confidence.

As nearly as possible one hundred miles west of Macao is a large island called Chang-chuen in Chinese, and St. John's in English. Several bays run deeply into the land, cutting the island up considerably. A few small villages of the poorest class of fishermen or farmers are here and there found. A very miserable lot of people these villagers are; but as the island is visited by none but pirates, no other class of Chinamen would care to live there. I doubt much if the Government ever knew of this place. It was a very frequent resort of mine when cruising along this wild coast, and many a stroll with my gun have I enjoyed on it, always managing to bag a few partridges, quail, or pigeons. One day, when wandering about in this way, I came upon a large flat slab of stone, almost concealed by grass and herbage. A great rock rose close to it, and a few bushes and some screw pine plants grew near. Thinking it rather queer-looking and tomb-like, I cleared away the rough grass, and almost the first thing I saw were two words, "Francis Xavier!" Scraping off some more rubbish, the whole inscription came out quite clear. Here, then, was the spot where this great man died. A more out-of-the-way, God-forsaken sort of place to end one's days on could scarcely be found. I asked some Chinese of the half-dozen wretched huts which clustered together a short distance from the spot what they knew about it. "Oh," they said, "one big priest makie die there, a long time since. He come from another country; not Chinaman, but very good man."

XAVIER'S TOMB.

CHAPTER XVII.

THE SAME, AND A FEW INCIDENTS WHICH HAPPENED IN THE LAST CHINA WAR.

My friends the pirates were not always very polite. I knew, of course, they would have relished getting hold of me. Occasionally they managed to convey messages such as, " We'll skin him;" " We'll blow him out of the water," and so on. The latter considerate inclination came so decidedly in April 1866 that I thought they really might mean something, and the Admiral, who happened to be in port, rather reluctantly gave me permission to go out. He was at first anxious I should take two gun-boats, but I knew my only chance of teaching them a lesson was to go alone. Puckshui, which I had previously burnt to the ground, was the spot these bits of pleasantry came from, and the following morning, as usual, at daylight I arrived there. The place had been entirely rebuilt. My three guns were loaded and run out on one side, and steaming in I anchored abreast the battery. But not a movement of course was made. Seven or eight long snake-boats were drawn up in a side creek; these I destroyed, and landing with four men, the inhabitants took to their heels, and once more I burnt the place to the ground.

Not very long after this an expedition was got up on a great scale. A combined Chinese and English force was to proceed to utterly destroy this renowned stronghold. It consisted of fifty-three war-junks, sixteen hundred Chinese troops commanded by numerous Mandarins, and one very big man in charge of all. There were, besides, four English vessels, three being gunboats, and a hired steamer. I was sent in command. The British contingent was supposed only to support, or act as moral force. We rendezvoused just off the entrance between the two islands, which I have described before, and I said to the gallant Chinese General—

"Go in and win! If need be I will come to your support, but I see nothing in the way."

This celestial warrior, however, positively refused to attempt any such bold design unless I went first, which ultimately I did. I then pointed out where the Chinese troops had better land; in the place I had with my two boats done so months before. This, after blazing away with his junks at the village for some time, he did, the troops looting the village, which had been again restored, and burning it for the third time. Then the opposite side had to be taken; again I showed him where to land and take the place on the flank. About eight hundred men were told off for this, who advanced helter-skelter across the fields in front of the village. The pirates here, however, had concealed themselves in the wooded banks and low hills just behind the houses, and peppered the imperial troops as they approached. These worthies blazed away in return, but in the most indiscriminate manner, and as for advancing further, that idea they lost sight of altogether. The General now hurried off to me, and prayed for assistance.

"Look," he said, "my troops cannot take the place."

"I have been watching you all the time," I answered, "but this sort of thing is utterly absurd; go in at them, and they will run as fast as their legs can carry them." But the poor man could not, or would not credit such a thing; it was utterly beyond his comprehension.

"Very well," I said, "I will come with a few men and help you."

I therefore landed, taking this paper commander-in-chief along with me, one marine, and a blue-jacket; then leaving him with his troops I walked ahead with my two men, close up to the cover where the pirates were potting at the troops, and opened fire at them. It was quite enough; they cleared out and went over the crest of hills like a flock of sheep. The Chinese soldiers now flocked in and looted every nook and corner, their usual mode on such occasions, and afterwards burnt the village.

It will be easily understood from what I have just related why piracy in China was a trade practised with such impunity. The whole proceeding I have endeavoured to describe seems so entirely ridiculous and almost fabulous, that if I had not been rather more than an eye-witness, I should have hesitated before repeating it. There was another small village destroyed without the pirates showing, and then we dispersed, the junks and Chinese troops returning to Canton, and the gun-boats to Hong-Kong. The fifty-three junks I have mentioned as part of the force, mounted at least ten 12 or 18 pounder guns, or about five hundred and thirty in all.

I shall only relate one more adventure after pirates. This time I was looking along the east coast, when I picked up information from some fishermen that three large junks were anchored in a snug bay about six miles away at a place I knew well. On my way thither I conned over in my mind the mode of attack. The gun-boat I knew could not enter the place they were in, the entrance being exceedingly narrow, and at low tide much too shallow. I also felt quite certain that the pirates were as well aware of this as I was, and might in that case give us a warm reception, as we entered in the boats, and bolt immediately afterwards, in plenty time to reach the cover of the hills long before we could get near them. I decided to surprise them if possible, though the chances were against us, as probably look-outs were on the hills watching us. Approaching as near the rocks as possible, I quietly left the gun-boat with seven men, and landed; the little vessel steaming on, with orders to appear off the entrance to the bay, as close in as possible, and to send another boat to my assistance when she reached her position.

We had hardly three hundred yards of scrubby bushes and grass to go through before the low ridge which overlooked the little bay was reached. On peering cautiously over I found we were within a hundred yards of the junks, which were below us, and evidently aground in the middle of the bay. They all were broadside on to the entrance, and the crews, who were standing about the guns watching the opening to their snug stowaway anchorage, appeared quite prepared to resist attack from that quarter. Two were very fine junks, with nine or ten guns each; the third was smaller, mounting about seven. Between twenty and thirty men were in each; I calculated roughly they mustered something like ten to one of us. Just below where we were, a few houses clustered together under some large bastard banyan-trees, and a small sanpan lay hauled out of the water on the beach in front of them. On this sanpan my hopes centred. It was most amusing to watch these free-and-easy gentlemen, who little thought how near we were; all their movements convinced me they were at any rate bent on saluting us with a broadside as we pulled round the rocky point of the channel, scarcely a hundred and fifty yards off. I laughed to myself as I thought how awfully taken in they would presently be. Afterwards I found all their guns loaded to the muzzle with grape, and pointed straight for the entrance. The gun-boat now showed, and for a few moments I waited to see if any effect was produced on those in the junks. They all stood still, but showed no signs of clearing out; quite the contrary, they clustered closer round their guns, talking hurriedly amongst themselves.

Quietly topping the crest, we quickly passed through the few yards which intervened between the coveted sanpan and our position, and, pushing off with three men, made for the junks. The scene that now took place was too absurd. To the ruffians' utter consternation, four dreaded beings appeared within a few yards of them, three more were moving round the beach. Probably in their confused minds we were only the first of a large party. Into the boats alongside the junks they jumped, tumbled, and fell; half of them missed their mark and went into the water. The splashing and excitement were most ludicrous. Our wretched sanpan would keep turning round and round, and the more we tried to catch some of the terror-stricken pirates, the more the thing would go as if on a pivot. It resembled a duck-hunt in a tub much more than a piratical capture. In came one of my boats to assist, which added considerably to the confusion already produced. By the time most of the Chinamen had reached the shore, we had captured seven or eight; the rest were very soon in safety amongst the bushes and other cover. The junks we of course destroyed.

It may appear, from what I have said, that Chinamen are the most despicable cowards. This is not, however, exactly the case. I have seen them fight well, and be cut down at their guns before attempting to move. This was the case at Fatchan, and at one of our attacks on the Pei-ho Forts, they beat us off most signally. Our amount of killed on that occasion was enormous. At the capture of the Bogue Forts they returned our fire for two hours steadily; and there are many other instances which I could mention of their fighting well. What they never did appreciate was close quarters this I knew from experience, and in all my piratical adventures invariably acted on it. The consequence was, much bloodshed was prevented, and things were done easily and quickly, generally without a shot being fired on either side. A Chinaman very soon loses his presence of mind, which, at the best of times, is of the most meagre description. Then again he is no fool, but quite capable of drawing comparisons between his own wretched arms and ours, and realising the utter folly of attempting to stand against them.

I found my little pirate boy very useful; he knew his old friends at once, and could pick out a piratical junk with ease and certainty. He soon understood English, and became a good servant. I was often offered a couple of girls in exchange for him, and one

Mandarin offered to take him, educate him, and make him a Mandarin in time; but until I left China, notwithstanding these tempting offers, I kept him. Girls and boys in China are looked upon as two very different articles, the former being comparatively of no value. The baby towers, or deep pits in some instances, which are found near all large Chinese cities, receive, as a rule, only girl children, **which are flung** into these receptacles and allowed to die. I had a vivid description of one of these places by a Chinese artist, in **the** shape of a print, wherein the poor, wretched little new-born babies were shown being torn to pieces by snakes, dogs, etc. The mother of one of the children was gazing over the side of the pit, watching her two or three days' old child being fought over by several brutes of dogs.

During the China War in **1856,** a few days after we had taken the last fort near the Boca Tigris, some midshipmen roaming about the fields behind the fort in quest of quail or pigeon, came upon an earthenware chatty, and looking in, found it contained a baby girl, alive and kicking. She was brought on board at once, when the doctor pronounced her only **two** days' old. What was to be done with her; the demand for the poor little motherless thing was very great. The weather-beaten old Master, who had been forty years at sea, wanted to have her; he was sure he could rear her. Others were equally anxious to "bring her up." What a pet she would make! The doctor laughed at all the professions of ability which came from so many rough old tars, and sent on shore by the Chinese bumboat-man to see if a more effective nurse could not be obtained. In a short time he returned with a Chinese woman, who, for a small sum, agreed to take care of the wee thing. Every Saturday while we lay about the river blockading Canton, the baby was brought on board and passed about the ship, whose property it was now considered. On our return to Hong-Kong, the child was given over to the Sisters of Mercy there; and on the vessel leaving the station for England, a subscription was got up, and a good sum raised for "*our*" protégée, who, at the same time, was christened Victoria Nankin.

Five years after this, in 1862, I again returned to the East, and the first thing I inquired about, on reaching Hong-Kong, was the baby, but the poor forsaken little thing had gone to a better world some two years before. It is possible this child was purposely put in our way, and also that it was its own mother we got to nurse it, and that she was delighted at her offspring being not only saved, but provided for; but it is far more likely that the child was put there to die, in the usual way or custom of the country.

During the time I was particularly employed in looking after pirates—about eighteen or twenty months—I took in all fifty-four junks, and about two hundred prisoners. **As for the number** of guns, and people liberated, I hardly know, not having kept any regular list. The guns were all of good manufacture, most being made in England, the others in Germany or Belgium.

At the time I speak of, Hong-Kong was a **hot-bed** of piracy and villany. Chinamen generally, but Cantonese particularly—and of all Chinamen I suppose there are no greater rascals—who had made their own country too hot for them, congregated on this rocky piece of English soil for **protection**. **The Chinese population** was then about 115,000. Headmen of pirate gangs resided there, and piratical junks anchored with impunity in the harbour; they used actually to have the coolness to come to, and take up a berth close to my gun-boat, but usually they remained amongst their fellow-craft at the other end of the harbour. **An** English brig, or **schooner, or the smallest,** most insignificant craft sailing under **these vaunted** colours, on anchoring in this *English* port, was at once boarded, by not only one authority, but by two or three; certainly by the harbour-master and the guard-boat of some man-of-war at anchor in the port. She had to sign papers, deliver others, and generally give an account of herself, her whole crew, arms, contents, and other items being entered in printed forms. Possibly her crew consisted of five or six men, the captain, and a boy, and she may have had a couple of small swivel-guns on her after-bulkhead. A junk, or a dozen junks, coming in, were never even looked at. I have seen these vessels come sailing along in sixes, or more, mounting ten or twelve guns each, and with crews of forty or fifty men, large enough and perfectly able to take the finest merchant vessel afloat. These junks were not pirates, but honest traders, or ostensibly so; but honest traders were by no means above doing a bit of piracy when trade was slack. However, this is not the point of my remarks. What I objected to was that these junks could come and go without any notice whatever being taken of them, whereas our own vessels were very differently treated; and as I have said before, pirates were often anchored in the port, which seemed a queer arrangement, to say the least of it. On one occasion I saw a small English vessel leave the port, and a fine big junk follow her; they both went round the point together and disappeared from view. Before they had gone very much further, our countryman was attacked and robbed, I believe by that very junk. On another occasion, I actually took a pirate junk and all her crew from under the very nose of one of our police stations, at the eastern entrance to the harbour. All these things I pointed out in the proper quarter, and they have been, if not altogether, to a great extent, rectified; junks are now registered and numbered, and Chinamen prevented from entering Hong-Kong without a passport.

Most of the circumstances relating to the China War of 1856-8 have been ably described by Mr. Cooke in his *China*. A few little incidents, however, which happened before he arrived on the scene of action, may still be of interest.

We had attacked and taken the Bogue Forts, which are situated on the Pearl River, about half-way between Hong-Kong and Canton. The river narrows at this place, there being two islands in the centre of the passage, and on these islands forts were erected; in the north island 180 guns were mounted, and in the south one 120. On the mainland, guarding the east passage, the Annunghoy Fort mounted 140 guns; and on the opposite side of the river, guarding the west channel, were two smaller forts of twenty guns each. We took the island forts one day, with a small loss of killed and wounded, and the following morning the large Annunghoy Fort; and now the passage was clear.

The day we took the latter forts I was left on shore to guard the east gate, which was situated on a hill about 200 feet high, and commanded the extensive plain running to the south. A higher range ran along behind the fort, completely commanding it, and the renowned celestial soldiers kept sneaking back to this ridge and taking cool pot-shots at us, which began to get unpleasant, although at 200 yards they were not to be much feared. Still as a stray shot is supposed to have effect even on his Satanic majesty, I planted three or four men behind big stones half way from the gate to the ridge, who, whenever a Chinaman showed his nose, let fly at him. I was wandering over the ground myself, looking for wounded or dead Chinamen, when I saw a wretched man on his back, apparently by his moaning and movements in great pain; he had one of their long daggers stuck in the ground beside him, and knowing instances where they had feigned being wounded, and attacked their intended relief, I judiciously stalked him, through the rough grass and boulder rocks, and quietly from behind possessed myself of his dagger. The unfortunate man was shot through the thigh, and going back to the gate, I had him brought in and his wound dressed. The coolest of all the Chinese officials now actually walked up from their side of the ridge and stood clear on the top, perfectly unconcerned, shading his head with a large umbrella. My men lying behind the rocks fired away at him, but without any effect. I never saw an individual so indifferent to bullets whizzing about his ears. At last one touched him on his leg, which seemed to remind him that he might just as well get behind the ridge once more.

From my elevated position I could see everything that went on in the fort below, as well as miles away down the plain. I noticed a party of officers walking round the battery examining the guns, most of which were very large, and coming on one not yet spiked, I saw my own captain put something in the vent (a nail), pick up one of the shot lying by the gun, and standing on the step of the carriage, began to drive the nail down the vent with the shot. Off went the gun, recoiling several feet, and tumbling the gallant captain head over heels, fortunately without hurting him much. The shot, a twelve-inch one, went booming along and struck the water right under the *Hornet's* stern. A few feet more to the left would probably have sunk the little craft.

Towards dusk a poor woman came along the plain to the foot of the hill on which the gate where I was stationed stood; she perpetually called a certain name, by which I concluded she was looking for her husband or some relative, who had been engaged in the action during the forenoon. Going on her knees and holding up her hands every half-dozen yards, she approached by the steep path to the gate where I was, apparently in a most distressed state of mind. I pointed out to her the dead bodies, which she uncovered and examined, but evidently without finding the one she wanted, so I then took her inside and showed her my wounded friend. Yes, this was the one. After a little conversation, and giving the man some water to drink, she ran away down the hill, in the direction of the village, and soon returning with assistance, took her husband, I suppose, away with her.

Shortly after we took these forts, one of the passenger steamers running between Hong-Kong and Canton was destroyed, by the native passengers rising, murdering all the officers and crew, and burning the steamer. This happened a few miles above the Bogue Forts, and in consequence all but one steamer thought it high time to leave off running. We were short of ships at this time, and from the Bogues to Whampoa, a distance of fifteen miles, there was no ship guarding and blockading the river. The Mandarin junks had, therefore, numerous safe outlets, as well as retreats, by the different creeks which opened into the river in that distance. The little passenger steamer, which still stuck to the river, had comparatively safe work of it until she reached the Bogues; but from there to Canton was the ticklish part. However, as I said, she stuck to her work. One day she had rather more than her usual number of Chinese passengers, and the captain, a plucky little man, obtained leave from the Admiral, then at Hong-Kong, to ask for a guard of men from the ship stationed at the Bogues. I was sent on board with twelve men to guard the steamer. I first saw all the passengers—of course Chinese—passed under hatches, and put a sentry over them to watch their proceedings. We then steamed away up the river.

Two o'clock came, and with it dinner; and I now found we had two young ladies amongst three or four other European passengers. These two girls were going to Whampoa, where their father had some business in connection, I think, with the docks at that place. We had hardly commenced our repast when the report of a gun reached us, and looking out in the direction from whence it came, I saw a few junks stealing quietly out from a creek which entered the river just under the shadow of some low hills on which the pagoda marking the second bar stood. Another shot now followed, then a third, all falling short of the steamer, but in a very good line. In less time than it takes to relate it, no less than forty-four junks had opened out, each pulling eighty or ninety oars, and armed with ten or twelve guns. There was no turning back; our only chance lay in our speed, and being able to run past without the machinery being damaged. The engineers sat on the safety-valve, or did something equally effective. I got the one 12-pounder gun, which was mounted on the forecastle, trained for the thickest mass of junks. The other men, except two who were on guard over the Chinese passengers, opened fire from aft, and we returned John Chinaman's cannonade as hard as we could load our one gun. Their guns soon found our range, and the little steamer was riddled. The boiler was struck where two plates overlapped, and just started sufficiently to let the steam and water come spitting out. Three inches on either side it must have broken the plate, and then, of course, it would have been all up with us. The chief officer was a Portuguese, and was steering the vessel. He, however, entirely lost his head through sheer fright, and putting the helm hard over, ran the steamer for the bank. If we had touched, not a soul would have escaped. Fortunately, the captain saw this little episode of his chief man, rushed to the wheel (I don't know what he did to the Portuguese), and altering the helm, we just shaved the bank, only stirring up the mud; but it was a very close thing. For twenty minutes we were under fire, and got remarkably well peppered. I would not have believed Chinamen could fire so well at a quickly moving object; but then there was such a number of junks, and about 450 guns, half of which, I suppose, were firing. Steam told against manual propulsion, and in the above-mentioned time we were out of range, and very soon afterwards snug under the guns of a forty-gun frigate lying at Whampoa.

The two young ladies behaved during this sharp twenty minutes in the most admirable manner, making neither noise nor fuss. As soon as we were clear of their guns, the little skipper's wrath burst forth against his chief officer, and he was not only ready, but anxious, to shoot the wretched coward who had so nearly done for us; I thought, however, probably the man would receive ample punishment in his own mind, without our having to resort to such extreme measures, and he may be alive now for all I know to the contrary.

The whole of this incident was seen from the ship at the Bogues; but owing to the dense smoke occasioned by so much firing the result of the engagement was not known. My captain assuming the worst, expended much unparliamentary language against Chinamen generally, and walked furiously up and down the deck, lamenting the loss of his officer and men. Up into the main-top he went, thinking from there he could see better. When the firing ceased, and the junks disappeared again from view up the creek in which the rascals had previously been lying in wait for us, it became an undertaking how to get the captain once more on deck. It was a good many years since he had been aloft; I doubt his ever having had much to do in these airy places, owing to a natural defect in his feet. However, I believe, with the assistance of two or three blue-jackets, he was in time safely deposited on deck.

I had the satisfaction, not very long after this, to be at the attack and capture of most of these junks up Escape Creek. The remainder joined the Fatchan fleet, and again it was my luck to assist in their destruction.

At both of these places they fought well. Our loss, particularly at the latter place, was very severe. At Escape Creek one in ten of our force engaged was killed or wounded.

CHINA

CHAPTER XVIII.

RÉSUMÉ.

HAVING been several years in the East, spread over a period of a quarter of a century, I have of course seen many changes in that part of the world. To begin with, China was not, when I first visited it as a youngster, what it now is; and Japan was little known beyond being represented on the map of the world, or stuck into the corner of that of China: though in the latter country a few phlegmatic Dutchmen endured imprisonment on one island, for the sake of being allowed to send four or five ship-loads of lacquer, etc., to Holland.

I remember well when we arrived at Nagasaki in 1855, the trepidation in which we found the Governor. This was a few months after the visit to Hakodadi before mentioned, and a new English Admiral had taken command. **The** Admiral had visited the place **a** month or so previously, and had been treated in an off-hand, contemptuous way. This sort of thing was no longer to be endured, and as for only being allowed to remain in an outer roadstead, **two** miles from the proper anchorage, **not allowed to land**, and not **granted** the small privilege of buying fresh beef or vegetables; also of having a two-sworded Yakonin, with a boat-load of soldiers, pulling round the ship day and night, —these little peculiarities, as I say, were not to be endured any longer; so the line of guard-boats drawn across the harbour's mouth to prevent any vessels entering **had** to retire, as the two British ships, one towing the other, proceeded into the excellent inner harbour. Taking a guard of fifty marines, our Admiral **went** for a country walk. Ultimately the Governor paid his respects by calling on this wonderful man who had dared to beard him, and fresh beef and vegetables were provided, besides presents being exchanged. The ship in which I was, reached the place soon after this little episode had occurred, and we profited by the **new** order of things. Every civility was shown **us; complimentary** visits were exchanged; presents, tea, and sweetmeats flew about in all directions; we were shown all over the place, and a great store was filled with all kinds of Japanese productions, from which we could select what we wished, paying a very small price for anything we took. From this period the Dutch traders on the island of Desima led a far happier life. I remember how they hailed with delight our arrival, and told us of the difference that took place in their treatment immediately after our Admiral had acted so promptly and wisely.

In the days I speak of also—twenty-five years ago—fortunes were made in China rapidly. The chief trade, particularly that of opium, by far the most lucrative of all, was in the hands of a few. Mails from England arrived once a month, and during the interval, rest, shooting, racing, and amusement were the general routine. On the peak of the island of Hong-Kong there was—and still is—a signal-gun to announce the approach of the English mail-steamer, which from this elevated position can be seen at least forty miles off. As the mail-day drew near, the excitement in the place became general; anticipation was on every one's face, hardly anything else was spoken of, and if a steamer was reported from the peak, heavy odds were freely offered on its being the mail-boat. But directly the boom of the gun sounded from this elevated station, the place appeared like an ant's nest that some one had just kicked. I have seen the male part of the congregation in the cathedral get up and walk, or rather hurry out of that uncathedral-looking edifice, during any part of the service that happened to be going on, almost before the echo of the report from the signal-gun had died away.

Some of the chief merchant-houses had fine brigs, armed to the teeth, and manned by Lascars, to carry their opium from port to port. Then came their steamers, magnificent boats in their day, which used to run between Calcutta and Hong-Kong, and being much faster than the Peninsular and Oriental Company's boats, they generally left forty-eight hours after these slower craft had departed, bringing so much later dates as to the price of opium, and arriving at least a day or two before them. They anchored in some bay outside, and sent a boat into Hong-Kong with all the latest news to their owners; who thus had ample time to work on, before the public and smaller men had a chance in the markets. These wealthy merchants lived in the greatest luxury, nothing was too good for them, but their days for monopolising the chief trade in opium were numbered. First, in 1856, came the China War, and with it the necessity of a fortnightly mail instead of only a monthly one. Then followed the telegraph, which at once put every one on an equal footing. The splendid steamers soon fell into disuse.

Ultimately some were glad enough to cart coal about, or any other cargo; while others were sold to the Japanese, who were just then beginning to buy all the obsolete and greatest coal-consuming craft offered them.

The Suez Canal was like the last straw to the overladen camel. Some houses collapsed altogether. The remaining firms reached level ground, and instead of their representatives giving two or three thousand pounds for a horse to vie with their neighbour opposite, they were content to appear on the racecourse with their hard-mouthed, ugly, but strong China ponies. The cry went forth—trade was done for. Germans came to light, and not only to light, but steadily to the front. Commencing on a small scale, they gradually worked their way on until their clubs and mode of living almost equalled ours. Steamers took the place of sailing vessels; the first teas were despatched by these more speedy vessels; the great clipper race of the year with the spring teas was no more; the betting and premiums on the first arrivals of those beautiful yacht-like craft were things of the past, and, in fact, a revolution in trade took place. Profits were less, and fortunes came less speedily. But as for trade being lessened, it appeared to me, an uninitiated hand, to be only spread over a larger field. I believe comparatively few people in England have much idea of **the** enormous interests we have in **the** East—I mean leaving India and Australia out of the question, and speaking of China, and China alone. Japan, of course, is to be considered, but in trade it is as a molehill to a mountain when compared with China; rather **may it be thought of as a pleasant, a beautiful** country, with charming inhabitants, a fairy-land, where one feels inclined to live without thinking of the morrow, but there, comparatively speaking, it ends.

China, with its vast resources, resources which have never yet been brought into play, and its teeming industrial population, must go on improving, and becoming of more and more importance. The Chinese character is thoroughly conservative, **and having taken so** long before introducing changes, **which are now being** gradually brought about, **they are not likely to** do things rashly, hurriedly, and unadvisedly. Step by step they have taken to new modes of warfare. Their old jingalls, and guns with a few inches of windage, are things of the past, and instead, good rifles, torpedos, and **breech-loading** guns are either purchased or **made.** At the Kiang-nan arsenal last year, twenty 40-pounder Armstrong guns were turned out, equal in manufacture—so the European engineers reported—to any of the Woolwich or Elswick guns. Much larger guns 150-pounders, have also been with equal success manufactured there. And as regards their small arms and torpedos, they have the latest and best patterns. Steamships have been built, and gun-boats purchased. The latter particularly are most formidable little vessels.

Suffice it to say, very great progress has been made in their arms since the last war in 1860. I remember how amused we used to be watching some half-dozen braves sneaking up behind cover to have a quiet pot shot with their absurd rockets fired from a bamboo tube. The things, certainly, if they managed to hit, might prove fatal, but it had to be at very close quarters; and at a hundred yards or so, it was easy enough to get out of their way, as they skipped along towards you. The first breech-loading gun I ever saw was in the shape of a jingall in China. The whole *breech* came out, was loaded and replaced, the arrangement being both perfectly effective and simple. As to pluck, I have previously said, I consider the Chinese have sometimes shown themselves to be by no means devoid of that element.

I think, considering the conditions under which the Chinese fought us, and the immense disparity of arms, that they showed great pluck in fighting us at all.

Their forces were badly fed, absurdly armed, clothed in a queer sort of nondescript dress, ragged, and of any colour; always in arrears of pay, and if knocked over, had nothing to look to as far as being cared for, neither surgical treatment, hospitals, nor pensions being known. Such circumstances or conditions are not conducive to the manufacture of soldiers. The northern men are fine big fellows; and that they have the animal courage and contempt of danger, has over and over again been proved; but they are badly led, or more properly speaking not led at all, for the General and his subordinates prefer squatting behind a wall and saying, "Go ahead" to his soldiers. The idea of leading them never seems to strike the officers. Armed with good weapons, which they now are, if officered properly, and with proper discipline instituted, I firmly believe they would be most formidable troops against any enemy. As for foreign officers entering their service, they might do so for a time, but I don't think the Chinese will ever retain the assistance of outside help in any way. One of their traits is a settled jealousy of all foreign help. To supply themselves whatever may be good for the country, is far too inherent in their nature to allow foreign aid ever to become a permanency.

The day must come, sooner or later, when Russia

will have to be confronted by China. The great gateway to their western provinces is now threatened by the former. All the commerce and traffic between China and central Asia passes through the Kiayu Pass, and leads across the desert of Gobi to Kulja. It is their weakest point, and has of late years been watched with vigilance. Russia desires, or prefers, to hold a part of Ili, that once belonged to China, as well as Kulja, which naturally the Chinese consider as a menace. This part of the world is a long way from any base of operations Russia could arrange—probably the Caspian—and to move troops to the frontier of China would be a matter of excessive difficulty. But as for China, a thousand miles or so is of no moment; and if one army got knocked all to pieces, another would immediately take its place. A check or defeat to the Russian arms so far away from their starting-point would, however, be a very different matter. China, properly managed, I mean of course in regard to her armies, might defy Russia, and the sooner she prepares to do so the better.

A few years ago Chinamen would have been perfectly thunderstruck if told the time was at hand when their ambassadors would be sent to the different European capitals; but so it now is, and the ambassadors'

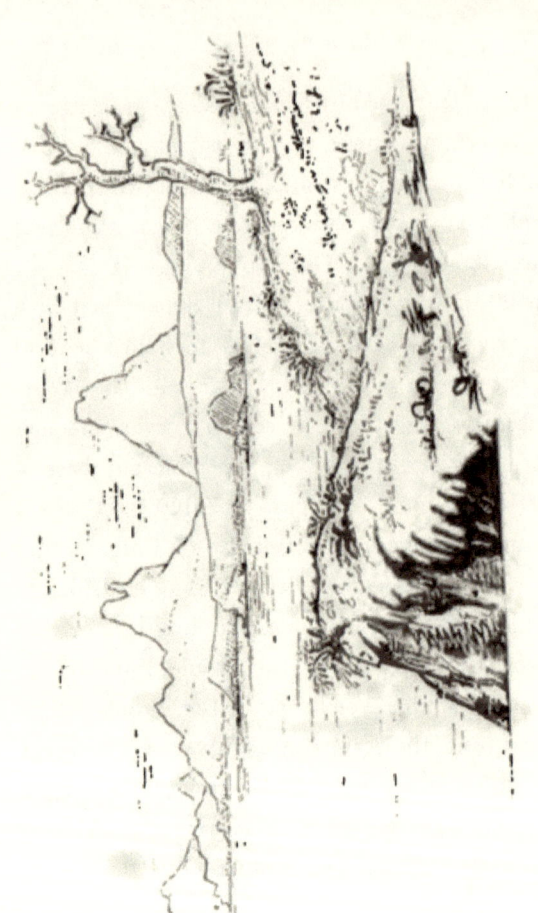

TWO VOLCANOES IN YESSO, 8000 FEET HIGH.

wives give receptions, though the male sex is carefully excluded.

If China was but well and honestly governed, her position might be one of the first in the world; gradually, I have little doubt, she will creep up to this, as her destiny to hold a great place in the universe appears more than probable. Patience, perseverance, and soberness, are three great essentials to success, and these virtues the Chinese most certainly possess.

The system of squeezing[1] amongst the Mandarins is terribly pernicious. As for religion, I don't consider the Chinese really have any, although hardly a room in a Chinaman's house is without its joss or josses. They are cynical to a degree on this score. When the ground is dried and parched up, their custom is to haul the god of rain from his resting-place, and set him down on the hot dry ground, so that he may feel the state it is in, and how very much rain is required. I doubt if Western people can form a conception of what the Chinese character is, and as for their manners and customs, pages could be filled on this score. It is all very well to suppose Western powers are so superior

---

[1] By "squeezing" is meant the system of forcing the poor to pay unfair fines, taxes, etc.

in every way that necessarily they must get the best of the day in any question that may arise to disturb peaceful relations. China is only now, and very slowly, beginning to break the skin of her chrysalis; when developed, it will be very different. The very idea of their numbers is astonishing. A nation mustering three hundred million, all of pigtail renown, is a serious thought. Combined and well governed, and taught rightly the art of war, Russia's constant encroachments would be heard of no more. Since I have known the East, Russia has gained two extensive acquisitions to her territory; from the Amoor she has come down to the forty-second parallel, representing a coast line of five hundred miles, with a width of one hundred and twenty. The forty-second parallel brings her to the borders of Korea. Along this extensive stretch of coast there are excellent harbours, but not one which is free from ice during the winter; the most southern, Vladivostok, is not open to navigation until the end of April. Then she has also acquired the remaining southern half of Saghalien, the northern part of the island having previously been in her possession, but here again there is no harbour. It is unlikely, almost impossible, as I have elsewhere said, for her to stop adding, by hook or by crook, to her already great extent of coast line, until at **any rate** one or more **good** and open harbours form part of her territory. **It is** simply a necessity which follows the acquisition of territory, and would stand good with any nation as well as grasping Russia. She has **long had her eye on** Hakodadi in Yesso, indeed **on Yesso entirely, and is now only separated from that island by the narrow straits of La Perouse;** but for the present further encroachment in that direction—in **other words, against** Japan—is postponed.

Tsu-sima would be an excellent position for Russia to acquire, possessing a magnificent bay or sound, with splendid harbours running off it. It is midway between Japan and Korea, and in the fair way from the south to their own territories **in the north; commands the south entrance to the Sea of Japan, and** is capable of being made perfectly impregnable; points which, I have no doubt, are well known to Russia. **On** one occasion, when Japan was as yet young in Western ideas, Russia actually placed her foot on the island; and if it had not been for the prompt measures taken by the English Admiral at the time, she in **all probability** would be there now. Korea appears **to me** her most legitimate locality to break ground, or in the way of encroachment; indeed, I can see no reason why she should hesitate in so doing: an unknown peninsula, standing isolated, it has no friends. Formerly Korea was under some sort of protectorate, or, at any rate, in some way came under the wing of China; but this is not now the case, and there is little doubt she would have to fight her own battles in any dispute with other nations. This was clearly shown to be the case when Japan, in 1877, singly, and uninitiated by string-pullers, made her own terms in a treaty which they insisted on Korea signing. She is the only nation that has been able to do so. *Able* appears an absurd word to use in relation to a semi-barbarous people and any Western power; none other, however, is applicable to the expeditions both of the French and Americans, which these two great nations attempted with and also against the Koreans.

As for ourselves, we have never done more than send an occasional ship to waste her time in trying to survey their coasts. A similar result attended each and all of these ill-advised expeditions; we were always insulted, and had to leave the coasts without being able to carry out any thoroughly done work, and to this day we know nothing regarding the south coast except that a magnificent sound, which I called "Sylvia Basin," exists a short distance to the westward of Chosan harbour. No finer bay have I ever seen, nor do I believe one of greater capacity, and possessing to the same extent the points essential to a natural harbour, exists in the world. We, I suppose, would be very jealous of any attempt on Russia's part to make a treaty with Korea, either by good-will or force. But there, probably, our objection would end. Nothing would be easier for Russia than to force Korea into troubled waters, when, of course, she could, and no doubt would, make her own terms. Every mile further south Russia comes, so much the more easy will she find it at any time to hold a menacing hand over China. It appears to me it is really from this quarter that China might with greater ease and success be attacked vitally by Russia.

The Koreans are, in features and figure, like the northern Chinese or Tartars; they are rougher perhaps, and more uncouth in manner, but physically are much the same.

Japan, though so near China, and with a true Mongolian type of inhabitants, is yet literally and entirely different. A few years ago no country in the world, barring Korea, was so completely shut to all outsiders. A wise Emperor,—I forget now when he reigned,—observing that his people began to show tastes for foreign articles of trade, for more communication with the world, and notably with China, from whence junks both went and came; became very much perturbed, and for some time he brooded over the probability—the certainty, in his mind—of the corruption of his people, but without seeing his way through the difficulty. At last he hit upon a plan. It was easy, he said, to stop the foreigner from coming in, but not to prevent his own people from going out, and in this way learning new ideas, and becoming discontented; and now, after nights made sleepless by conning over how so much evil to his people could be prevented, he had come to the conclusion there was only one way of averting it, and that was by constructing a certain kind of vessel which would answer to coast along their own shores, but would be utterly unfit to launch out into the open sea in. This decree was carried out to the letter, and to the present day this great Emperor's model of a junk may be seen in every craft that sails over Japanese waters,—an unwieldy mass, almost as high out of the water at the stern as they are long, with a single huge sail and one mast,—an article in no way adapted for seafaring purposes. Certainly they get along before the wind, so would a hay-stack, if it happened to find itself on the water; but as to beating to windward or weathering a gale, two points usually considered of some importance on the ocean, nothing of the kind could be attempted: a more effective way to prevent his people from getting abroad he could not have devised, and well it answered until we came upon the scene. Now, steamers which they have bought do most of their trade.

Suddenly this wonderful country flings all its old customs to the winds, and rushes headlong into the newest inventions and ideas that the Western world can send her. I think it may be safely said no such rapid and complete metamorphosis ever occurred before or since the world has been understood to go round. The success of the operation appears almost equally strange, for no reaction has taken place, and it is now not at all likely that any ever will. Japan does not abound in wealth and resources within itself like China. Gold a few years since had no value in the country, and the inhabitants were unable to comprehend our great craving for the yellow metal. Their mistake, of course, in time came home to them; but it was not before a large quantity of their big plate-like coins had been passed through a very different manufacture. Foreigners quickly relieved the Japanese of their great coins, by giving in exchange their weight in silver. Their exports are feeble. In 1878, roundly, they amounted to four and a half million pounds from all the ports, and the imports to five and a quarter million pounds sterling. Tea and silk are the two chief articles that are exported; cotton, grey shirting, and muslins, the principal imports.

My own impression is, Japan was pretty well worked out before any foreigners came on the scene. Every inch of the country that is capable of being utilised is so, and probably has been for centuries. I have over and over again remarked, when coming upon some cultivated spot, so situated that it appeared utterly worthless on account of the labour necessary even in reaching it, that only Japanese would utilise such extraordinary patches of ground. As to substituting one crop for another, changing a home consumption article into an export one, this, of course, could be done. Tea, for instance, might be substituted for sweet potatos, both flourishing best in similar latitudes and situations. A limited trade may be done in rice; but as, frequently, Japan cannot supply its own wants in this article, but has to depend on foreign supply, it must be considered uncertain as an export.

I remember one year (1870) when this great article of food failed in crop. China merchants made a good haul; but the supply sent from Rangoon and the south of China at last glutted the Japanese market, and the price, which had been forced up to the highest pitch, fell so low as to be quite unremunerative to the sender. The natives on the out-of-the-way parts of the coast took to deer flesh, a queer substitute, but not a bad one; and I was told by these poorer people that this was invariably the case when the rice crop fell short. I mention this to show that the want of rice, their mainstay, was, if not often, still frequently felt; and, therefore, although in some seasons it is quite possible to export rice, there is no certainty about it.

To my taste, there is no rice like the Japanese; it is large, full, and dry in grain, and very white. The Japanese young ladies who cross the water to China to act as housekeepers—a situation they fill most admirably—always make it a stipulation that they are to be supplied with rice from their own country. In 1878, twenty-eight million pounds of tea were exported, nearly all of which went to the American market.[1]

An attempt was made for two years to manufacture black tea for the English trade, but the result was only

[1] In the United States Japanese "oolong" is preferred to all other tea. At an hotel, if you want black tea, you must ask for "English breakfast tea." The Japanese "oolong" is much more stimulating.

disappointment, and I do not think will again be tried. There is a small export in copper, which in the year named amounted to, roundly, £45,000. A good deal is now coined; but I have seen this useful article heaped up into small hillocks, and left for years just as it was flung into these heaps from pits or holes, long since abandoned.

A few remarks on the direct trade between Japan and England will best show how our interest compares with that of other countries in this far-away land. In 1878 the total imports amounted to 26,000,000 dollars, out of which 21,000,000 were from Great Britain alone. The exports from Japan to Great Britain were 4,000,000, and to British colonies 3,000,000.

Japan may be rich in mineral wealth for all that foreigners yet know: I doubt its being so. Coal is fairly plentiful; out of the six or eight different kinds I tried for steaming purposes, that from Taka Shima, near Nagasaki, was incomparably the best. In the year I have previously quoted (1878), 141,772 tons were raised from this mine alone, averaging in price about seventeen shillings a ton. Good iron is found in Yesso, but so far only in small quantities. We know there is silver and gold, but in what quantities the Japanese alone can say. Up to the present day, all knowledge that the Japanese possess regarding the mineral wealth of the country is kept entirely to themselves.

Once when returning from an inland mountain peak, to get to which I had crossed numerous high ranges, I observed a sort of rough settlement on the side of one of the mountains, and on asking my Japanese guide what was done in such a queer, wild spot, he told me it was a gold mine, and that the workmen employed in digging out the precious metal lived in these rude dwellings. There were about one hundred men employed, so he assured me, but from my own observation I thought there might have been half that number. This was the only thing approaching a mine, or where mineral of any description was worked, that I ever came across in all my peregrinations, which extended over a large area. I consider, therefore, that if I had not actually come across mines or other mineral workings, that I must have heard of such things if they had existed to any considerable extent.

When the art of saving or prolonging life is more thoroughly understood and brought into play, the population, already quite sufficient for the country, will increase, and probably rapidly. What will become of the extra population is a question not easy to answer. An island without colonies, or ground for her people to stand on, has a difficult problem to solve. She might then, indeed, be ideally compared with ourselves: cut off the safety-valves for the enormous increasing propensities we show, and we should very soon eat each other. At present there is no immediate fear in Japan under this head. The strong, robust, and healthy only reach maturity, and of these, certainly not half that are born.

When the day comes, if it ever does, that she has to look round for breathing space for her extra population, where will she find it? Barring numerous small islands dotted about the Pacific Ocean, there remains at the present day, under native rule, the eastern half of New Guinea, the northern part of Borneo, and the north-west end, or nearly half, the island of Sumatra; among which are large tracts of rich and beautiful lands.

One of the greatest mistakes we ever made was to give up to Holland Sumatra and Java, the two most productive spots in the East. The Dutch have done well for themselves by Java, and are now striving hard to gain the north end of Sumatra. It is impossible to say what we might not have done with these grand islands; it is quite impossible to understand our folly and short-sightedness in not keeping them; it is equally impossible to conceive the ignorance we must have shown in the matter; and still more impossible to take in what object we had in giving them up.

It can only be a matter of time, and no great length of time either, when all the East not yet taken **under the wing of some Western power, will be absorbed by one or other of the higher civilised nations.** The being **we call the savage must go down** before the other we call civilised. **No** sooner do the two meet, than the one **gives way,** is absorbed, gradually disappears, and is heard of no more. It is the inevitable hand of fate. Therefore it appears infinitely more wise on our part to forestall other Western claws. This certainly should be done with regard to the northern part of Borneo and eastern half of New Guinea. The importance **of the north end of that wonderfully productive island Borneo, situated as it is half way up the China** Sea, and possessing good harbours and coal, cannot be over-estimated. It is in about the same **parallel as** Ceylon, and as it has high mountain **ranges and** low undulating hills, besides fine **plains, and is** well watered by both **large and** small **rivers**; probably no more prolific **spot exists.** Its climate, of course, varies from the great heat of **the lower tropical** latitudes **to the temperate and cold, even to a** greater extent than is **found in Ceylon,** owing to the higher mountain ranges. The large island of Formosa has had many jealous eyes on it for years, but, so far, no opportunity has been obtained by any to give a fair excuse why it should change hands. China, of course, prefers retaining it in her own hands. The greater part of the island is mountainous and wild, and to this day is in the hands of the aborigines of the land, who are of a Malay type, and not Chinese or Mongolian. On the east side are magnificent plains teeming with sugar-cane. The extraction of the saccharine substance is done in the most wasteful and pitiable manner possible. A large field for European enterprise may be found here if only the island were in other hands. One drawback, by no means a small one, is the great want of harbours; the few that there are, are all on the west side, and these are only small and indifferent ones.

H.M.S. "SYLVIA."

APPENDIX.

ROCK IN AWASI BAY.

APPENDIX.

There is, as far as I am aware, no catalogue of the Japanese birds published, except that in Siebold's *Fauna Japonica*, a work now out of print, and unattainable by the public generally.

I found it very inconvenient myself, when in that country, being without a list, however imperfect; and thinking that possibly this volume might fall into the hands of some naturalists who also may wish to collect the feathered tribes of Nipon, I add a list of those named in the above-quoted work, which, so far as it goes, is no doubt correct. It is, however, more to be depended on as referring to the birds of the southern parts of the country. Siebold's opportunities for collecting, etc., lay almost entirely in the south, and considering the up-hill work it must have been in his time for a foreigner to do anything of the kind, the *Fauna Japonica* is a most excellent and valuable work. I add to this catalogue a list of the birds I collected myself, which almost all were from the north of Nipon or Yesso. Ornithologists, I hope, will excuse any inaccuracies I make in the nomenclature. I am quite aware that all naturalists will not agree with me.

Some of the birds I have named differ slightly from their British or foreign congeners. For instance, the bird

I call *Fringilla chloris* is, in my opinion, the same as our own. Its habits, note, and character generally are exactly similar, the only observable difference being in the plumage, which in the Japanese bird is much richer.

Cinclus Pallasii is, I consider, the same bird as *C. aquaticus*. The Japanese bird is entirely dark, having no white horse-shoe mark on the breast, as in our bird; but in note, habits, food, and favourite localities, there is not the slightest difference in the two birds. The Japanese species I have closely observed for several years.

Several other species differ in some slight and similar way from those mentioned.

SIEBOLD'S LIST OF JAPANESE BIRDS.

Falco candicans.
... *communis.*
... *tinnunculus, var. jap.*
Astur nisus.
... *gularis.*
Spizaëtos orientalis.
Circus cyaneus.
Aquila fulva?
Haliaëtus pelagicus.
... *albicilla.*
Pandion haliaëtus orientalis.
Milvus melanotis.
Buteo japonicus.
... *hemilasius.*
... *poliogenys.*
Pernis apivorus.
Otus semitorques.
... *scops japonicus.*

Strix hirsuta japonica.
... *fuscescens.*
Hirundo rustica.
... *alpestris japonica.*
Caprimulgus Jataka.
Lanius bucephalus.
... *excubitor?*
Muscicapa cinereo alba.
... *gularis.*
... *hylocharis.*
... *mugimaki.*
... *narcissina.*
... *cyanomelana.*
Muscipeta principalis.
Ficedula coronata.
Salicaria turdina orientalis.
... *cantans.*
... *cantillans.*

LIST OF BIRDS.

Salicaria brunniceps.
Lusicola **cyanura**.
   ... **akahige**.
   ... **komadori**.
   ... **aurorea**.
   ... *calliope*.
Zosterops japonicus.
Saxicola rubicola.
Anthus arboreus, var. jap.
   ... **pratensis japonicus.**
Motacilla boarula.
   ... **lugens.**
Turdus Naumanii.
   ... **daulias.**
   ... **pallens.**
   ... *chrysolaus.*
   ... *cardis.*
   ... *sibiricus.*
   ... **manillensis.**
   ... ?
Orpheus amaurotis.
Cinclus Pallasii.
Accentor modularis rubidus.
Troglodytes vulgaris.
Regulus cristatus.
Parus minor.
   ... **ater.** ?
   ... ?
   ... **trivirgatus.**
   ... **varius.**
Certhia ?
Sitta ?
Picus awokera.
   ... **Kisuki.**
Jynx torquilla.

Cuculus canorus.
Alcedo coromanda major.
   ... *ispida bengalensis.*
   ... *lugubris.*
Corvus macrorhynchus.
   ... *corone.*
   ... **frugilegus.**
   ... **dauricus.**
Pica varia japonica.
   ... **cyana.**
Garrulus glandarius japonicus.
Nucifraga caryocatactes.
Bombycilla garrula.
   ... *phoenicoptera.*
Sturnus cineraceus.
Lamprotornis pyrrhogenys.
Upupa epops ?
Alauda japonica.
   ... ?
   ... *alpestris* ?
Fringilla montifringilla.
   ... **Kawarahiba.**
   ... ... **minor.**
   ... **linaria.**
   ... *spinus.*
Passer montanus.
   ... *russatus.*
Coccothraustes vulgaris, var. japonicus.
   ... **personatus.**
Pyrrhula orientalis.
   ... **sanguinolenta.**
Loxia curvirostra.
   ... **bifasciata** ?
Emberiza elegans.

Emberiza variabilis.
... *rutila.*
... *fucata.*
... *rustica.*
... *cioides.*
... **personata.**
... *sulphurata.*
Columba gelastis.
... **janthina.**
... *Sieboldii.*
Coturnix vulgaris japonica.
Phasianus versicolor.
... **Sömmeringi.**
Lagopus mutus.
Charadrius pluvialis orientalis.
Vanellus cristatus.
... *squatarola.*
Lobivanellus inornatus.
Tringa crassirostris.
... *variabilis.*
Actitis hypoleucos.
Totanus pulverulentus.
... *glareola.*
... *ochropus.*
Strepsilas interpres ?
Numenius major.
... *minor.*
Scolopax rusticola.
... *gallinago.*
... *solitaria.*
Rhynchæa maderaspatana.
Limosa melanura.
... *rufa.*
... *recurvirostra.*
Hæmatopus ostralegus.

Ardea cinerea.
... *alba.*
... *egrettoides.*
... *garzetta.*
... *russata.*
... *nycticorax.*
... *stellaris.*
... *goisagi.*
... *scapularis.*
Ibis nippon.
Grus cinerea longirostris.
... *leucogeranos.*
... *leucauchen.*
... *monachus.*
Platalea major.
... *minor.*
Fulica atra japonica.
Gallinula ?
... *erythrothorax.*
Rallus aquaticus.
Podiceps rubricollis major.
... *auritus.*
Colymbus arcticus.
Uria umizusume.
... *antiqua.*
Alca torda.
... *monoceros.*
Cygnus musicus.
Anser hyperboreus.
... *albifrons.*
... *cygnoides ferus.*
Anas boschas.
... *poëcilorhyncha hybr.*
... *falcaria.*
... *galericulata.*

LIST OF BIRDS.

Anas crecca.
... formosa.
... penelope.
... strepera.
... acuta.
... clypeata.
... tadorna.
... rutila.
... clangula.
.. fuligula.
... histrionica.
Mergus merganser.
... serrator.

Mergus albellus.
Carbo cormoranus.
... filamentosus.
... bicristatus.
Sula fusca.
Puffinus leucomelas.
... tenuirostris.
Diomedea brachyura.
Larus melanurus.
Sterna fuliginosa.

APPENDIX.

Pitta nympha.
Biophorus paradisiacus.

The following list of birds, not named in Siebold's *Fauna Japonica*, with few exceptions, I collected myself.

Hirundo urbica.
Cypselus apus.
... vittatus? or
Acanthylis cauducata, Schrenk.
Acanthylis gigantea.
Calamodyta phragmitis.
Pratincola rubicola.
Alauda arvensis.
Fringilla chloris.
Turdus aureus.
Parus palustris.
Certhia familiaris.
Sitta roseilia.
Dryocopus martius.
Picus major.
... leuconotus.
Garrulus Brandtii.
Phasianus. (Sp.)

Bonasi sylvestris.
Charadrius minor.
Tringa Temminckii.
... alpina.
... canutus.
Totanus calidris.
Numenius tahitiensis.
Phalaropus hyperboreus.
Scolopax gallinula.
... australis.
Gallinula chloropus.
Anser ferus.
... segetum.
... albifrons (small).
... leucopsis.
... torquatus.
Oidemia nigra.
Fuligula ferina.

LIST OF BIRDS.

Fuligula cristata.
Hærelda glacialis.
Procellaria Puffinus.
Puffinus pelagica.
... (Sp. ?)
... (Sp. ?)
Larus canus.

Larus ridibundus.
... cachinnans.
... argentatus.
... islandicus.
... fuscus.
Lestris (Sp. ?)
Sterna nigra.

EAGLE'S NEST, KUNASHIR.

PRINTED BY T. AND A. CONSTABLE, PRINTERS TO HER MAJESTY,
AT THE EDINBURGH UNIVERSITY PRESS.

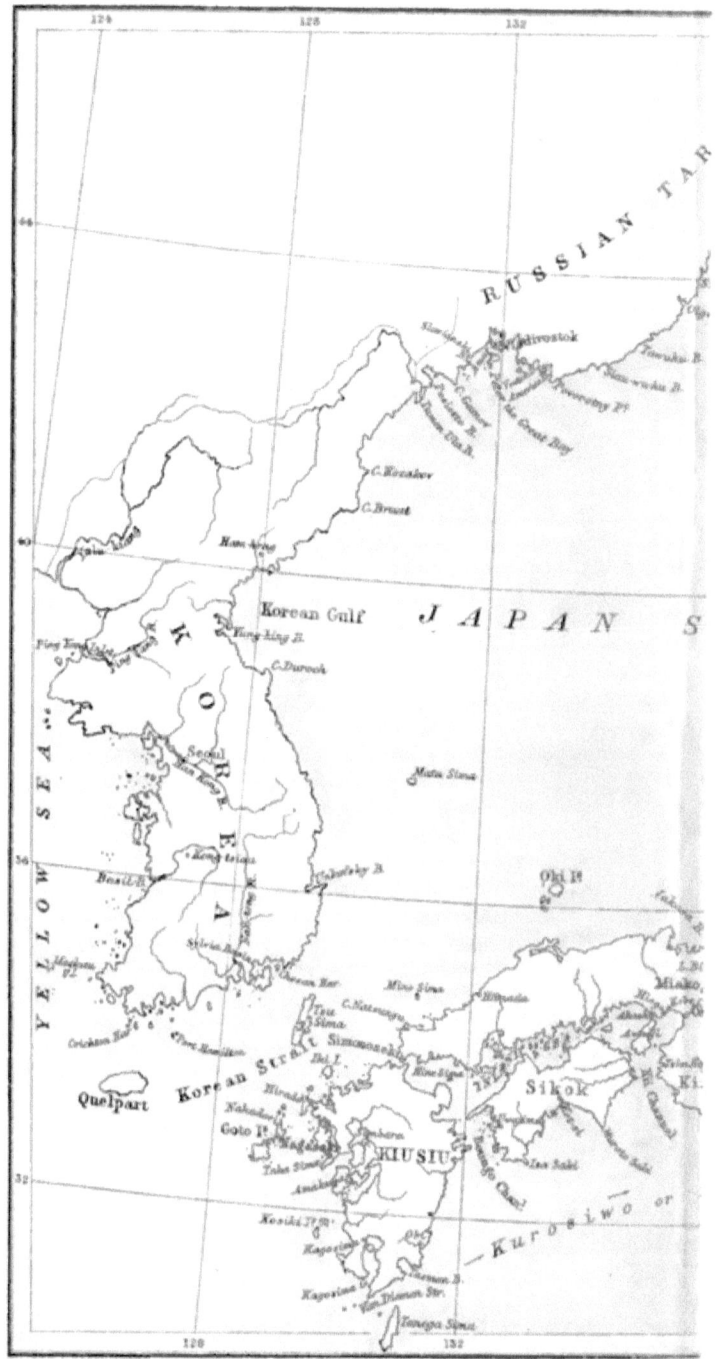

www.ingramcontent.com/pod-product-compliance
Lightning Source LLC
Chambersburg PA
CBHW032140010526
44111CB00035B/636